T0358558

Routledge Revivals

The Business Side of Agriculture

The Business Side of Agriculture

Arthur G. L. Rogers

First published in 1904 by Methuen & Co.

This edition first published in 2018 by Routledge
2 Park Square, Milton Park, Abingdon, Oxon, OX14 4RN
and by Routledge
711 Third Avenue, New York, NY 10017

Routledge is an imprint of the Taylor & Francis Group, an informa business

© 1904 Taylor & Francis

Publisher's Note
The publisher has gone to great lengths to ensure the quality of this reprint but points out that some imperfections in the original copies may be apparent.

Disclaimer
The publisher has made every effort to trace copyright holders and welcomes correspondence from those they have been unable to contact.

A Library of Congress record exists under ISBN: 5015549

ISBN 13: 978-1-138-60172-7 (hbk)
ISBN 13: 978-0-429-46194-1 (ebk)

THE BUSINESS SIDE OF AGRICULTURE

BY

ARTHUR G. L. ROGERS, M.A.

EDITOR OF THE LAST VOLUME OF THE
"HISTORY OF AGRICULTURE AND PRICES IN ENGLAND"

METHUEN & CO.
36 ESSEX STREET W.C.
LONDON

First Published in 1904

CONTENTS

CHAPTER I

CHAPTER II

CHAPTER III

CHAPTER IV

THE BUSINESS SIDE OF AGRICULTURE

CHAPTER I

INTRODUCTORY: THE FARMER AND HIS MARKET

IT was customary with writers on agriculture in the eighteenth century to comment in the opening pages of their works on the multiplicity of labours that attend the life of the farmer, and the extensive knowledge that he ought to possess in order to practise his art to the best advantage. Professor Bradley, who taught botany in the University of Cambridge, and published about 1726 a book called *The Country Gentleman and Farmer's Monthly Director*, says in his introductory discourse: "I consider a Farmer as a Person whose Business depends more upon the Labour of the Brain than of the Hands; that is, his Contrivance and Wariness will prove much more beneficial to him than the working Part. . . .

B

'Tis not hard Labour alone will fill the Sack ; but in the Business of Husbandry there must be Experience and Judgment as well as Industry : for consider the vast Variety the Farmer has before him." He then proceeds to detail at some length the many duties of the farm, including some things, such as the management of fish ponds, and the care of carp, tench, pike, perch, etc., which we should hardly consider nowadays belonged to agriculture.

Some ninety years later Sir John Sinclair, founder of the Board of Agriculture, as he styles himself, published a work, entitled *The Code of Agriculture, including Observations on Gardens, Orchards, Woods, and Plantations*, the opening words of which run as follows : " Agriculture, though in general capable of being reduced to simple principles, yet requires on the whole a greater variety of knowledge than any other art."

Both writers agree on the great store of information an agriculturist should possess, and both set themselves to inform him as to the particulars. And yet Bradley was able to satisfy himself that he had given all that was generally necessary in a hundred and ninety-one pages, while *The Code of Agriculture* is contained in less than five hundred, exclusive of an appendix, which covers another sixty. In the years, now nearly ninety, since the latter book was published the development of scientific agriculture has progressed apace, and it would require a book of some thousands of pages to contain all the scientific and practical knowledge a farmer ought to have at his command.

From the opening years of the nineteenth century, when chemistry was utilised in solving some of the problems of the farm, down to the present day there have not been wanting men of science who have applied their learning for the benefit of agriculture. Some have investigated the nature and properties of the soil, or the life-history of the plants that grow in it; others have studied the beneficent and harmful micro-organisms, and the place they take in the economy of agriculture; while the researches of students of natural history have added enormously to the volume of information that a cultivator of the soil and a rearer of cattle ought to possess.

Nor can it fairly be said that all this learning has been offered to an unintelligent class of men who persist in neglecting the teaching of the science that has busied itself in their behalf. The English farmer has adopted in many instances the teaching of the professors, and has often assisted to carry out their experiments. It is indeed customary to talk as if the agriculturists of Great Britain were a backward, unenterprising race, content to follow the practice of their fathers without endeavour or desire to improve on their ways. But it may be doubted that those who criticise them are aware of the great skill and versatility shown by the farmers of this country and the high standard of efficiency to which they have brought their profession, and that in the teeth of a fierce competition and severe depression which would have sufficed to crush out many a manufacture or business. At the Industrial Exhibition in Paris in 1855, as well as on similar and more recent occasions, as Mr. John Wilson wrote in the *Encyclopædia Britannica*, the one department in which Britain confessedly outstripped all her rivals was not in any of her great staple manufactures, but in the livestock of her farms and in her agricultural implements and machinery. This position has not been lost in more recent times. Agricultural statistics show that a greater number of bushels of wheat are grown to the acre in the United Kingdom than in any other country in the world, except perhaps in Belgium. Large quantities of seeds are yearly exported from these islands to sow in foreign countries, and it is to this country that breeders of cattle come to buy the stock that they want to improve their own herds. So far as the soil and climate permit, there is no equal to the British farmer in either hemisphere.

In spite of all this it is universally admitted that agriculture does not pay. We hear on all sides of reduced rents and declining values of agricultural land; we are told that the landlords of this country have lost in the last twenty years a sum exceeding the National Debt. The debaters at the Farmers' Club declare that the cause of the decline in the number of sheep in Great Britain is the smallness of their bank balances, and the utmost that any one of them will admit—in public—is that by unremitting toil and special circumstances he is just able to keep his head above water. It is a lamentable spectacle. The most enterprising, hard-working men, whom the whole agricultural world regards as the pattern and standard of their profession, cannot make their business pay. Surely there is something fundamentally wrong.

Every business that is conducted for gain has two sides, the practical and the economic. On the former of these the man of business endeavours to produce the best article he can, the one most suited to the customer's requirements. On the second he tries to make his incomings exceed his expenses by discovering means of cheapening his processes, or of increasing his values. Agriculture forms no exception to this rule. A farmer must, in order to lessen his expenses, produce as cheaply as possible the best article he can contrive to put on the market. This is the first element of profit-making. The farmer, like any other business man, has got to decide when it is most profitable to expend money, and when he will best be served by reducing his outlay. It is the more difficult in his case inasmuch as his turnover is slow (in respect of much of his produce only once a year), and the wisdom of his expenditure is often dependent on the weather or other circumstances over which he has no control. But it is generally held that in this respect, as in that of those already mentioned, the English farmer has exercised discretion, foresight, and enterprise. Experience has taught him in which direction he should not venture, and in which he might embark with caution. He has readily adopted labour-saving machines and devices for increasing the value of his products as well as for reducing his expenses. No little ingenuity has been employed in bringing cattle to maturity at an earlier age than was the case half a century ago. The competition with fruit and vegetables for the early market, at a season when prices rule high, is extremely keen, and, as is well known, extraordinary prices are often given for special plants or seeds having a tendency to ripen early or resist disease. The public have repeatedly been startled in the last year or two by reading in their newspapers of sensational prices given for small quantities of some new potato, and have been inclined to draw wholly false conclusions as to the profitableness of that class of agriculture.

All these instances, however, relate chiefly to functions of production; the successful conduct of a business requires, in addition, economic abilities of a different class. The object of a manufacturer of cloth or cotton goods is obviously not merely to make what he can, but also what he can sell. But agriculture in England is as much a business as any of the staple manufactures, and is governed therefore by very much the same rules. It has indeed been pointed out by many writers on English agriculture, in comparing its characteristics with the husbandry of the Continent, especially of those countries nearest to our own shores, that the object of the English farmer is to make money, by which is meant not merely to make a profit, but to produce something that he can sell for cash. He is not, as so many of the occupiers of land in other countries are, dependent on the produce of his farm for his daily sustenance. Many of the articles that appear on his table may be brought direct from his farmyard, but not only do many things appear there which he cannot grow, but it has become customary with him to deal with tradesmen for many things that he could, and perhaps does, produce. Probably few farmers in England bake their own bread, and still fewer brew their own beer. On the other hand, a large number of peasants and small farmers in France and Germany maintain themselves and their families on what they grow, and send but a small proportion to the market. To such people money is a scarce, and hardly a necessary commodity.

The English farmer, therefore, seeks to make money exactly as the manufacturer of cloth or cotton goods does. The reasons for this are two. In the first place, owing to a variety of causes, which may be found discussed at length in books on history and economics, land in England, especially agricultural land, has passed into the hands of very few owners. The process, which was mainly political at first, has now an economic reason. The general want of capital, the great amount required, and the variety of uses to which it could profitably be put in a large English farm, have led many men who owned land to sell it and employ the money in the purchase of stock, manures, and machinery. This has had an important effect on agriculture in Great Britain. It has reared a race of tenant farmers who are able to move from one part of the country to another in a way that the yeoman could never do. And in the second place it has made them regard the land as a kind of loan out of which they must make the best rate of profit they can. It has also elevated the payment of rent into a matter of first importance. Now it has been customary in England for many hundreds of years to pay rent in money, and, therefore, the tenant has to see that he has sufficient money in cash, or at his bank, to pay his rent every half-year, or whenever it may be due. For a tenant who has to pay £200 or £500 in rent all transactions whereby he is able to turn his products into money have the utmost interest.

While, however, it is customary in England to pay the landlord in money, it is compulsory to pay labourers who do not live in the house in that way. The Truck Acts are not so strict in the case of farm labour as they are in the case of artisans, and money wages are generally supplemented by allowances, whether special, as in harvest, or general, such as the potato-patches, the fuel, or the other additions that a farm-hand gets to swell his income. But in every part of England some money is paid over, even to the children; and as—in the south, at any rate—wages are paid weekly, sales must be made of the farm produce for the coin that is to be given. The need, therefore, for replenishing the bank balance is periodical, in small amounts for wages, and in large amounts for

rent. A farmer has, over and above these, a variety
of expenses. There is the cake and manure merchant,
the machinery maker, the seed merchant, and a number of other tradesmen with whom he has transactions.
It may be that some of these will also be customers
of his and will write off the value of the corn he
sells them against the value of the cake he buys,
and so no money will pass at all ; but at all events
that is a commercial transaction, the advantages or
disadvantages of which he has to consider. It may,
therefore, be asserted that the profitable disposal of
farm produce is quite as important an item in the
successful management of the business as the profitable production of it is.

Now the multitude of a farmer's cares in the production of his saleable commodities, as has been
already mentioned, forms the theme of the opening
chapters of many books. Few have even referred to
the variety of troubles that he has in disposing of
them. And yet they are not much out of proportion.
If the farmer has to sow and reap wheat, rear and
fatten oxen and sheep, and attend to all the minor
branches of his trade that are recommended in the
text-books as sources of profit, he must have a
corresponding number of articles to sell. He has
this additional difficulty, that he has to sell them by
different methods and to different people. He has to

know not only at what price such articles as he has to offer are selling at any given market, but he has to know whether it will pay him to sell them at that price. He has to exercise his judgment as to whether prices are likely to rise or fall, and to use his ingenuity in finding out whether, by going further afield, he can get a better offer, and whether the cost of taking his produce to that market will not extinguish the advantage he might hope to gain. Then it is to be remembered that he is dealing with men who confine themselves to one branch of his industry; for the butcher does not buy wheat, or the miller beef, and consequently he is dealing with men who may be expected to know the details of the trade better than he does. Add to these that he is face to face with a fierce foreign competition, and the sum of his difficulties as a trader will be found to equal, if not surpass, the sum of his difficulties as a producer.

A book of this size is obviously too small to contain a description of all the operations in which a farmer is engaged, and it may not be considered amiss, therefore, to confine it to an examination of the various methods that are in vogue in England for the sale of farm produce, giving some attention to the people with whom a farmer has to deal, and the means by which the prices current of the day are ascertained or recorded. In the course of doing so we may notice some recent changes and the tendency of these developments. The extent to which new ways of transacting business have been adopted is the measure of the skill that has been shown in this part of a farmer's occupation. That the agriculturist is deficient in this quality there is no reason to suppose, though the specialisation of employment, which has led to the great increase in the number of middlemen, has led many people to deny it. The middleman is, of course, a necessary part of modern civilisation. He performs a useful economic function, and has as much right to the gratitude of the community whom he serves and to the protection of the State as the producer, to whom he stands in much the same relation as a sovereign does to a pound's worth of goods. He is essentially the outcome of the modern system of rapid communication. In the old days, when travelling was slow and difficult, the market town was the centre to which most agricultural produce went, and at which the consumer was to be found. The quantity of produce exhibited at the market was limited by the productivity of the immediate neighbourhood, except in the case of some of the large annual fairs. But with the advent of railways and telegraphs the small markets have been deserted for the larger towns, where transactions are greater. A farmer must therefore spend more time at the market or arrange for the sale of his produce by a middleman. On the other hand, the complexity of modern agriculture has made the presence of the husbandman on his land more necessary than ever, and his absence for a large part of a day at a market a source of wastefulness. It may be that this development is regarded with disfavour by those whose natural inclination is towards the trading side of a farmer's life. A recent writer, recounting the visit of our countrymen abroad to learn the ways of the foreigner, declares: "The English farmers are intensely commercial; the bartering at the weekly market, the sale of corn by a farmer at sixpence a quarter better than his neighbour, or the purchase of seed at sixpence less, is the bright spot in an otherwise monotonous existence, and all wish of sharing with others the advantages of profit sharing and co-operative undertaking is absent from a farmer's breast." However this may be, the constant pressure of home duties and the increasing intricacies of trade are acting as a perpetual incentive to the practising agriculturist to devote his energies to production, and delegate the duties of sale. How and to whom the charge is to be entrusted, whether the trustee is acting as an agent for the farmer or as an independent trader, and whether the results are advantageous, must be the object of inquiry. It is proposed, therefore, to begin with the customary methods of selling which have been in vogue, with modifications, since farming became a business, and to deal with the two divisions of vegetable and animal products separately. Afterwards we will examine some of the schemes that have been devised in recent years by persons or organisations interested in the prosperity of the agricultural classes to assist them to dispose of their produce to better advantage.

CHAPTER II

TRADITIONAL METHODS OF MARKETING CEREALS, HOPS, FRUIT, AND OTHER VEGETABLE PRODUCE

THE word agriculture, which is now used to comprise all the operations of the farmer, means properly the cultivation of the soil, and though the livestock interest has gradually eclipsed that of tillage, it has always been customary to give the precedence to the latter in all books on husbandry. It will be natural, therefore, to begin with an account of wheat, since of all the vegetable products of the farm that plant ranks first—not only in the public estimation, but even among farmers themselves. The consumers as a body, and especially those who live in towns, naturally attach the highest importance to the grain which figures at every meal of nearly every inhabitant of the kingdom. With the producer, however, the reasons are more numerous and complex. Apart from the sentiment attaching to the growth of wheat, it is a valuable crop in the economy of production, since it takes a leading place in the system of rotation of crops which is usually practised here, and with which the fame of English agriculture is closely bound up.

In recent years, when wheat has become almost unremunerative, many efforts have been made to find a satisfactory substitute without success, and therefore it retains a certain value, apart from its use as a food product. From the commercial and economic point of view there are other arguments for its continued production. It is a crop which can be depended on to produce approximately equal results every year, while it forms a palatable and nutritious food for animals as well as men. It is a crop which, when harvested, will keep without great difficulty, and which does not rapidly deteriorate like soft fruit or animal products. It has a ready sale at all times, and the demand for it is equal at all seasons and in all years. It has, in fact, many of the economic qualities which have made gold the usual medium of exchange throughout the world. In spite of these advantages it is, however, well known that the acreage of wheat in Great Britain has been substantially reduced in the last thirty years. At the beginning of that period some three million seven hundred thousand acres were sown with that grain; at the present time it is to be found in a little over a million and a half, while the price has fallen in the meantime from forty to twenty-five shillings. Barley has suffered a proportionate decline, both in acreage and in price, while oats, which are only a shilling or two below the price of those days, have actually increased the area devoted to their cultivation.

There are a number of kinds of wheat, each having its special good quality, but as they are valuable chiefly in accordance with their productivity or their power of resisting the influence of bad weather, it will not be necessary to enumerate them. For general purposes we need only remember that all English wheats, whether white or red, belong to the "soft" variety, and depend for their price upon the quality of the grain as put on the market. For purposes of the present discussion it will be convenient to make three classifications—seed wheat, and what are commonly known as "head" and "tail" wheat, the latter of which is always consumed on the farm. It is needless to say that the first is the best, and that only a very small proportion of the crop, probably not more than 8 or 9 per cent.,[1] is used for the next year's seed. Now, as is well known, wheat sown continually on the same soil tends to deteriorate, and farmers therefore change their seed periodically. But it does not follow that the seed is brought from a different locality, and a farmer who has both

---

[1] *Farm Revenue and Capital*, by R. H. Rew, p. 11.

C

light and heavy soil to plough will not need to buy seed from outside for two or three years. When, however, he does think it advisable to have a change, he usually buys from a farmer living some distance away, where the nature of the soil is quite different and these negotiations are not conducted through the usual public channels of exchange. The amount of wheat therefore that passes through the market will be correspondingly reduced. Sales by private treaty of this kind are not regarded quite in the same way as other business transactions, and the seller may have to wait a very long time for his money and only get it with some little trouble. There are, however, a certain number of transactions of this class at the regular corn markets, though a farmer with seed wheat to sell will not look for the same sort of purchaser that he would seek if he had the bulk of his harvest to dispose of. He may on such occasions sell to the merchants, especially to the representatives of the large companies or firms that deal in seeds, who, it is interesting to note, send a considerable quantity abroad, where the great productivity of English wheat, and its cleanness from rubbish of all kinds, including the seeds of weeds, are naturally highly valued.

Before we go on to discuss the sale of English wheat for consumption in the form of bread, we must spend a little time inquiring into the special qualities of English and foreign wheat, and to the place which each holds in the market. The reader is probably aware that the average crop in England is nearly thirty bushels to the acre, that of Wales about twenty-four, while Scotland, on account of certain exceptional districts, can boast of over thirty-seven bushels. The counties of Haddington, Linlithgow, Ayr, and Renfrew returned more than forty bushels to the acre in 1902, while the county of Edinburgh gave forty-five. Even better results than this are sometimes obtained, and a gentleman at the meeting of the Farmers' Club, in November, 1901, declared that on one occasion, admittedly exceptional, he had obtained fifty bushels of seventy-five pounds per statute acre. On the other hand, the average return per acre in foreign countries is small. Some European countries, like Germany, Denmark, and Holland, give twenty-five to twenty-eight bushels, but France returns only eighteen. Canada grows over eighteen bushels to the acre, but the United States have an average of little more than thirteen, the Argentine Republic eleven, Roumania twelve, Russia (excluding Poland, which gives fifteen) no more than eight to ten, and Australia barely over seven.

It will readily be understood that wheat grown in such different countries is not all of the same kind or quality, and that although in many places the deficiency is due to bad management, the wheat grown in some of the districts where a very small crop is produced has counter-balancing advantages. Such indeed is the case, and it is to these peculiarities that so much of the foreign wheat owes its place in the English market. The " red winters," as some of the American wheats are called, some of the Polish, and of the River Plate wheats, are very much of the same character as the English grain in the amount they contain of that substance known as gluten, in which much of the nutritive property of bread exists.[1] These wheats are what is known as "soft," though of a good colour, and of a high, or, at any rate, fair " strength." Others are of a totally different character. The greater part of the American wheats, such as those known as Duluth, Minnesota, Chicago, Spring Milwaukee, the famous Manitoban, most of the Argentine, the Australian, the Indian, and most of the Russian and Egyptian wheats, are " hard," sometimes even to brittleness, often with great strength, and they give a very different kind of flour from the English wheat on being milled. The bread which we eat in England is generally made from a mixture of several of these flours, and the art of combining them is one requiring no little skill. The proportions differ in places, but

[1] National Wheat Stores Committee, Reply 97 A.

in the big towns near the sea there is usually more foreign wheat, while in some inland places bread is made almost entirely from home-grown flour. " The finest wheat," said one of the witnesses to the National Wheat Stores Committee,[1] "that you get in England is No. 1, hard, Duluth wheat (Australian wheat would also be very fine). It is a very strong wheat, and by itself is too strong, as it makes the bread tough : you can only use a proportion of it. The average loaf of a Londoner would be composed of, say, not more than 10 per cent. of English wheat, about 20 per cent. of American wheat, about 30 per cent. of South Russian wheat, and the balance made up of the various qualities of other wheats." In spite of the small proportion used, it must not be supposed that English wheat is inferior. It is admitted on all hands that for colour, flavour, and texture there is no wheat to equal the home-grown wheat when the harvest is good. It has also the incidental advantage of being far better cleaned when offered for sale than most of the foreign wheats, some of which are full of other seeds and impurities of all kinds.

The object of this digression from the subject under discussion is to show that foreign wheat is to a certain extent supplementary to home-grown

[1] Reply 214.

wheat, and does not merely supplant it. But it will naturally occur to the reader to wonder if the foreign method of selling wheat is the same as that which is practised in Great Britain, and whether the organisation in each case is so highly developed. The sale of so many million quarters of foreign wheat in England, coming from so many parts of the world, is no small affair, and it is of immense importance for the miller or merchant to know what he is buying, or where he can get the quality of wheat that he wants out of so many harvests gathered under such different conditions, and at prices subject to so many influences. The plan adopted in America is as follows. The wheat which has been thrashed by the farmer is sent by railway to one of the big towns which form the grain centres, such as Chicago, St. Louis, Minneapolis, or Montreal, consigned to one of the granary companies, whose "elevators," as they are called, are capable of holding some two or three hundred thousand quarters. The grain is inspected on arrival by the officers of the Board of Trade, by whom it is "graded," according to its quality, into one or other of three classes, and stored in the buildings of the elevator company, a certificate being given to the consignor for so many quarters of No. 1 Manitoban or Duluth, according to the district from which it comes. The buildings in which the wheat is stored are specially devised, and are thus described by the chairman of one of the largest:[1] "They are buildings on stone foundations built of wood, and covered with corrugated iron, being carefully built to guard against fire. They have automatic sprinklers, and the top of the elevator is decked in like the deck of a ship, so that in the event of a fire water can be thrown all over it without injuring the grain." The bins in which the grain is kept do not come to the bottom of the floor of the elevator, but terminate in wooden pipes. When the wheat is sold and delivery is claimed, the bins are opened and the grain pours forth into the receptacle in which it is to be transported, with the least possible amount of labour and expense. Both incoming and outgoing grain is inspected and graded by a State inspector, and weighed by a State weigher, so that complete accuracy is ensured. Wheat so treated becomes a kind of coin, and the system works with the ease and rapidity of a bank. By this means the farmer is no longer troubled with the storage of his wheat, and his certificate is as good as a draft on a commercial house, while English dealers can buy American wheat without any uncertainty as to the general quality of the stuff they are buying. No such system prevails in England.

Other foreign countries sell their wheat on the

[1] National Wheat Stores Committee, Reply 110.

basis of " fair average value." In this case a more careful examination of the grain is necessary before the quality can be known and a price agreed upon. This entails delay, and possibly loss and disappointment, to the farmer, who cannot be so sure that he is fairly treated. Russia and other eastern countries sell their corn to us by the system in vogue in England—that is, by sample. It now remains to give some description of this method of selling, which is usually carried out at a public market.

Although we know what the number of quarters of wheat, barley, and oats raised at home every year is, the amount that is sold for consumption cannot be accurately ascertained. Various estimates have been formed at one time and another; but it is most improbable that more than 80 per cent. of the wheat, 70 per cent. of the barley, and 40 per cent. of the oats grown in Great Britain find their way into the hands of that part of the public that is not engaged in agriculture. At least half of these amounts, and probably nearly the whole, is sold in this country at markets, to which some part at least of the grain is brought and offered for examination at the time of the negotiations. What the total number of markets in Great Britain may be there is no way of discovering, nor is it easy to say what constitutes one. The Icelanders were taunted by Thangbrand, in Longfellow's poem, with the jeer that "three women and a goose" made a market in their town. But there are many places in this country where there is scarcely more than that amount of business done in what was at one time a busy trading centre.

These declining places of sale may, however, be disregarded, and the term market confined to those centres, as far as England and Wales are concerned, in which sales of British corn are required to be notified to the inspector under the Corn Returns Act of 1882. The law which was amended by that Act is more than a hundred years old, and it owes its existence to the following cause. During the period of the earlier corn laws the amount of the duty on imported corn was regulated by a sliding scale, varying with the price of native corn. In order to ascertain this figure all buyers of grain were bound under penalty to register the amount of their purchase and the price at which the bargain was struck. From these returns an average was prepared for the kingdom for the use of would-be importers. When the Tithe Commutation Act of 1836 was passed, the statesmen of the day, fearing that the value of money might be liable to the same disturbances that it had been subject to a few years before, and anxious to secure as steady a rate as possible for the commutation of the tithe, fixed on these prices as the best available standard, and the value of the tithe rent charge is still calculated by this means. The number of towns from which returns are required has varied from time to time. In 1842 it was 290, and remained so till 1865, when it was reduced to 150. It was raised to 187 in 1883, and to 196 in 1890; but in 1901 the number became 190, at which point it remains. The number therefore is considerable, though all are not of equal importance. Corn markets may be considered from several points of view, but the most obvious distinction to draw in the first instance relates to their size. They may, therefore, be roughly divided into three classes, which we can call (1) the small or ordinary markets; (2) the larger or junction markets; (3) the largest or controlling markets.

The distinction in the size of the markets is of comparatively modern growth, and is due to the development of general trade and the improved means of communication that have done so much to affect English agriculture. Sixty or seventy years ago matters were different. Farmers sold their grain in the nearest market, and the miller who bought it had his mill in the immediate neighbourhood. Long journeys were out of the question, and few people thought of sending their wheat far afield in hopes of a better sale. To-day it is often as easy, or easier, to send all grain to the big towns as to the small ones, and the millers have moved to the centres where the most business is done. The introduction of the system of roller milling from Hungary and the competition with American flour have resulted in the destruction of a large number of country mills and the construction of large roller mills at seaports. Wheat, therefore, even if sold in the first place at the small towns, cannot be ground there, and is resold at the second class of markets and possibly transmitted again to the third. The flour may eventually be returned to the town in which the grain was originally purchased.

Out of 190 markets scheduled for the return of corn sales some are quite insignificant, making practically no return at all. Thus in 1902 Ludlow, Kendal, Llangefni, Carnarvon, and Cardigan appear to have had no sales of British wheat at all. Cockermouth returned only 5 quarters 5 bushels, Penrith 34 quarters 7 bushels, Haverfordwest 99 quarters 3 bushels, Alnwick 64 quarters of wheat. Other markets recorded similarly small transactions in barley and oats. At Preston, which, however, cannot be called a small town, no barley or oats were returned, and only 281 quarters 7 bushels of British wheat. At Garstang 12 quarters 4 bushels of barley were sold, but no oats. At Bishop Auckland no barley and only 37 quarters 5 bushels of oats. In both these cases the amount of wheat sold was small also. But it is not necessarily the case that where one class of grain is poorly represented there is no demand for the other classes. There were some which recorded large sales of wheat or barley and very little in the way of oats, or the converse was the case. Southhampton, for instance, reported the sale of 3,125 quarters 5 bushels of wheat, and only 98 quarters 3 bushels of barley, and 411 quarters 5 bushels of oats in the year. The position is altered at Shrewsbury, where 7,705 quarters 7 bushels of wheat, 27,377 quarters 7 bushels of barley, and 6,502 quarters 1 bushel of oats were sold, and at Carlisle, where 139 quarters 7 bushels of wheat, 779 quarters of barley, and 15,234 quarters 5 bushels of oats found purchasers. It must be remembered, however, that these figures cannot be taken as an exact measure of the amount of corn delivered, as the same parcel of grain may be sold more than once in the same market, and may then be resold in another. Be this as it may, there are some markets to which a great deal of grain is sent that is not grown in the immediate neighbourhood. Salisbury and Devizes, for instance, return some 35,000 quarters of wheat each, Basingstoke 24,000, Reading 22,000, Birmingham 15,000, and Banbury 14,000, while other markets close by return only 1,000 quarters or so, being not so favourably served by the railway. We see from this that the volume of trade does not necessarily vary with the size of the town in which the market is held, though as these figures refer only to British wheat they afford no clue to the amount of foreign wheat sold in those places.

Finally, there are the big controlling markets, which do a continuous and steady trade, and which influence the price of grain throughout the kingdom. These are Chelmsford, Colchester, Cambridge, Norwich, Lincoln, Hull, Peterborough, and London, the last holding, of course, quite a peculiar position in the matter of importance, though the amount recorded as sold in 1902 was only 71,837 quarters, a total surpassed by Chelmsford, Cambridge, Norwich, Lincoln, and Peterborough, which last is the only market at which more than 100,000 quarters were sold. Both home and foreign grain are usually bought and sold in the same place in the controlling market, though not necessarily by the same class of dealers. In Mark Lane, according to a witness before the Corn Averages Committee of 1888, there would be at least 4,000 to 5,000 persons buying and selling corn on a market day, and of these many would be dealing only in foreign wheat.[1] On the other hand several witnesses before the same Committee replied, in answer to the

[1] Reply 501.

question put to them, that they dealt only in English wheat.

Home-grown wheat is offered at all seasons of the year. It used to be said that a farmer who had no wheat to sell was looked on with suspicion as a man who had been pressed by his creditors and forced to realise. But in modern times very little wheat is kept more than a year, and the greater part is sold before the summer. The first week in October, when the first thrashings are being sold, or some weeks towards the end of winter, when bad weather, perhaps, is keeping the farmer from getting on the land, and there is little or no work to do at home, are the seasons when the market is most active. Barley is sold rather later in the autumn than wheat, and in any week in November there are twice as many quarters of barley sold in England as in the six months between the end of March and the beginning of October. But the sales of barley in all the markets put together drop to a hundred quarters or less during July and August. With oats the difference is not so marked, and the sales are much the same as in the case of wheat. During harvest, as may be supposed, practically nothing is offered except the stocks that are held by dealers. A change in price, moreover, takes place corresponding with the seasons. Wheat not unfrequently rises slowly but steadily during July and August, and generally falls rapidly on the introduction of the supplies of the new harvest. Barley, on the other hand, is usually highest at the time when there is most in the market, and the price rises above the level of wheat. This is, of course, due to the greater value of the malting barley which is offered at this time. Later on in the season, when it is finished and the grinding barley is brought into the market, the prices decline.

It will assist in understanding the vagaries of prices if we can picture to ourselves the appearance of a market, and have a description of the different men who frequent it, as well as the way they do their business there. In many towns the transactions will be carried out in a large hall expressly built for that purpose and capable of accommodating hundreds of persons. But more often business is done by groups of farmers and dealers talking outside in the market square, or perhaps trading with one another more sociably in some frequented public-house. "They sell it anywhere," says one witness to the Departmental Committee on Scottish Prices, "at the corn exchanges, auction markets, travelling in the train, and meeting at local shows."[1] Even when a hall is provided a great many of the negotiations are carried on this way. The discussions that precede a bargain

[1] Reply 1138.

are often prolonged through the day, and at times the business is not settled till just before the train leaves, and one or other of the parties is carried away. This, however, is mainly confined to country places, and in the more important centres affairs are conducted with more system and regularity inside the authorised precincts of the corn exchange. Many classes of persons attend these markets—farmers, dealers, millers, maltsters, jobbers, and factors—all more or less expert in the art of buying and selling corn, and acquainted by long practice with the conditions likely to affect prices, though their local knowledge may be supplemented by telegrams received in the course of the day describing the movements of trade elsewhere. As a rule each dealer has his regular customers, for business tends to run in the same channels, and there are reasons why certain people trade continuously with each other. A farmer will sell his wheat to the man from whom he buys his cake ; and a dealer tries to persuade the farmer to purchase his fertilisers or seeds.

On the other hand, there are men who avoid dealing with third parties, and many a miller or maltster goes into market and buys his grain direct from the farmer. This is especially the case with barley, and a maltster generally makes a careful inspection of the available stocks, and selects the class of grain he requires at first hand. The big brewers, again, have their agents or buyers in all these markets, and the Burton representatives usually buy direct from the farmers, and have the barley sent straight to their place of business. The other purchasers are dealers who buy to become sellers again, so that a stock of grain may change hands more than once in the day, usually, of course, at an enhanced price. The increase in price caused this way is generally very small, no more than threepence a quarter, and it stands to reason that the increase may be due to more than one cause. A miller with a quantity of grain of a low order, or if he is grinding foreign wheat of a dry nature, may be willing to give an extra price for a small quantity of special wheat which will enrich and give quality to his flour. But the grain is not necessarily delivered every time it changes ownership. It may be sold twice or thrice in the same market, or in two or three successive markets, and the producer may receive eventually instructions from the purchaser to consign part of what he sold to one railway station, and the rest to a railway station in a different direction. Now in such an assemblage a farmer, unless he is exceptionally capable, or has a special class of grain to offer, seems to be at a disadvantage. The dealer is a trader who specialises more or less in his business, whereas the producer has a variety of things to sell,

D

and cannot spare so much time to the study of the market. The miller or maltster knows what grain he wants, and can inspect and choose his samples. The agriculturist can only offer what he has got, and if his wares are below the level of those of his competitors he suffers accordingly. In order to surmount this difficulty, a custom has arisen in some parts of the South of employing factors, who act as agents for the farmers, and meet the purchaser on his own ground. These gentlemen hold often very influential positions.

There is one person of importance to be found at each of the markets scheduled under the Act of 1882, who, though he is not a trader, must not be overlooked—the Corn Inspector. He is, except in London, an officer of the Inland Revenue Department, and it is his duty to attend the market and receive from each buyer of British corn a return showing the amount of his purchase and the price at which it was effected. He has a desk usually in a conspicuous place in the market, furnished with forms for making returns, and during the course of the day he goes round the market inquiring prices and asking the purchasers if they have made their returns. The total of the amount sold and the average price must be calculated at the end of the day, and the result published in a conspicuous place in the market and forwarded to the Board of Agriculture. It is no pleasant task always to collect these figures, and great tact, judgment, and ability are required. It must be remembered that, though the purchaser is bound by law to make the returns, there is a natural disinclination on the part of the dealer to say what price he has paid. "It is naught, it is naught, saith the buyer : but when he goeth away he boasteth." Besides, there are some small dealers who buy infrequently or in small quantities, such as horsekeepers or corn chandlers, and these are not easy to recognise or notice, and the inspector's work must thereby be rendered more difficult.

The different persons referred to above are probably to be found in nearly every market of repute and size, but the way of doing business is not in all cases alike. In order to judge markets from this point of view we must divide them into two classes, the "pitch" market and the "sample" market. In the first of these it is customary for the farmer to bring a sack or a given quantity of grain to the place of business and to "pitch" it on the floor for full examination by the intending purchasers, who come round to the sellers with their offers. In the second case a sample of the grain only is offered for inspection, the bulk, which is to be delivered after the bargain is complete, being guaranteed of the same quality. The samples are usually carried about in small bags that can be put in a greatcoat pocket, and the would-be seller goes to seek a purchaser among the dealers or the millers and maltsters. The latter pass about in the crowd, but the dealers have fixed stands where they are to be found during business hours.

Of these two systems the pitch market is undoubtedly the older, and was probably at one time the prevailing type everywhere. It has now given way to the newer method in nearly all places, and that for sundry reasons. In some towns a toll was levied on all corn coming in for sale, and even in the middle of the nineteenth century this was sometimes taken in kind—a handful from each sack. No toll, however, was taken on samples, and so there was a distinct material advantage in the more modern plan; while the expense of carriage and the possible damage from exposure are two serious objections to exhibiting corn in bulk. As an example of this, we may take Edinburgh market, though it is not a pitch market in the strictest sense. "The practice in Edinburgh," says a witness before the Corn Sales Committee of 1893,[1] " is that the farmers bringing in their grain to market bushel the grain at home, that is to say, find out the natural weight per bushel, and they measure the grain up (taking, for instance, oats)

[1] Replies 646–52, 678.

four bushels in the bag; then they bring it into market
in a bag, and go to the market clerk, and tell him
what the weight of the imperial half-quarter is;
and they get from him a ticket, such as I have here
(producing a ticket), giving the particulars of it.
Then the man pitches his bag on the market floor,
and at a certain hour, when the oat market comes
round, he stands by his bag, and the buyers come
round and buy from him. He guarantees the grain
to weigh naturally what he has stated on the ticket.
The tickets are of different colours, according to the
different kind of grain. In East Lothian and Mid-
lothian the same practice prevails. In Roxburghshire
and Berwickshire the same practice prevails generally.
Then when you go further north in Fife, Forfar,
Perthshire, and Aberdeenshire, you have a different
sort of market. You have more a sample market
than a stock market. A farmer comes in and shows
his samples to two or three men," and a certain
amount of discussion and bargaining goes on before
the sale is completed.

Another witness before the same Committee gives
us a striking picture of such a discussion. In this
case[1] it is a Kentish farmer justly proud of the
quality of his wheat, who takes a sample to market.
"I have had forty-five years' farming," says he. "I

[1] Reply 148.

have never allowed anyone to take a sample of my corn but myself, and I always weighed my corn before I went to market, because I fortunately lived in one of the best districts and grew the best quality, and therefore I always went prepared with the weight of my barleys and the weight of my wheats. We take a small sample, about a pound, say, and put it into our factor's hands or sell it ourselves; if it is weighted the miller will come up and take it and look at it, and examine it, and all that sort of thing. 'This is nice wheat!' 'Well, what do you think it will weigh?' 'Oh, I do not know; about sixty-four, I think.' 'No, a good sixty-five.' Of course, a miller is a judge, and if the farmer does not take sufficient care of his own business and of himself in weighing his corn before he goes, and takes a sample himself so as to be perfectly certain what he is about, very likely half the millers would buy a sample of wheat of his 65 lbs. a bushel at the same price as they would another man's 63 lbs., because the man who has got 65 lbs. did not know what it would weigh, and would leave it entirely to them. But the man with 63 lbs. would have weighed it, and come prepared with the weight to back it."

Now, of course, when business is conducted on sound lines and between men of care and accuracy, there is not much ground for mistakes and misapprehension ; but unfortunately everyone is not so methodical, and wheat is often bought after a mere examination of the sample. The miller judges by the appearance of the grain how much it will weigh, and there are some who can judge by sight and feel to within half a pound of its weight per bushel. But it must be remembered that a sample carried about in a bag in the pocket is apt after a while to get drier, and as dry grain weighs bulk for bulk more than moist, it becomes heavier in proportion. A miller or dealer may find himself deceived when the consignment is delivered. It is customary, therefore, to demand a guarantee that the wheat shall be of so many pounds to the bushel, and the bargain is concluded on the understanding that the final settlement is to be adjusted on that basis. The greater part of the purchase money may be paid over at once, leaving a tenth or other small percentage to be paid subsequently, or delivery of bulk may be required before any payment is made. But before we examine the methods by which the adjustment is carried out, we must understand what is meant by wheat of 65 or 63 lbs. weight. This will lead us to an inquiry into the different weights and measures by which grain is sold in various parts of the country. It is important to try and reduce these to some order before going any further, for they are so many and so diversified that a farmer in one town is often quite unable to understand the ways of the market in another place not very far off.

In olden times wheat was always sold by measure. But about the middle of the nineteenth century this system began to break up, and, as is the case in the sale of nearly every other article of farm produce, the element of weight was introduced into the calculation. There are still a few markets where wheat is always sold by the imperial quarter of eight bushels, as in the days of old, or by some measure which is purely local but probably of great antiquity, and there are some where it is sold only by weight. About all of these we shall have something to say later on. But in the vast majority of markets wheat is sold by what is known as "measure and weight," or "weighed measure." There are many ways of using either system, and some are extremely complicated. For not only does the way of practising either system vary from town to town, but more than one system may be in vogue in a market, while as each custom is in a state of transition, it is unsafe to say that a certain system prevails in a certain district because it was found there some years ago.

For the purposes of the corn averages all weights and measures are reduced to a common standard. Section 8 of the Corn Returns Act of 1882 provides

that, where returns of purchases of British corn are
made to the local inspector of corn returns in the
scheduled markets already referred to in any other
measure than the imperial bushel or by a weighed
measure, that officer shall convert such returns into
the imperial bushel; and in the case of weight or
weighed measure the conversion is to be made at
the rate of 60 imperial pounds for every bushel of
wheat, 50 imperial pounds for every bushel of barley,
and 39 imperial pounds for every bushel of oats.
These numbers were chosen because it was believed
that they represented the average of the natural
weights of the different classes of grain sold in the
markets. But in a great many towns a different
standard has been adopted, and a bushel of wheat
is expected to weigh more or less than that amount,
as the case may be. In all these cases where the
bushel is understood to imply a certain weight, corn
is said to be sold by "weighed measure." In about
75 per cent. of the markets returned to the Corn
Sales Committee[1] wheat is sold by the assumed
weight of 63 lbs. to the bushel, and in about 18
per cent. at 62 lbs. to the bushel. There were, however, forty-six different weighed measures in all,
by which wheat sales were returned, varying from
52 lbs. to 90 lbs. per bushel. There were twenty-six

[1] Select Committee on Corn Sales, 1893, p. 125.

different weighed bushels for barley ranging from 42 lbs. to 70 lbs. apiece, but 94 per cent. of the quantity returned were at 56 lbs. A somewhat similar tale is told as regards oats. There were thirty-eight different weighed bushels, ranging from 17½ lbs. (at which three quarters were returned at Mark Lane) to 75 lbs. (by which denomination 28 quarters were returned at Ludlow). Seventy per cent. of the oats sold by weighed measure were returned at 42 lbs. per bushel. Altogether there are said to be one hundred and twenty different ways by which corn is sold in England.

Now it is obvious this must be extremely perplexing to a stranger attempting to deal in any given market. He is unaware if the bargain is made in weight or by measure, and this must limit competition, unless the purchaser stipulates that the bushel is to weigh a certain amount. This, in fact, is what is usually done, as we have already seen.

Now let us return to the case of the farmer who has not weighed his wheat before taking the sample to market. Let us assume that the purchaser requires the wheat to weigh 63 lbs. The sample is approved as far as colour and quality go, but the farmer finds it will only weigh 60 lbs. What is he to do? He could perhaps treat it, so as to bring it up to the required weight, but that would be a difficult and

expensive process. It could be raised to the required
standard by careful screening perhaps, but that would
leave him with an additional amount of tail corn,
which he certainly does not want. The way out of
the difficulty is usually found in the terms of the
bargain, which is to deliver so many quarters of
corn which is to weigh up to 63 lbs. The plan
which is common in many parts of the eastern
counties is to weigh the first bushel of corn, and,
having ascertained the number of pounds, to trans-
late the bargain into terms of weight, and deliver, not so many quarters, but so many hundredweight. In this case the bushel measure is used
merely as a shovel, and the grain is rapidly shovelled
into the sack. The result is, of course, that a larger
measure than was bargained for is delivered, while
the weight remains constant. This is the system
known as sale by "measure and weight." Under
certain circumstances it may suit the miller or dealer
very well—he gets more than he bargained for, but it
is not always the case. The lighter weight of the
grain—some 3 per cent. in the case we have assumed
—may take away from its value as much as 5 per
cent., and the greater the falling off from the standard, the greater would be the consequent loss of
value; for it is admitted that if texture, colour, and
other properties are the same or not very different,

heavier grain is worth more than lighter. It may be, however, that he does not wish for a large amount of corn the weight of which is perhaps affected by its moisture. He has bought it for a definite purpose, and it will not suit his mixture. In this case two courses are open. He may repudiate his bargain and return the corn on the farmer's hands—a course naturally seldom adopted unless the bulk is much below the weight guaranteed in the contract—or he may demand a reduction in the price.

Here is a case described by a witness before the Corn Sales Committee of 1893.[1] He says: "There is just one case that came under my observation. There were 48 bags of wheat sold to a customer, and the natural weight was stated to be 59 lbs. per bushel. The buyer said he wished the wheat weighed up to 63 lbs. into four-bushel quantities. That is our standard. This dealer sold the grain to another dealer, and when the grain arrived at its destination he wired the first merchant he had bought it from that the wheat turned out only 55 lbs. the natural weight, while it weighed 63 lbs. per sack. The aggregate weight was right enough according to the second buyer, and the weight per bushel was 4 lbs. lighter than the seller said he had put on. Consequently the first buyer wired the seller that the wheat was

[1] Reply 2099.

lying at Dundee at his risk, and would not be taken delivery of. At the same time the first buyer sent his own man to Dundee to investigate the matter, and he turned it over and weighed several bushels of it, and found out the average weight, as the first buyer had said, to be 59½ lbs. per bushel." The result in this case was fortunate, but cases must occur in which a mistake has been made, and some arrangement must be agreed upon. Everything in that case depends on the standing of the dealer, and the relations that exist between him and the farmer. Probably as a rule the settlement is made amicably, but it is unlikely that it tends in the long run to increase the farmer's profit.

There now remain the cases in which grain is sold simply by measure or simply by weight. The first of these will be found to resolve themselves into cases where, as in Kent, the practice of selling by weight is making headway but slowly, or a few cases where abnormal and local measures are used, or in certain instances where the very best and the very worst grain is sold. The places in which weight alone is used belong mostly to the latter category, of which the sale of barley in certain counties forms a striking example. It is generally known that the barley that is put on the market is broadly divided into two classes—the malting barley, which often sells at a higher price than wheat, and grinding barley, which is frequently cheaper than oats. The latter class is sold by weight, as the question of quality does not come into the calculation at all. On the other hand, malting barley, the best of which is grown in Norfolk, is usually sold by measure, and without reference to weight. There are many parts of England where such barley is sold by weighed measure, but such barley, being generally thick-skinned and rather coarse, is not used for the best beers. Norfolk barley, on the other hand, which is eagerly bought by the " Burton " brewers, and maltsters of high reputation, is thin-skinned and light, and its quality depends on these attributes. Not only therefore do buyers of this barley never ask what the weight is, but the lighter qualities actually sell at a higher price than the heavy ones, owing to their colour being better as a rule. So firmly attached are the Norfolk farmers to the system of selling by measure, that they have strenuously opposed all proposals to introduce the practice of selling by weight in any form. The argument adduced against the change is that the dealers would compel the farmers to bring their barley up to a certain weight, as they do their wheat. This would mean that they would have to deliver a greater amount, when, as is usually the case, the grain is below the stipulated weight.

Reference has already been made to the number of different ways of selling wheat in England, but this does not mean that a different terminology is used in each case, though the use of local expressions gives an appearance of complication which is possibly not justified. Wheat in the Midlands is sold by the bag, generally of 186 lbs. In Cumberland the Carlisle bushel, equalling 3 imperial bushels, is used. The eastern counties reckon by the coomb of 4 bushels, or 18 stone, while in parts of Lancashire the windle of 220 lbs. is customary. In Lincolnshire it is weighed by the sack of 18 stone, that is 252 lbs.; in Newcastle by the boll of 27 stone. The men of Flint sell by the hobbet of 168 lbs. These variations, though they are troublesome to a visitor, are probably found convenient in the districts where they are used for the reason that in many cases the unit represents approximately what a strong man can carry on his shoulders, and it is therefore more suitable for calculation than the bushel, which is too little, or the quarter, which is too much.

In Liverpool, where little, if any, English wheat is sold, though a great trade is done in American wheat, a curious arrangement is in force. Wheat has been for some years past sold there by the cental of 100 lbs. The system has been enthusiastically supported by the merchants of that city, but it has not spread to any important market outside Lancashire. It was tried at Mark Lane and abandoned. Why it is so popular at Liverpool it is not easy to see, as neither Russian nor American wheat is bought by that weight there, and wheat is not so sold in any other market in England.[1] Railway rates are made out by the hundredweight and not by the cental, and though it is no doubt easy to make calculations by decimals, yet as people do not usually buy odd quantities of grain, it cannot be of much assistance in that respect. To be able to reckon rapidly in percentages is, no doubt, a great advantage in paper transactions that lend themselves so readily to gambling. But that, of course, cannot be the reason why it is so popular.

There remains, finally, the determination of price to be considered. By this is not meant the method by which the amount that is offered and accepted by two bargainers for any particular sample in the market is settled. That is arranged according to the opinions of the two parties as to the quality of the grain offered. But as the prices in one place are in the main dependent on the prices ruling in other quarters, it is of first importance to know what rates are current throughout the kingdom ; and of course the only way of doing this, unless the trader is in possession of special information, is through the state-

[1] Corn Sales Committee 1893, Replies 549-51.

ments in the public press.   These are of two kinds—
the unofficial, collected by the trade papers, and the
official, published in the *London Gazette*.   The first of
these takes usually a general form : prices are quoted
as ranging from so much to so much per quarter
or per local measure or weight, and in most cases
some description of the state of trade is added.   The
market is said to have been quiet, or steady, or,
perhaps, firmer.   Occasionally comment is made that
better prices ruled for best samples, other sorts
neglected, or some such descriptive account is given.
Sometimes a little more distinctiveness is given by
quoting the weights of the grain sold as well as the
prices, the test thus afforded being of great assistance
to habitual traders.   Thus the quotations in Edinburgh market give the number of quarters of wheat
sold at each weight and the prices at which they
parted hands.   The wheat in this case is " graded "
after a fashion, and though not absolutely satisfactory
the system gives no small amount of information to
the student of prices.   The agricultural papers which
devote pages to notices of this kind every week take
a good deal of trouble to get trustworthy intelligence
through their special correspondents, who are frequently men of considerable standing and absolute
integrity.   The details which are supplied are possibly
sufficient for the wants of business men trading under

E

the conditions and according to the ways that prevail in this country. They are, however, perplexing to the members of the general public, and too vague to be made the basis of a calculation.

The official figures that are published weekly are, however, clear and definite, and apparently readily understood by everyone. They are therefore generally employed in making computations about the price of English grain, and although the returns are only taken from English markets, it is commonly assumed that they represent the true prices all over the United Kingdom. The inspector of corn returns to whom, as has already been said, all sales of corn in certain towns are bound by law to be reported, prepares from the data sent in to him the true average by dividing the aggregate values by the total quantity of grain. From this an average for the whole kingdom is made out by dividing the sum of the prices thus obtained by the number of the places making returns. Thus we learn that the average price of wheat in, say, Norwich market in one week was 29s. 6d., and that the average for the kingdom was 29s. These figures, which are adequate for the purpose for which they are obtained—the determination of the tithe averages—are exceedingly useful as a basis of economic and statistical study, but are misleading if employed improperly. To begin with, people are tempted to overlook all variations of quality, and assume that because the average has fallen for the week that the price of all wheat has fallen, though the demand for high-class grain may have gone up, and the market been well supplied with wheat of a lower standard, the sale of which has brought the average down. Thus we find that the average frequently rises in July and August, when there are comparatively few sales, and that no doubt of the best grain only, and falls rapidly in September and October, when the wheat of the new harvest, which is perhaps damp and is certainly soft, is offered. Thus we can get no standard of "wheat." In one year the harvest was extremely bad, and the price fell to 17s. 6d. per quarter. A few years afterwards it touched 40s., but it is difficult to believe that the wheat that changed hands at the lower figure was of the same fineness as that which brought such a much better return. Finally, as we know, it is the duty of the inspector to convert all returns made by weight at the rate of 60 lbs. per imperial bushel for wheat. Now it was found to be customary in 75 per cent. of the markets to sell wheat at 63 lbs. to the bushel, and though in a large number of cases the weight was "made up" to that amount, there must have been a great many cases in which the wheat actually weighed that, or more. In all these cases, therefore, the quantity returned as sold will be greater, and the price at which it was sold will be lower proportionately. The conversion will make no difference to the two traders, who pay and receive the same sum of money in either case, but the average published for the market will be affected. The misunderstanding that has arisen from the imperfect knowledge of the limitations of this method of collecting prices has caused a good many farmers to make reflections on it. They regard it as valueless because its results do not accord with their own local information, or they draw deductions from it which cannot be sustained.

It has been already mentioned that this system is confined to England and Wales, and that in Scotland there is no uniform official method of ascertaining the average prices of grain. There is, however, a semi-official method which has been practised for nearly three hundred years, known as the striking of "Fiars Prices," the original significance and precise meaning of which are not known. The prices are supposed to have their origin in an attempt to fix the Crown revenue, but they have been used for some time past almost entirely to regulate the stipends of the ministers of religion. The practice of ascertaining these prices has varied from county to county at all times, in spite of an Act of the Court of Session passed in 1723, with the object of securing uniformity and regular procedure. The custom, however, usually is as follows. About a month before the Fiars Court is held, which is in the month of February or March, except in the case of Orkney, where it is held in May, the sheriff clerk sends out schedules to a certain number of witnesses who are thought most likely to be acquainted with the transactions in the county—that is to say, farmers and dealers. Each schedule is ruled in columns to show the different kinds of grain for which prices are required, and they are filled up and returned to the sheriff clerk. When the Court is held the witnesses are summoned, and swear to the accuracy of these returns before the jury, which consists of "fifteen men having knowledge and experience of the prices and trade of victual, whereof not fewer than eight shall be heritors." These men are required to "return their verdict upon the evidence underwritten, or their own proper knowledge concerning the Fiars for the preceding crop." This practice is adopted in every county except Haddington, where no jury is summoned, a different system having being in vogue there since about 1749. The nature of the evidence and the character of the witnesses, however, differs very largely. In some counties, as, for instance, Ayr,

Dumbarton, and Haddington, all the evidence is taken from farmers, while in Perth none but grain merchants are summoned. In the majority of counties, however, a certain number of farmers, grain merchants, millers, brewers, distillers, etc., are called before the Court.[1]

There are two important circumstances which must be borne in mind before the prices which are thus ascertained can be accepted as truly representative of the prices of the grain harvested in Scotland in any given year. In the first place it has long been the custom only to tender evidence as to the sale of grain since the first of November preceding the Court day. Although the greater part of the barley grown in Great Britain, and in Scotland perhaps even more than in England, is sold between the beginning of November and the end of March, it cannot be denied that a good deal is sold at other times, and that perhaps of a high quality. It is certainly so in the case of oats. A comparison of the estimated quantity of wheat, barley, and oats grown in each county with the amount returned at the Fiars Courts shows that only 9 per cent. of the wheat and oats and about 30 per cent. of the barley is accounted for, and though it is of course true that a fairly accurate average may be ascertained without

[1] Report of Departmental Committee on Scottish Prices, p. 7.

taking the whole produce sold, there are many cases where the quantities are so small as to preclude all probability of a satisfactory result. Indeed, Mr. Nenion Elliot, the Clerk of Teinds, in his pamphlet, *The Position of Fiars Prices*, goes so far as to say : " Fiars prices might now quite well be dispensed with. They are, in fact, no longer required for the purpose for which the Court of Session originally intended to make provision. As a statement of prices which have been current during any one year the Fiars are of no value. They are not the prices which have been current, neither are they, taking one county with another, to be relied on as the proportionate values for each county, because each county deals with its Fiars prices in its own manner."

Even, however, if it were not for these difficulties the prices could not be compared with the figures collected according to the English method, on account of the divergence in the weights and measures in use in the two kingdoms. Southern prices, it will be remembered, when quoted by any other standard than the imperial bushel, are adjusted so as to make wheat, barley, and oats weigh 60, 50, and 39 lbs. per bushel respectively. In Scotland, however, a different standard prevails. Thus we are informed:[1] " It is no

[1] Evidence taken by Departmental Committee on Scottish Prices, Reply 319.

longer possible to strike the Fiars as they were in 1723, and ought still, theoretically, to be struck. In Forfarshire, at any rate, no grain is sold at the natural weight—that is to say, the grain is no longer sold by quantity but by weight. A standard weight per bushel has been adopted, which is now 56 lbs. for barley and 42 lbs. for oats, and what is sold is not a bushel, but a parcel called a bushel, which is in reality a weight of 56 lbs. or 42 lbs., as the case may be. If, then, the farmer's barley naturally weighs 54 lbs. per bushel, he has to throw in 2 lbs. extra to make up the weight. Now in the county of Forfar, except in extraordinary seasons, neither barley nor oats reach the standard, and every farmer has what is termed to ' weigh up.'" But even in this case some result might be achieved if the standard were kept the same ; but it does not appear that this is so. According to another witness, the standard was at one time 52 lbs. for barley, then 53 lbs., and then 54 lbs. For the two or three preceding years it had been 56 lbs., so that there is no certainty that the bushel has the same value from one year to another. It is, however, in every case, some 3 to 6 lbs. heavier than the bushel as calculated according to the Corn Returns Act.

We must now pass to the discussion of hops, a plant which holds a most important position in the husbandry of some parts of England, though it is not of the same universal interest as wheat or the other cereal crops. Its cultivation is carried on under very different conditions to that of corn. Wheat is seldom sown successfully year after year on the same field, and on most arable farms it is customary to change the course the next year. Hops, on the other hand, give no return the first year, but when once planted a hop garden remains under the same cultivation for years together. There are, indeed, certain spots in Kent where hops have been grown continuously for eighty years' running and more. Wheat is not only of general demand, but can be utilised for stock feeding as well as for human consumption. Hops are useful to no trader except those connected with brewing. It must, however, be remembered that though we could find substitutes for wheaten bread, the greatest ingenuity of man has been unable as yet to find any product which will take the place of hops in the preparation of beer. The services which this plant renders are fourfold: " first, to precipitate or render insoluble certain nitrogenous ingredients of the wort; secondly, to preserve the beer by preventing a renewal of fermentation during the time before it is fit for consumption; thirdly, to give it the bitter taste to which the public have become accustomed; fourthly, to give it a delicate aroma."[1] The quality of the hop, and consequently its value in the market, depends upon the extent to which it excels in the two latter categories.

There are said to be one hundred and sixty varieties of the plant in the world, but the number grown in England is small. They are known by names which recall the original discoverers, or the improvers of the variety, but which do not convey much to the ordinary citizen. It is, however, admitted that the Golding hop, with its bright, straw-coloured, filbert-shaped cones, is the best, and is succeeded by the Bramling and the Fuggles. Other sorts are known as Colegates, Grapes, Jones, Meophams, and have qualities which caused them to be extensively planted at one time. An early crop, a prolific yield, a power of resisting disease, recommended these and other sorts in former days when the demand for a high quality was not so important, and when science was less developed. But they are nearly all now superseded. Continuously with the disappearance of the commoner varieties the area of cultivation has decreased. Thirty years ago hops were grown in Scotland and Wales, as well as in many counties in England, from which they have long since vanished. The last acre was grubbed in Scotland in 1871, while Wales ceased to rear them in 1874. But as recently

[1] Report of Select Committee on Hop Industry, p. 6.

as 1884 they were to be found in Berkshire, Essex, Herts, Notts, and the East Riding of Yorkshire. The fall in prices and the foreign competition have been potent factors in causing the farmers of these counties to abandon this form of husbandry, but the most important cause has been the great change which has taken place in modern brewing. The year 1882 produced an exceedingly short crop. The average price for English hops was £21 2s. per cwt., nearly three times that of the average of the years 1865 to 1884,[1] which was £8 0s. 10d. This induced brewers to turn their attention more closely to the chemistry of their manufacture. By the use of ice it was found to be possible to brew all the year round, and it was no longer necessary to keep large stocks of beer for many months. The right proportion of hops to malt was accurately determined, and as the taste of the public for a lighter and brighter beer increased it was found possible to dispense with a large proportion of the hops that had been at one time used. The inferior grades were driven out of the market, and it became profitable to grow the better qualities only. The cultivation of hops is now principally confined to six counties in England—Kent, Surrey, Sussex, Hampshire, Worcestershire, Herefordshire—though in 1902 there were 46 acres in Glouces-

[1] Select Committee on Hop Industry, Appendix iii.

tershire, 125 in Shropshire, and 4 in Suffolk devoted to that plant. But though the number of counties in Great Britain has diminished, the number of acres in the chief counties has not fallen in a like degree. There were still in 1902 nearly 30,000 acres of hops in Kent, and though that is a great falling off from the area so cultivated thirty years ago, the district in Herefordshire and Worcestershire is considerably greater than it was in those days. Kent, however, which for hop purposes is divided into three districts, the East, Mid, and the Weald, still ranks as the premier county, not only in extent of acreage, but in excellence of quality. It is said that the finest Goldings can only be grown in East and Mid Kent, and even the latter district cannot grow such perfect specimens as those of its neighbour. These fetch the highest price in the market, and if harvested in good condition are preferred to the produce of the finest hop gardens of Bavaria or California.

For a description of the method of planting and gathering hops the reader is referred to the many text-books on the subject of practical agriculture. As is well known, they are picked in the early autumn, and after being dried in the " oasts " or kilns, are packed and despatched to market. " In no branch of hop management," says Mr. Charles Whitehead in his article in the *Royal Agricultural Society's Journal*,

entitled "Fifty Years of Hop Farming," "have such
radical alterations been made as in packing. Hops
were in old times put into bags and pockets. The
former were 7 feet 6 inches long, and 4 feet wide, of
material nearly an inch in thickness, made of hemp,
hay, and tow woven together. About 2 cwt. were put
into these, especially brown, diseased, and inferior
qualities. 'Brown bags' formed the tail end of most
growths. Pockets are now alone used; they are
between 6 and 7 feet long, and 3 feet wide, holding
1½ cwt., and being made of coarse canvas. Planters
are particular to get bright, heavy qualities of
'pocketing' to preserve the hops, and that the pockets
may look well." After the pockets have been filled
they have to be marked. This law, which dates
back to the days when there was a duty on hops,
requires each pocket to be stamped with the name of
the grower, the parish in which they were grown, and
the year,[1] the weight,[2] and the number of the growth,
that is from 1 to 100, or whatever the number of the
pockets may be. The effect of this system of mark-
ing on the prices realised by the produce is remarkable. According to several witnesses before the
Select Committee on Hop Industry, the pockets
marked with the name of an East Kent parish will

---

[1] Select Committee on Hop Industry, Reply 4694.

[2] *Ibid.*, Reply 2508.

fetch several shillings, and according to one member of the Committee, who "knew to his cost," 20 or 30 per cent. more than the same kind of hop grown in the immediate vicinity in Mid Kent.[1] While according to another witness the simple brewer buying pockets marked East or Mid Kent assumes he is getting Goldings or hops of a good character, "whereas you will very often find that there is a number of wild hops which are not Goldings at all, and you will often find Henhams—a fraudulent hop having no qualities common to the real hop in it. That hop is merely grown for quantity and appearance. It is worth 80s. per cwt. to-day in the market, whereas to the brewer it is worth nothing."[2] It is presumed that the speakers in this instance refer to the cases in which the producer has attempted to negotiate direct with the brewer, a proceeding which has at no time been very common, but which is coming more into vogue in modern times. The usual method of selling hops is conducted on a more elaborate principle.

In former times hops were very commonly sold at the great annual fairs, among which the Weyhill Fair took a leading position. "Hops from the Hants and Surrey plantations were taken and pitched there

[1] Select Committee on Hop Industry, Question 477.

[2] *Ibid.*, Replies 4693–5.

for sale in whole growths. Some thousands of pockets were sent to this fair in good seasons. The hop fair was divided into the 'Farnham Row,' for the hops produced in the celebrated Farnham district, and the 'Country Row,' for Hants hops and those grown in other parts of Surrey. More recently the planters have sent the ordinary samples of their growths, or sample pockets. The business done in hops at Wey-hill Fair is now, comparatively speaking, very small. The greater part of the hops, at least from Kent, Sussex, Surrey, and Hants, is consigned for sale to the Borough, the great hop emporium of the world. There was a hop fair at Maidstone and other Kentish towns, where hops were sold by sample; also at Robertsbridge, in Sussex. These now exist only in name, no hops are sold there."[1] The method of selling hops in the open market is, however, still practised in the west. There is a special building in Worcester, where the hops of Herefordshire, Worcestershire, and Gloucestershire are sold. The hops are carefully weighed, and tested either in the market or the warehouse; but in this district they are as a rule sold by the owners direct to the hop merchants, who store them and sell them according to demand to the brewers. A few, however, are sold according to the Kentish method, that is, through

[1] "Fifty Years of Hop Farming," by Charles Whitehead.

factors, a system which is so remarkable that it deserves a lengthy study.

We have already seen that it is customary in Kent for some farmers to sell their corn through agents. If this method is advantageous in the case of wheat, which can without serious loss be kept by the farmer, it is not surprising that it is yet more frequently adopted in the case of hops, which are liable to deteriorate in the damp and uncertain atmosphere of England. Pockets kept in store-rooms or other buildings on farms develop a crust of mould, which gradually eats into the bulk and takes away from its value. In order to avoid this loss planters usually send their produce directly it is picked to the store-houses of the factors in the Borough, where specially built houses are maintained in which risk from deteriorating is avoided. The whole growth is, or was till recently, so consigned, and in former days the planter sent his produce regularly to the same factor year after year. Not infrequently, and in bad years, the factor made advances of money to the producer, and, by thus financing him, and using his skill to secure the best prices for him, ensured keeping his customer. The factor, however, did not sell direct to the brewer, but to another intermediary—the merchant. This trader, however, bought the crop, whereas the factor, who was only an agent, sold on commission. Thus between the grower and the brewer there were two parties who were supposed to act in the interests of their clients, the chief difference being that a brewer was able to deal with another merchant if he did not feel satisfied with the offers that the first made him. This system has grown up from the necessities of the trade. The sampling of hops is a delicate operation requiring great care and nicety,[1] and is no doubt a matter of great importance. Many considerations enter into the determination of the quality of a good sample. The purchaser must know the colour, the thickness and quantity of seed, the condition and state of maturity at the time of picking. The cones should be whole, and the lupulin or gold dust should adhere to the bracts. The peculiar smell of the hop should not be tainted, and the sample should be elastic under pressure.[2] But the chief feature is the "rub." Hops, when they have been examined in other respects, are tested by being rubbed on the hand. From their smell, and from the nature of the resinous deposit that is left on the fingers, the quality is decided. It is not surprising that so delicate a test has called forth a set of experts, in whose hands the

---

[1] "Hop Cultivation," by Charles Whitehead, *Royal Agricultural Society's Journal*, 1893, vol. iv., third series.

[2] *Ibid.*

business rests. The prices, moreover, of hops vary immensely from year to year, though they are steadier now than they used to be. A factor, therefore, who is able to advise his client as to the probable course of the market and tell him the moment when to sell may be of great service to him, and secure for him a profit not only greater than the grower would obtain for himself, but far in excess of the charges and commissions that are deducted. On the other hand, the system seems to have outgrown its usefulness. The hop market is now highly organised, and the course of business and prices are to be learnt through trade circulars and newspapers. The anxiety to sell leads the planters to press their factors, and the trade suffers from the desire to speculate and the fear of foreign competition. The farmers are isolated and almost without combination in matters of selling. They do not see the purchaser of their hops, nor do they know where their produce ultimately goes to. The grading is done by the merchants, who secure the ensuing advantages, while the value of the consignment is not even known by the farmer when he sends it to the factor. Mr. Charles Whitehead, whose writings on the hop industry are well known, declares that the present system is essentially wrong,[1]

[1] "Fifty Years of Hop Farming," *Royal Agricultural Society's Journal*, 1890, vol. i , third series.

and though he has a long list of improvements to chronicle in the cultivation and management of hops in the fifty years from 1840-1890, at which date the pamphlet already quoted was written, he is obliged to say that not very much alteration has taken place with regard to the method of selling them. His final judgment is thus expressed : " Unfortunately, in almost all instances, farmers are mulcted, directly and indirectly, by the charges and intermediary profits of middlemen in the disposal of their produce. Hop-growers are worse off than any other producers under the sun in this respect. The modern sale of hops is costly, antiquated, and one of the reasons why hop-growing in England is in a depressed condition."

In addition to the crops already referred to, there are a large number of other vegetable products which are consumed by the inhabitants of this country either raw, cooked, or preserved. Potatoes form an article of diet in every household, from the highest to the lowest. Other kinds of vegetables appear in their seasons on the tables of all but the very poorest, while fruit is grown and sold in such plenty that few even of the dwellers in the heart of the biggest towns are altogether unable to enjoy it. In addition to this, many thousand tons of hay and straw are annually produced for the food of animals. In certain districts special crops of chicory, mustard, and herbs are gathered, and every market in the kingdom has its exhibits of flowers, cultivated and wild, which are plucked in the country for the pleasure and adornment of the towns. These may be sent in large consignments or in small quantities. They may be sent to special markets, as in the case of hay and potatoes, or to general markets, as in the case of fruit and flowers ; but they are for all practical purposes sold by the same method and under the same conditions. It will be better, therefore, for present purposes to treat them all under the one head, making such allowances for individual cases as may be necessary.

The quantity and value of these vegetable products are very great. According to the agricultural statistics, in 1902 there were over 400,000 acres planted with potatoes in England alone, 31,000 in Wales, and nearly 130,000 in Scotland. There were 2,000,000 acres under roots, cabbages, rape, vetches, and other such crops in England, 80,000 in Wales, and nearly 500,000 in Scotland. All these are cultivated by persons occupying over one acre. But it is quite impossible to estimate the amount of land cultivated in small areas, with these or other vegetables, or to form any opinion of the annual value of their produce, owing to the immense number of allotments, gardens, and patches tilled by artisans and labourers who do not belong to the agricultural classes, and who make no return to the yearly agricultural census. A large part of the fruits of these small fields, however, is sent to market, and competes with the produce of the farmer ; and even when it is not sold, but is consumed by the grower and his family, it reduces the demand which the farmer has to meet. There are nearly 6,000,000 acres of land in England mown for hay, nearly 700,000 in Wales, and nearly 550,000 in Scotland ; and as very little hay is grown on allotments, this probably represents the whole produce of Great Britain, though there are over 14,500,000 acres under grass, which is not destined for that purpose. Great as the produce of all this area must be, it is insufficient to meet the requirements of the nation. A reference to the agricultural statistics shows that 357,000 tons of hay were imported in 1902, though it is fair to say that this is greatly in excess of the imports of the previous four years. There were 5,700,000 cwts. of potatoes, of which, however, a million and a half came from the Channel Islands, while 7,600,000 bushels of onions, 780,000 cwts. of tomatoes, and immense quantities of apples, pears, cherries, strawberries, currants, plums, and gooseberries found their way into these islands.

On the other hand, every visitor to the country knows that great quantities of English fruit and vegetables are wasted, given to the pigs or not gathered because of the difficulty of getting them sold, or on account of the unremunerative prices obtained for them in the market. I have been told by the cultivator of a small parcel of ground by an important railway junction in the West Riding of Yorkshire that, being quite unable to get any price for the turnips he had grown, he had been forced to cut them up and use them as manure. Stories were common some years ago of the bushels of plums that were allowed to fall from the trees because they did not pay to gather and send to market. While one of the leading firms of English grocers has pointed out that in 1893, when many apples were wasted because there was no sale for them, the price of evaporated apples imported from America was from 45*s.* to 50*s.* per cwt. in consequence of a short apple crop in America.[1] "One of the greatest obstacles," says Mr. Riger Haggard,[2] "with which the little farmer, the small holder, and, indeed, all agriculturists have to contend is the impossibility of delivering their produce in markets that are eager for it, because of the overwhelming difficulties of collection and delivery, and the overwhelming charges of its transport. The other day, in my own garden, I saw some hundreds of particularly fine Cos lettuces which

[1] *Journal Board of Agriculture*, 1895, p. 267.
[2] *Rural England*, vol. ii. p. 557.

were beginning to bolt, that is, go to seed. I told the gardener he had better sell them, to which he replied that there was no local market, and that they would not pay to send away by train. . . . This, of course, is but one very insignificant instance out of thousands, since the case applies to every sort of agricultural produce that is grown in small quantities, and more especially to fruit." Perhaps after this it will not be thought extravagant to say that on the proper organisation of the sale of fruit and vegetables the success of that form of agriculture depends.

Although it may occasionally happen that an enterprising grower may discover fresh openings for his produce, there are practically three ways in which articles of the kind just referred to are usually disposed of commercially. Fresh fruit and vegetables are either consigned to a salesman in one of the wholesale markets in the large towns, or they are vended in small quantities in the retail markets that exist in most urban centres ; while considerable quantities, that are destined for preserving, are bought direct by the great jam and pickle makers throughout the kingdom.

The business of selling in the retail markets, which are widely distributed throughout the kingdom, is very similar, whether the produce is part of those minor vegetable or animal articles which figure so prominently on the table, and it will be convenient to postpone the examination of the advantages and disadvantages of this system to a later place in this book.   It is proposed at this point merely to notice the two methods of dealing with merchants or manufacturers capable of taking large quantities.   Transactions between farmers and the great firms of seed merchants, jam and pickle makers, are not usually carried out in the open market, but by private contract, and the arrangements may be made before the produce is ready for sale or at the moment of harvest. There are some farmers who undertake to grow certain seeds for the merchants, who, in addition to the business done at home, export a considerable quantity every year.   In the case of apples another plan is sometimes adopted.   In recent years the cider industry in the West of England has undergone great development.   The best qualities of this beverage are no longer made in the farmer's own homestead, where the conveniences for its preparation are few, but in well-equipped factories using the latest appliances and the most recent scientific discoveries. The cider-maker is unable to grow all the requisite apples himself, the more so as several kinds of trees are cultivated for the purpose, each having its special qualities.   It is customary, therefore, for the brewer to enter into engagements with certain farmers, and to visit their orchards just before the fruit is ripe, for the purpose of buying the apple harvest while it is yet on the trees. It is not infrequent for whole growths to be purchased in this way, the fruit being picked and sent to the factory subsequently.

Another industry that has developed in recent years is jam and pickle making. Some of the best-known makers have fruit farms of their own, but there are others who buy great quantities from English growers. The best fruit is generally picked and sent to market, and it is only when the season is well advanced and the price for ripe fruit has fallen, or the quality begins to be such that it is no longer attractive on the table, that the remainder of the crop is sold to the confectioner or jam-maker. The vegetables that are grown for pickling have, however, no sale as fresh fruit. They are usually cultivated for a special purpose, such as the silverskin onions, which are grown in the district near Biggleswade, in Bedfordshire, for pickling by the London manufacturers.

By far the greater part of the fruit and vegetables that are sold wholesale passes through the hands of the salesman or merchant on its way to the shopkeeper and the small dealer, who sell it to the consumer. Hay, straw, and potatoes are treated in the same way, though allowance must necessarily be made for the uses to which the produce is to be put. The markets in which these traders carry on their business are of three kinds. Hay and straw are sold in markets specially devoted to that purpose; potatoes are of sufficient importance to have a place of sale of their own ; fruit and vegetables are commonly sold at the same place and time. Except in the retail markets the three classes are seldom found in combination. In theory the salesman is an agent acting between seller and buyer, selling solely on commission, which varies with the price he is able to get for his client. The merchant is a dealer who buys the produce outright from the farmer or producer, and takes, of course, all the profit he is able to make out of such a transaction. It frequently happens that the two occupations are combined by one person, with all the attendant advantages that such a union gives ; but it is not so common for one of these dealers to undertake business outside the class of produce in which he is accustomed to trade. He will, however, deal in foreign as well as home-grown goods, although there may be many points of difference in the way the business is carried on.

We will begin with the sale of hay, which is not a subject that is brought frequently before the public eye, and seldom takes any prominent part in the discussions on agricultural economics that from time to time appear in the public press. It is, of course, mostly carried on by a special class of farmers, and the buyers are generally horsekeepers, cab, tram, and omnibus proprietors. The ordinary householder rarely visits the market. As a rule the course of business follows the usual lines of the large wholesale markets without much variation. There is, however, an exception in the case of the Whitechapel hay market. This market, which is of old foundation, was a flourishing place of business in the eighteenth century, when the wilderness of houses that now form East London had not yet been built, and it shared with Smithfield market the whole trade of the metropolis after the hay market near St. James's waned in importance. At the present time passengers through Whitechapel are sometimes astonished to see the broad street, which, however, is scarcely capable of accommodating the ordinary traffic, packed with hay carts from end to end, to the great disturbance of all other kinds of business. It is a piece of country life suddenly appearing in the thronged streets of London.

The peculiarity of this market consists in the fact that its transactions are strictly regulated by statute. The Act of 1796 (amended by a later Act of 1851) relates in its preamble that many and great abuses are committed by salesmen and other persons selling hay and straw in the city of London and adjoining places. It prescribes, therefore, that all hay and straw shall be made up and sold in bundles or trusses, which are to weigh in the case of new hay 60 lbs., old hay 56 lbs., and in the case of straw 36 lbs.; while every load of hay or straw is to contain 36 trusses. The bands with which they are bound are not to exceed 5 lbs. A register is ordered to be kept, in which every sale of hay or straw is to be entered, together with the names of the seller, the salesman, and the buyer, and the true price at which the bargain was made. This register is to be open to general inspection on payment of the fee of one penny. Penalties are imposed on fraudulent dealing, including the offence of buying to sell again in the same market, and failing to bring into the market on the ensuing market-day hay or straw exposed on any occasion but not sold, or bought for sale between two market-days and lodged in the neighbourhood. The hours of the market are notified by the ringing of a bell, and no produce may be sold after the prescribed hours. Furthermore, no common salesman, factor, or agent may buy or sell on his own account, or of any person or persons in trust for him, any hay or straw whatsoever; while he is bound, within seven days, to deliver to the vendor a "just and true account under his hand of the place where, time when, and the price for which the same was sold, and also the name and place of the purchasers thereof." This statement is made on what is known as the "home note," which is delivered to the seller's carman, and is supposed to contain an account of the salesman's charges. It appears, however, from the reports of a legal case that was tried in the High Courts some years ago, that much of this had fallen into abeyance, and that another system has gradually taken the place of the statutory method. The salesmen who frequent the market, following a practice customary elsewhere, became merchants of hay, and invited large consumers, such as railway companies, vestries, and carrying contractors, to enter into an agreement with them for the supply of hay at a certain price for periods of six months or more.

They then took the hay which was consigned to them as salesmen, and sold it in their capacity as merchants to the other contracting parties, crediting the farmer with "the price of the day," a figure which is arrived at by a calculation based on the average of all the sales. It was asserted that this plan was advantageous not only to the merchant but to the farmer, for it enabled him to make sure of selling his goods, whereas if he had to depend on finding a purchaser each market day he might find himself in a slack season compelled to hold his hay over till the next market at, of course, considerable expense.

Whitechapel market is in no very prosperous condition, and the business of selling hay has perhaps outgrown the bounds set by the Act of 1796, just as the demands of housekeepers in London have far exceeded the capacities of the market-place. When the Act was passed all hay was brought in by cart, whereas nowadays the greater part is sent by railway. It was asserted on the occasion of the trial already referred to that the market was in the hands of three salesmen, and whether this was accurate or not, it is clear that many transactions must take place outside the market. Much of the hay consigned to London is sold in the railway yards, and a great deal of what is sold at the market is only a sample, the bulk being delivered by the farmer or contractor direct to the purchaser, much in the same way that has already been described in the case of corn. Whether the system of selling hay and straw as required by law in these markets of London is to the advantage of the farmer or not is, of course, a matter of dispute. The size of the bundles or trusses is convenient for carrying, and the method of conducting the business is simple, even if stereotyped. But it must be remembered that a good deal of foreign hay and straw that is sent in years of drought to England is packed in a different manner and subject to no restrictions, and that an inelastic system is liable to prove a burden when in competition with a method that can be adapted to circumstances.

The sale of potatoes in large quantities is of comparatively recent growth, and the markets which are devoted to that purpose are usually quite new. Potatoes, moreover, are a bulky commodity, and do not depend on their appearance for their price so much as other kinds of vegetables and fruit. They are therefore sold in markets near railway stations, often in the stations themselves, and where they are sold in the central market, it is more often than not that a sample only is exhibited, the bulk being consigned either from the farm or the depôt. They are usually sold by weight, but in the case of new potatoes they are taken by the acre occasionally, in much the same way as fruit. With fruit and vegetables of other kinds the case is very different, the utmost importance being attached not only to the fresh, attractive appearance of the individual articles that make up the consignment, but also to the neatness and artistic effect of the way in which they are presented for inspection. For this reason skill and care in packing and growing fruit for market is of the highest importance. A publication of the Board

of Agriculture and Fisheries on the subject begins
with these words :—

" Intensive cultivation has been carried in many
places to a high pitch of excellence, and British
horticulturists pride themselves, justly, upon their
skill as producers. Admirable and necessary as the
highest cultivation must always be, yet something
more is required to ensure complete commercial
success, namely, the conveyance of the produce in
the best possible style to the market or to the
consumer. It is at this point too many fail, and a
material proportion of unprofitable sales is mainly
attributable to neglect in presenting goods in the
most satisfactory manner. Proofs of this defect are
evident in every British market, and commonly the
produce of the home grower may be seen in direct
contrast with that of his foreign competitors, to the
conspicuous disadvantage of the former."

As a general rule, producers of fruit simply despatch it to the various markets, where it is sold for
their account. It has been largely the habit in Kent
for proprietors to sell their crops at auctions, but a
large number of them are giving that up now, and
are marketing their own fruit ; instead of selling their
fruit to the little dealer they are distributing it all
over the country and selling it in the various markets.

Let us therefore return to the traders in the

market, taking Covent Garden as the best example we can find. A large amount of foreign stuff is sold there as well as English, but the foreign is usually sold by auction, while the English is generally the subject of negotiation by private treaty. This is probably due to the smallness of the market-place and the necessity for clearing it rapidly in the case of the foreign goods which are all sent into the market. The English is often only a sample. Of the two kinds of traders there is no doubt that the merchants are the more prosperous. It is customary with them to go down into the country and buy up whole fields of fruit and vegetables, and whole orchards of fruit, and have such quantities consigned to them as they require. Strawberries are often dealt with in this way ; pears, plums, and damsons follow when the soft fruit is over, and apples are purchased after the others are gathered. Some merchants travel round from farm to farm picking up small quantities, and making their profits out of the reduced railway rates they are able to get when they send the whole of their purchases to London. Such a system may suit the small farmer, but the large important growers naturally wish to get all the profit on their produce, and in their case the fruit and vegetables are consigned to the salesmen, who dispose of them to the high-class shopkeepers

G

of the West End, who are able to exact a high price from their customers. The volume of trade that passes through the market in this way, the number of persons who consign their goods to the salesmen, as well as the number of persons who flock there to buy, must be taken as a proof that the system works satisfactorily on the whole, and it is indeed unreasonable to suppose that a trade could exist for very long if it did not in the main meet the wants of the producers and consumers. But the complaints that are made about it are many and bitter. Stories are rife which tell of fruit and vegetables consigned to a salesman in considerable quantities with no better return than a shilling or two of profit, and a bill showing how the saleman's commission, the market charges, and the cost of carriage and handling have swallowed up the remainder of the price. Consignors assert that they are unable to make out how the market charges are calculated while the prices quoted in the daily and trade papers are very different to what they received. The answer given is that, owing to the supplies of fruit from abroad, there is often a scarcity one day and a glut the next; that the changes in the weather have an important effect on the demand for fruit as well as on its keeping qualities; that it is impossible to sell small and irregular consignments as profitably and as easily as large and constant supplies; and, above all, that the inferior packing and insufficient grading of much of the English produce compared with the arrivals from abroad lower the selling price of the home-grown article. As pointed out above, attention has repeatedly been called to this last point, and a most notable example has recently been made public. The silverskin onions consigned from Bedfordshire to the pickling firms in London would not command any sale at all, if they were not carefully graded, and yet in spite of the English farmers' skill the Dutch peasants have succeeded in taking part of their business away. "The organisation of the brining industry in the Netherlands," says Mr. Crawford, in his report on the Dutch brined vegetable industry (page 11), "has enabled the factories, by collecting their supplies of raw onions from a large number of growers, and by the use of improved apparatus, to send to this country large consignments of onions in brine, possessing greater uniformity in size, shape, and colour than it seems possible to obtain by the methods at present adopted at Biggleswade. It is just this uniformity in the bulk which the great pickling firms in this country desire, and for goods possessing it they are prepared to pay a higher price than for produce which is deficient in this respect."

If so much importance is attached to these qualities in a factory, it may readily be supposed that they are yet more requisite in a crowded market where business is rapidly transacted. The most prominent English growers therefore have a mark on their consignments by which their goods are distinguished, and they are in this way able to avoid the ill-effects of the plan which is adopted to clear the market, and which is known by the name of "averaging." All the produce consigned to any salesman is sold, the best at the highest prices of the day, the rest at what it will fetch. At the end of the day the returns are made out, and an average is taken of the prices realised, a rough method by which substantial justice is done from the salesman's point of view, but which injuriously affects the consignor of selected articles. The owners of fruit forwarded under a recognised mark are excepted from this procedure, and get the actual price their goods fetched. It is natural that the determination of the market price is difficult for the consignor, and the producers who have no standard of quality to which they invariably conform in preparing for the market are unable to tell at what price they ought to be remunerated.

A further complication is caused by the remarkable measures used in selling fruit and vegetables in Covent Garden which producers are expected to adopt. The very names are peculiar, and the number of different varieties is great and perplexing. Thus we learn from an article by Mr. W. W. Glenny, in the *Fruit Growers' Year-Book* for 1897, that "vegetables may be gathered and loaded direct on the wagon, cart, van, or barrow; may be secured in bundles with bass or rods, tied in bunches with rods, arranged in hands, packed in loads, flaskets, crates, hampers, pads, sieves, half-sieves, quarter-sieves, flats, molleys, prickles, feys, pottles, punnets, 2-cwt. sacks, 1-cwt. sacks, pea bags, ½-cwt. bags, besides foreign bags of no defined size, and barrels, boxes, trays of innumerable sizes and endless shapes." Of course, none of these are legal measures, and in many cases the words are easily recognised as common technical terms, but in other cases they are expected to imply a given weight or number. Thus, according to the same *Year-Book*, a sea-kale punnet measures 8 in. in diameter at the top and 7½ in. at the bottom, being 2 in. deep, while a radish punnet is 8 in. in diameter and 1 in. deep, if to hold six "hands," or 9 in. by 1 in. for twelve "hands." A mushroom punnet is 7 in. by 1 in., while a salading punnet is 5 in. by 2 in. A sieve contains 7 imperial gallons, while a bushel sieve holds 10½ imperial gallons. After this it is a relief to know that a bushel basket "ought" to contain an imperial bushel, two-thirds of which is contained in a "junk." We next learn that a pottle of strawberries should hold half a gallon, but never holds more than one quart, and that a "hand" of radishes contains from twelve to thirty or more, according to the season. A "bundle" of broccoli, celery, etc., contains 6 to 20 heads, of sea-kale 12 to 18 heads, of rhubarb 20 to 30 stems, according to size, and of asparagus from 100 to 125. A "bunch" of turnips is 12 to 25, of carrots 15 to 40, of greens "as many as can be tied together by the roots"! An imperial hundredweight is, of course, 112 lbs., but a hundredweight of Kentish filberts is 100 lbs.

Provincial markets are less perplexing, as fruit and vegetables are usually sold by imperial weights. But even here terms are used which are not commonly known. At Sheffield vegetables are sold by the bag; at Nottingham fruit is sold by the pot and by the strike, as well as by imperial weights; while at Glasgow the old-fashioned "sleek" or West of Scotland bushel is used, though its meaning has been changed so as to connote a weight, varying according to the class of fruit offered.

Truly, the industry of fruit and vegetable growing is a toilsome and perplexing occupation.

CHAPTER III

TRADITIONAL METHODS
OF MARKETING LIVESTOCK AND THEIR
BY-PRODUCTS

ALTHOUGH the vegetable products of the farm are entitled to the first place in any book on agriculture by right of tradition, the interests involved in the breeding and maintenance of livestock in Great Britain are in reality of more practical importance. Barely one-seventh of the supply of wheat consumed by the nation is grown in these islands, while more than a half of the meat eaten is home bred. In one half of Great Britain the amount of land under grass exceeds the amount of land under the plough, while many of the arable crops are raised solely for feeding cattle and sheep. Under these circumstances it is not surprising that the amount of capital laid out in connection with the livestock industry is far greater than that invested in that branch of farming which is engaged in tillage. A comparison between English and continental agricul-

ture will assist us in trying to appreciate the importance of our flocks and herds to us.

In France, out of a total acreage under crops
and grass amounting to eighty-five million acres,
about thirty-five million acres are devoted to growing
corn crops, of which sixteen million are sown with
wheat and spelt. Nearly four more million are planted
with potatoes, and another four and a half are covered
with vines. Grass meadows, however, only account
for nearly fourteen million. In the United Kingdom
we had in 1902 about eight and a half million acres
under corn crops, and less than two million under
wheat. One and a quarter million were under potatoes,
while twenty-eight million acres were under permanent
pasture, and this though the total cultivated area
with us is about half that of cultivated France. It
is true that the French have about fourteen and a
half million cattle, while we have scarcely eleven and
a half million, but we boast of thirty million sheep to
set off against a little less than twenty million belonging to our neighbours.

Germany has sixty-five million acres under arable
cultivation, thirty-eight of which are under corn
crops, chiefly oats and rye, and there are only some
fourteen and three-quarter million acres under grass
for hay, or, if rough grazings are included, twenty-one
millions. The Germans have not quite nineteen

million cattle, and less than ten million sheep. By
the side of these two great countries our island
appears to be one great cattle ranch and sheep
run. The comparison must not be pressed too far,
of course, or injustice would be done to the agriculturist. The cattle and sheep are not turned loose on
huge plains to be driven hither and thither by cow-
boys. The cattle are often stall fed, or kept in the
fold-yard in winter and in hedged-in meadows of no
great extent in summer, while the sheep are often
folded and fed on roots, and all are carefully tended,
studied, and looked after, even in those districts
where they roam at will on the downs or marshes.
Our cattle and sheep have been brought to a high
state of development, and not only are they, perhaps,
on the average, in a far finer condition than any of the
flocks and herds on the Continent, but they hold a
leading position throughout the world, for, in spite of
the great progress that has been made in the more
distant parts of the globe, it is still to this country
that breeders come when they wish to buy animals
of high quality to improve their breeds. Indeed,
the cattle and sheep that are bred and fattened in
America and Australia are for the most part de-
scended from the stock that is native in our islands.
Our country is, moreover, peculiar in the number
of breeds of cattle and sheep it contains. The

Shorthorn beast is certainly most widely distributed, but the eastern counties have their Red Polls, the western their Devons, their Herefords, and their black Welsh cattle known as Runts. Scotland has its Ayrshires, its Galloways, its Aberdeen Angus or Black Polls, and its Highland cattle, so well known for their shaggy hides and long horns. Ireland produces a breed known as Kerrys, and the Channel Islands have their famous and beautiful breeds of Jersey and Guernsey, commonly called by the uninitiated, for some extraordinary reason, Alderneys. There are other, though less well-known, breeds. All these cattle are chiefly to be found in the localities from which they are named, but they are distributed to other centres. They have their good qualities from a producer's point of view, as in the case of the breeds able to thrive on poor pastures, but for our present purpose we may divide them into two classes, those which are kept for the milk given with special richness or in large quantities by the cows, and those which yield the best and the most beef. Among the former class the Jersey ranks highest, for the cow yields the fattest and creamiest milk, though not the greatest quantity and the beef is barely fit to feed dogs with. Among the latter, perhaps, the Angus or the Hereford is chief, a beast which is scarcely regarded as a milker at all.

Sheep may be divided into three classes, long wools, short wools, and mountain sheep. Among the first class the Lincolns and Leicesters are perhaps the best known. The Downs belong rather to the second category, while the last class includes the black-faced and the Welsh sheep. There are, of course, other well-known breeds.

Sheep are less freely distributed than cattle, the different breeds being for special reasons chiefly confined to their own localities, and the quality of the wool being dependent on the nature of the soil on which they live. In the British Isles they are reared mainly for their flesh, though some of the breeds are more renowned for the wool they bear than for their mutton, which in these cases is rather hard and tasteless.

After cattle and sheep, the next most important place must be given to swine, which must not be omitted or relegated to an unimportant place among livestock of the farm. There are six chief breeds: the large, the middle, and the small white, or Yorkshires, the Black Berkshires, the small Blacks, and the Red Tamworths, though there are many varieties bearing local names, and the purity of certain strains is as carefully maintained as is done with cattle.

The breeding and exhibiting of these animals is a

pursuit in which all classes of the community take a lively interest. There are shows held under the auspices of national or local agricultural societies all over the kingdom, at which, as is well known, royalty is a frequent exhibitor and prize-winner, and in which great and small alike compete. Associations exist for the purpose of fostering and keeping pure almost every breed of cattle, sheep, and swine that has a special name, and the pedigrees of the typical representatives of each breed are recorded in the herd-book or flock-book of the society. The result of this is that the purity and high quality of British cattle are renowned all over the world, and the breeding of pure bred stock for exportation forms part of the business of many a high-class farmer. The number that are sold every year is necessarily not very high, but the value is considerable.

In 1902 the number of native cattle exported from the United Kingdom was 2,428 and the average value was £40 per head, while there were 3,596 native sheep exported of an average value of £8 2s. In each year of the quinquennial period from 1896–1900 3,345 cattle were on an average exported of the value of £34, while the average value of the 8,765 sheep exported was £11 9s. The country which takes the greatest number of these animals is the United States, which in 1902 took 760 cattle, 635 sheep, and 86

swine, though Canada took 574 cattle, 155 sheep, and
103 swine. The Cape took 215 cattle, Sweden 205,
Russia 126 and 151 sheep, while the Argentine took
104 cattle and 327 sheep. The prices paid for some of
these animals are very high : thus the 104 cattle sent
to Argentina in 1902 were valued at an average of £120
apiece, one sent to South Russia figures at £100.
They sometimes reach ten times that figure. The
management of pedigree stock forms therefore an
important department of agriculture, and offers occasionally large prizes to the successful breeder, as there
are numerous sales of animals in which the purchases
are not made for export, but for keeping up and improving the race at home.

There are two methods most commonly in vogue
by which the breeders dispose of their stock. The
first is by direct sale with the purchaser, whose
custom is sought by extensive advertising in the
agricultural newspapers, especially in those devoted
to the livestock industry. The pages of some of
these periodicals are filled with advertisements an-
nouncing that animals of a well-known strain, often
the property of some well-known nobleman or
country gentlemen, are to be had at moderate prices
on application to the manager of the home farm at
such and such a park or castle. Along with these are
found the names of farmers and breeders who, though

in humbler and poorer positions, often succeed in offering a finer animal to the judge at the show or the would-be purchaser. This method, however, is more used in the case of pigs than of other animals. The most usual plan in the case of pedigree cattle and sheep is for the owner to give instructions to some auctioneer to sell either at the farm itself or in the ordinary market, a number, if not all, of the cattle he has in hand. These sales are usually thoroughly advertised in the usual quarters beforehand, and as it not infrequently happens that the seller expects to find among his customers many of those rivals whom he has contended with at shows and previous sales, and with whom he is often on terms of friendship, preparations are generally made for their convenience and entertainment, which at times reduce considerably the profit realised at the sale. These auctions are not necessarily held at any particular time of the year, but take place at all seasons except when the pressure of business on the farm renders the attendance of purchasers inconvenient or impossible. Sales by auction also take place after many cattle shows, and, of course, at all such gatherings opportunity is afforded for purchase by agreement. But in nearly all cases the buyers are other breeders, whether home or foreign, and there is very little done by intermediaries except by the auctioneer.

The main trade of the country, of course, is not in these highly bred and expensive animals, and the fat stock that are slaughtered for food are generally cross-bred, or of no particular claim to distinction. The sale and purchase of these, as well as of stores, that is unfinished, half-fat, or nondescript animals, are usually effected at the markets, sales, or fairs that are held all over the kingdom. Nearly every large town has its market, some more than one, while many quite insignificant villages have their saleyards ; and other places are known entirely by the great fairs held there once or more often every autumn or spring. There are about nine hundred such places in Great Britain, of which nearly seven hundred are in England, a little less than one hundred in Wales, and the remainder in Scotland. This includes places as great and important as the Islington cattle market, at which most of the London butchers make purchases of home-grown cattle, and as small and inconsiderable as a little sale or fair in an island among the Orkneys, or on a Welsh hillside. Some are magnificent build-ings paved with stone or concrete, supplied with iron hurdles or pens, and fitted with a water-supply that enables them to be spotlessly cleansed within a few hours after use. Some are neat little saleyards owned by the auctioneer who sells there, fitted often with every proper contrivance, though on a small scale.

Others are markets held in the street of a country town, or a fair held on a grass field, or a bleak hillside, where the rain of an autumn day turns everything in an hour to a ghastly swamp. At the first, and at the last of these, large numbers of cattle and sheep change hands, the former being held once a week, the latter, perhaps, only once a year. The large markets are often the property of the corporation of the town in which they are situated, and a considerable income is derived yearly from the tolls which are levied on the animals exhibited for sale, for the markets are open to all sellers on payment of the tariff fixed according to the animal exhibited.

Stock, especially store stock, is often brought from great distances to these markets, and buyers come from a long way to make their purchases. Thus in Norwich market a large number of Irish cattle are sold every autumn to the farmers of the eastern counties, who sell them at the same market, when they are fat, to the London butchers. Leicester is a great market for sheep, and stock are sold there which are distributed all over the kingdom. Northampton, on the other hand, is a place where great numbers of Hereford and Welsh cattle are to be found, and the morning train brings many butchers from London to make their purchases of beef there. York is a centre at which not only Irish but Scotch cattle are to be found in great numbers, while rams are brought there in great numbers in the autumn from Cambridgeshire and East Anglia. These markets are for both store and fat stock, but at some places only stores are sold, and at others, chiefly in large towns like Leeds, only fat cattle for the butchers appear. But the reader will readily understand that there are all sorts of variations.

But just as there are many kinds of markets, so are there many classes of traders who frequent them, and there is naturally more than one method of making the purchase. Besides the farmers and the butchers, who form the great bulk of the sellers and buyers of fat stock, there are cattle dealers, great and small, and men who buy and sell on commission. Dealing in cattle is conducted under different conditions from dealing in corn, for the latter, as we have seen, is usually sold by sample, and the cattle trade has not been so organised that a herd can be sold on the sample of a single beast. All the animals that it is proposed to part with must be brought to the market, and no more, and it is very often a matter of some nicety to calculate how many beasts or sheep to send. If too many are offered for sale, the price is likely to be brought down, or the owner is put to the expense of bringing his animals home again or taking them on to another market. If too few are brought,

H

the price may be better; but the profit on the transaction may be so small as not to pay for the expenses and labour. To hit the exact amount, and to offer the exactly right price, both sellers and buyers must have considerable knowledge of the trade, a knowledge that can only come by constant attention to business.

It is not surprising, therefore, that in the big markets the dealers are substantial men, and that the small men keep away from such places. The dealer, moreover, is not a merchant, with an office or a stand at which he sits. He travels from market to market, and stands by the stalls where his cattle are, or mixes in the crowd of purchasers, while his drover attends to the animals, and exhibits them, or drives them as required. Dealing is mainly confined to store stock, and most of the dealers are connected with Irish cattle. Great numbers of these are bought at Irish fairs from small farmers, and, collected in big droves, are shipped to Liverpool, Glasgow, Bristol, or Milford, some to be sold at the markets in those towns, some to be sent right on to Ipswich, Norwich, Wakefield, or Leicester. If not sold at one of these places, they are retrucked and sent to another town, where the market is held a day or two afterwards. There are, however, large numbers of men who, though they deal extensively in cattle, combine with that trade the business of farming, or of fattening cattle, or other occupations. These men could not spare the time from their other business simply to travel with their stores, and superintend the sale of them in person, nor would it be profitable to do so. Their actual circuit is, therefore, perhaps comparatively small, and the final sale is entrusted to an agent. Accordingly, cattle purchased at a fair in the south or west of Ireland may be bought up by a dealer, sent by train to Dublin, shipped to Liverpool, and thence consigned to an agent in Wakefield or Ipswich, himself a dealer, who sells on commission for the first dealer to the Suffolk farmer. The cattle may even pass through the hands of one or more dealers on the way. Add to this the expenses of the railway charges in Ireland and England, as well as of the transit by sea, the cost of feeding and attendance, market tolls, and minor expenses of all sorts, and it will be realised that considerable skill and enterprise are required to make the venture profitable. It is not unusual to read in the daily papers complaints from some parts of the kingdom that store cattle fetch too low a price, and from other parts that such cattle are exorbitantly dear.

Considering the risks, difficulties, and expense attendant on this method of transfer, and the great waste of time and labour that it would entail in the case of small men, it is not surprising that a more expeditious and satisfactory way of buying and selling is usually adopted. Sales by auction occur even in the big markets, side by side with the simple sale by private treaty, and in many markets no other form of negotiation takes place. In some it is—nominally at least—forbidden. The system is not very different from that of auction sales of any other class of goods. The auctioneer mounts on a stool or board, so as to give a full view of his actions, as well as to enable him to see his customers. In many markets a broad plank is fixed along the sheep-pens, down which the auctioneer walks. Bids advance by a fixed sum, generally at least two shillings and sixpence, and the sale proceeds quietly or noisily according to the methods and inclinations of the auctioneer. At the end of the sale the money is paid to the clerk, or the auctioneer himself in his office, certain fees are charged, the seller is usually paid at once, and the transaction is complete. It needs considerable ability and knowledge of the market on the part of the agent to do justice to both parties, to keep up the bids till a fair price is reached, and to knock the lot down without wasting time when the price will go no higher. A clever auctioneer who can get good prices will have his yard filled with the best animals, and will command the custom of the highest class of butchers if the animals be fat, or of dealers or fatteners if they be store.

Unluckily the auction ring is not altogether a temple of justice. Animals crowded together in a pen so close that their backs only can be seen cannot be judged properly, and the throng of buyers and sightseers is sometimes so great that only a cursory glance of the stock can be obtained. It is a common enough sight to see the ring invaded by anxious buyers who seize the animal by the flesh of its back or plunge their fingers into the fat on its sides in an attempt to form a judgment of the quality of their intended purchase by something more definite than mere observation. It is needless to say that such an invasion does not make matters any easier for the others. The disadvantage is not all on one side. Even where the sales are conducted with the strictest fairness, the disadvantage of being first or last in the list of sales may result in an animal fetching a price far below its value. The butchers see a large supply of meat in the market, and may refuse to bid high for the first few animals offered, or they may make their purchases early, being perhaps anxious to get home, and the last few lots may be sold at a low figure with little or no competition. The hapless farmer prefers to sell at any price rather than fetch his cattle home again. The changes of weather affect prices seriously, warm, muggy weather, in which meat will not keep will lower the price, when a large stock is offered, to the great profit of the butcher, and perhaps ultimately the consumer. Shortness of feed induces sales, and a welcome shower of rain in the spring after a drought may lead farmers to hold back cattle for a more thorough finishing. Such proceedings are consistent with honest business dealings. Unfortunately there are other devices which cannot be so described. It is roundly asserted that certain auctioneers are in league with the butchers, and that they consider it more to their advantage to please that class of customer by selling cheap than to please the farmers by selling dear. They are reputed to favour certain customers unduly, and it has been found that a stranger sending his beast to auction will find no one to bid, and no effort on the part of the auctioneer to find a bidder. There is, however, a more serious evil, one for which no remedy can be found, though it may be ruinous for the farmer. The process known as "working a knock-out sale" is an arrangement between the buyers by which it is settled which person is to buy which article, and the others agree not to bid in competition with their fellow. This is sometimes carried on so openly that the operators may be seen directly after the sale arranging matters according to the agreement.

The next in order after these large markets are the small provincial marts and auction sales. Some of these are of great antiquity, and are held either in the street or in an open place in the town. Many of these provincial markets, though small, are prosperous, and a good deal of business is done with local butchers and farmers, to which may be added a few traders from some neighbouring town. They do not differ materially from the larger markets, except that business is slower, the wealth of the traders is less, and the sales are more generally conducted by some firm or firms of auctioneers. The auction sales are, however, held in private yards belonging to an auctioneer, and no other dealing is allowed in them. They are frequently well fitted up, and business is often brisk. Occasionally they are the medium of sales direct to the butchers of the district. But a large number of these auction sales are, as has already been stated, situated in villages or hamlets so small that there is no local demand for the stock sold there. These rings are merely conduit pipes for the big markets, and they will usually be found situated at from about five to fifteen miles from them. The sales are held one or two days before the market-day of the big town, and the local farmers send their stock to these places to be bought up by small dealers, who drive them in by road if the distance is short and railway communication is insufficient. A beast under these circumstances passes through two auction sales in three days. The increasing number of these marts shows that the provision of a channel to the big markets is a useful function, and it is possible that the saving of time and expense to the farmer is an effective set off against the diminished price obtained for his stock. It is to be remembered that a farmer will only send a very few animals at a time to such a sale, enough to provide him with a little ready money to pay his wages and current expenses, and that the cost of sending to the large market might eat up a large part of his receipts.

The last kind of market that we have to notice is known under the name of a " fair." These institutions are of varying importance and diverse popularity, ranging from gatherings of hundreds of men and thousands of sheep or cattle to insignificant little meetings of a few dozen animals. They are the remains of the great mercantile gatherings at which, in the Middle Ages, traders from distant countries collected to dispose of their wares at a time when other means of purchase and sale were precarious and attended with difficulties and dangers of all sorts. As countries became more settled and communication easier, markets and shops grew up and supplied the wants of citizens more effectually.

Most of the great fairs became scenes of pleasure-making, which in the course of the day degenerated into rioting, to the disturbance of business, and led in some cases to the abolition of the institution. St. Bartholomew's Fair had long ceased to be a place of business before it was done away with. Many of the fairs which held important positions in the olden times are still continued, though shorn of much of their glory.   Weyhill Fair, now reduced to a meeting of trifling importance, was at one time the great centre where the Western cattle were driven to and sold to the farmers of the East, and where the hops of the Hampshire, Surrey, and Kentish farmers were sold to the West Country brewers. Stourbridge Fair, at one time perhaps the most important trading centre of England of its kind, has, I believe, ceased to exist. Others, such as Barnet Horse Fair, maintain a precarious existence. Out of the number which still are held those are the most important which are held least frequently and are situated at some junction where hill and dale farmers meet.   Thus in the North of England, and on the borders of the Highlands of Scotland, there are certain annual fairs at which a great amount of business is done, generally in store cattle and sheep.   But with a few exceptions, such as the fairs at Newcastle and Perth, or Lincoln, they have been destroyed or materially reduced by the growth of auction sales, where the transfers take place quicker and in a more orderly manner ; for the most primitive methods of selling are still in vogue on these occasions. Cattle and sheep are separated by rude movable hurdles, and there is no organisation for the transaction of business. They are, of course, very largely frequented by dealers, who, in distinction to the important dealers that have been described before, are sometimes men in a small way of business, and who are dependent on their wits and the chances of trade to make a substantial profit out of no very important transaction. It will not be surprising to hear that all kinds of ingenuity are practised, and that occasionally tricks not very creditable are played upon buyer and seller ; while the old practice of buying cattle or sheep on the road to the fair, that figures so often in the books on economics under the name of forestalling, though no longer attended with the same odium, is practised by enterprising dealers. How long these fairs will go on is very uncertain. The improved railway communication of the country, the greater and better organisation of sale, the better knowledge of the value of animals, of time and of markets, must tend, it would seem, to reduce their importance and their number. They serve at present as an opportunity for shrewdness rather than skill, and persistence rather than promptitude in business. It is remarkable that in a number of these fairs the sale of horses plays an important part, and that in spite of the innumerable opportunities that are afforded for the sale of these animals in more modern methods, the practice of horse-dealing at fairs does not seem to be dying out.

There is one fair which deserves to be specially mentioned on account of the remarkable manner in which is is conducted, and in respect of which it is believed to be almost unique. The great sheep and wool fair which is held every year at Inverness on the Friday and Saturday which fall nearest to the middle of July is known as the Inverness Character Fair, from the fact that no sheep or wool are exhibited by the sellers to the purchasers, the whole of the transactions being based on the reputation or character of the stock sold off the same farms in previous years.

The animals offered for sale are all store sheep, consisting of lambs, cast ewes, and wethers, bred upon the hill farms of the counties of Inverness, Ross, Argyle, Sutherland, Caithness, and the northern parts of Perth. The quality of the stock and of the grazing in each case is well known upon the market, and the owner or lessee of each farm or grazing is

careful to preserve the standard of the animals of
which he is for the time being the possessor. The
high pitch of excellence to which some of these
flocks have been brought has secured for their
owners that privilege which only sellers of high-class
articles can obtain ; but the system has been fostered
by two circumstances, which are not found in other
parts of the kingdom. In the first place, sheep are
in many respects tender animals, and the removal of
a flock from one district to another, or even from
a farm to which they are accustomed to fresh pastures, will result in the death of large numbers of
them. For this reason a special supplement is
generally added to the valuation of the stock on a
Highland farm for "acclimatisation," when, for any
reason, such as a change of tenancy, the worth of
the animals has to be calculated. It has become
customary in all leases of such farms to insert a
clause, making it compulsory for the incoming tenant
to take over the stock of the quitting tenant at a
figure to be agreed upon by the representatives of
both parties. In some cases this arbitration is avoided
by an agreement to take over the stock at the price
which the outgoing tenant took the stock of his
predecessor, irrespective of the fact that the market
value may in the meantime have sunk considerably.

The second circumstance is that although the fair

is held in July, none of the purchasers move the
sheep till September, in spite of the fact that prices
may have changed in the interval, or the cost of
keep—for which, of course, they have to pay—may
prove no inconsiderable expense. This makes the
transactions more or less speculative, and probably
tends to prolong the discussions that take place as to
the price before the bargains are finally settled.

The fair is held in the open market square, though
no doubt the final settlements are transacted under
cover ; and though it begins on the Friday, no business is done till after the dinner in the afternoon,
both buyers and sellers contenting themselves with
feeling the state of the market and urging reasons
for or against a rise or fall in prices. The bargains
are often not concluded till the Saturday morning,
but the town resumes its normal appearance as a
rule in the afternoon. Buyers come from a great
distance, it is said even from England, but the
majority are dealers of the locality, although there
are a certain number of farmers who wish to add to
their store. The method of dealing seems to be
chiefly by reference to previous year's prices, and the
records usually relate that wedders and ewes from
such-and-such a farm were a shilling up or down on
last year. This makes the prices a little difficult to
follow intelligently, and they are often rendered more

complicated by the habit of returning a "luck penny," a sum given back by the seller to the buyer, and sometimes not mentioned when the price is quoted afterwards. These prices are, of course, not official, but they have been carefully recorded since the year 1822, five years after the fair was started. The quotations are usually made by the "clad score" of twenty-one sheep, a figure which suggests that the purchaser expects to lose at least 5 per cent. of his stock before they are brought home. Wool is sold by the pound. The fair is still prosperous and well attended, the railways having brought as many new purchasers as it took away old ones; but there are signs that it is decaying. The growth of auction marts, the substitution of deer forests for sheep farms, and the low prices that have ruled recently for wool, have brought about a decline in the business. It is said that the fair begins later, and is over sooner than used to be the case, and if this is so it is possible that the diminution is more apparent than real.

Before we pass from the subject of dealing, another variant of this method must be noticed which does not come under any of the foregoing heads. The class of man who deals in pigs is by no means the same necessarily as the man who deals in cattle or horses. The animal is not only of less value and more easily negotiated by a man of smaller means, but it is also kept by a very large number of people who are not of the farming class at all. The pig dealer, therefore, has a much wider and much more ignorant circle of customers than the cattle dealer, and his methods vary accordingly. His commonest plan is to put a few pigs in a cart and to drive round the villages in a mining or manufacturing district, disposing of them as best he can. In a few cases the dealer buys the pigs from the cottagers and drives them to the next market, where he either sells them to the butchers or the other customers there, or, perhaps, puts them up under the hammer of the auctioneer. Others, in a rather larger way of business, go to Ireland and buy up swine at the local markets and fairs, and after shipping them to one of the Scotch or English ports rapidly dispose of them through the countryside. These gentlemen seldom remember from whom they have bought any of their pigs, and not infrequently cannot say to whom they have sold them.

A yet more ingenious and profitable course is pursued by some of the dealers who live in the district round Bedford, Cambridge, and West Suffolk. They advertise extensively in certain newspapers that are well known to those who barter or exchange domestic pets or other articles of no great value, or in the papers that circulate among the holders of allotments. But though their announcements are worded as far as possible in the same way as the owners of well-known herds and lead the reader to suppose that they have a great number of animals for sale, they usually do not own a single head. When, however, they receive an order for a pig of a certain age and at a certain price, according to the words of their advertisement, they drive round to the farmers with whom they deal and inquire if they have any pigs for sale. Thus they are able without any expenditure of money, beyond the advertisement, to have a large turnover in the course of the year. They are, in fact, commission agents, a business which is perfectly legitimate and is of service both to the farmer and the cottager. It is regrettable, however, that the advertisements are misleading, and that it occasionally happens that the animal is not of the quality expected by the purchaser for the money he has sent.

The methods that have been described so far have two points in common. First they are devised for the sale of individual beasts rather than of numbers, and, secondly, the success of the bargain depends on the skill of either party to judge the value of the animal sold. The two are, indeed, interdependent, for it would be almost an impossibility to make so accurate a calculation if twenty head of cattle were to be transferred as if one only was to be sold, and when there are more to be bought in one lot the greater must be the allowance made for taking an average. This may perhaps be done in the case of store cattle with comparative ease, but in the case of fat beasts, whose value is in the end the amount of meat they will give to the butcher, the weight of the ox on the scales must be the final test of merit. There are some men who have developed to an extraordinary degree the power of judging by the eye and hand how much a beast will weigh. They will calculate not merely the hundredweights, but even the pounds, and not be more than a pound or two out. Cases are on record in which the amount has been reckoned to within half a pound, when the expert has been put on his mettle. Such a power is, however, uncommon, and it is obvious that a weighing-machine must be a more accurate as well as a more rapid test. When large numbers are to be bought it must be the only test of real value.

It would be supposed that every farmer would wish to sell his fat stock by that method, or that at least he would be careful to ascertain either in the market or before arriving there how much each animal weighed, in order to know at once if the price offered is worth his taking, or if in accepting it he is letting the profit that ought to be his pass into the hands

I

of the butcher. It might be supposed that every butcher before buying an animal would insist on having it weighed, in order that he might reckon what he could afford considering the current price of beef. It is, however, the fact that in most parts of England, at any rate, both farmers and butchers are extremely chary of using the weighbridge, each preferring to trust to his judgment. It is not for want of facilities for weighing that this method has not become more popular. The advantages of the system, which is extensively practised in America, induced Parliament to pass in 1887 and 1891 laws requiring every market authority to erect in markets and fairs, where toll is taken for permission to expose the animals, a weighing-machine which shall be at the service of any person claiming to use it for testing the weight of cattle at a small charge. All auctioneers are required by the later Act to adopt the same course in their private marts, and exemption is only granted in those cases where the number exposed is small, and the sale held at infrequent intervals. The Government has power to require from certain scheduled markets a return of the number of animals exhibited, the number weighed, and the price at which they were sold. These returns, if complete and accurate, would be invaluable for statistical purposes, and afford farmers a valuable clue to the varia-

tions of prices in fat stock. Unluckily, although
the markets selected are the most important in the
kingdom, the number of cattle weighed in them is
small, and the number of sheep and swine almost
nil. The Scotch markets are those in which the
greatest number are weighed. In the year 1901 the
number of cattle weighed was only some 13 per cent.
of those entered in the scheduled markets, while only
1 per cent. of the sheep entered are weighed, and
0·5 per cent. of the swine. At Birmingham, Bristol,
Lincoln, Norwich, and York, the weighing facilities
under the Act remain practically unused. If this is
the case with the large markets, and those at which
fat stock are sold, it may be easily credited that
smaller markets are still less likely to give records
of weighing, and that at markets or fairs where store
stock only is sold the weighbridge, if provided, will
be allowed to rust in peace. As a rule this is the
case, in spite of the efforts of a certain number of
enthusiastic supporters of the policy who are endeavouring to popularise it.

At Falkirk, for instance, thanks to the enterprise
of a particular auctioneer, the bidding was actually
made per hundredweight of the beast exposed, so
that the calculations were made in terms of meat.
This plan was not adopted anywhere else, however,
and was dropped on the death of the auctioneer,

whose successor returned to the simpler method of asking for bids for the animal. Each beast is still weighed, and the weight in each case is written up on a board.

In another market a serious attempt was made to introduce the sale of store stock by weight, a system which though rare in England is commonly practised in Ireland and in America. Many Irish dealers in Scotland are prepared to sell by this method, and its adoption has at times led to some curious revelations about the economy of the farm. Thus several of the witnesses before the Departmental Committee on Scottish Agricultural Prices frankly admitted that they knew store cattle were selling at three to four and even more shillings per hundredweight than fat cattle. The following dialogue is given by one of them as if it had taken place between himself and some of his brother farmers:[1] "I have been to one or two sales lately. Some of my friends have said, 'What are we to do for cattle? We must go to the islands and try and get some there.' I have said, 'I will let you buy the cattle and summer them, and then in the autumn I will give you ten shillings a head less than you paid for them.' They have said, 'You will then have too much grass,' and I have answered, 'Yes, but I will have all the more hay. I will have it on hand to winter your cattle when

[1] Reply 3420.

I buy them. You will lose the ten shillings, and your grass will be eaten. I have not bought a beast this spring.'" A more frequent use of the weighbridge would no doubt lead farmers to avoid such errors.

It was the belief of the authors of the Act, no doubt, that if machines were universally provided the method would rapidly find favour, and it may have been hoped that a time would come when a farmer or dealer would buy a number of stores by live weight, having first settled on the price per hundredweight, and then weighing out the bulk, exactly as we have already seen is done sometimes in the case of wheat. Whether such a state of things will, or can ever come, it is not possible to say, but there is no doubt that weighing is gradually winning its way. The percentage of cattle weighed to the number entered in the big markets is rising every year, and as a number of auctioneers have adopted the automatic weighing-machine, by means of which every beast is automatically weighed on entering the ring, it is certain that the system is having a fair test in these marts. The obvious interest displayed by the buyers in the dial that shows the weight suggests that the purchasers at these yards are gradually becoming accustomed to this system, and will perhaps find themselves disinclined some day to make their purchases any other way.

The reader does not need to be reminded that, however important the meat of the livestock of the farm may be in the agricultural economy, the secondary products of his animals are what a farmer looks to for a substantial part of his income. Under this head we include the dairy produce, such as milk, butter, and cheese, the wool, hides, and skins, and lastly eggs. In his paper on farm revenue and capital, Mr. Rew calculates that these items bring in nearly fifty million pounds a year to the agricultural community, or about one-quarter of their entire revenue. Of this by far the greatest amount is due to dairy produce. In the mixed agriculture practised in England, especially in the proximity of large towns, which take large quantities daily, we may expect to find dairying distributed throughout every county or shire. But in those which lie on the west, where the greater part of the soil is under grass, it happens also that there are fewer large centres of population. It is also the case, whether nature or art has had the decision of it, that the breeds of cattle which are native to the west are generally those which are famous for their milking properties. Hence the surplus of milk has for many generations been used in making butter and cheese ; and with the exception of Stilton and Wensleydale, all the famous brands of cheese come from the west.

The changes, however, that have come over English agriculture during the last quarter of a century have profoundly affected the dairying interests. In the prosperous days of the old husbandry the farmer devoted himself to those branches which paid best, and the interests of his business were supposed to be bound up with wheat growing and fat-stock rearing. The progress made in these branches of industry was not shared by the smaller departments, which were contemptuously left to the women, with the result that certain well-known brands of cheese and butter fell into disrepute, or could not be purchased. Complaints were made that contracts were impossible with English farmers, because their supply was not equal in quantity or quality all the year round, and that they not infrequently left the contractor in the lurch. At first the deficiency was made up from France, and butter from Normandy and Brittany was placed on the London market in large quantities. The place was afterwards filled by Danish produce, prepared in factories under the co-operative system, which had meanwhile been carried to a higher pitch of organisation even than the French. The colonies and other foreign countries than those referred to joined in the competition, and added a rivalry in cheese-making. A great deal of this produce put on the market was distinctly inferior to English goods, but being of a uniform quality it held the field, and completely ousted the home-made stuff, which began to disappear. The introduction of the technical schools of the county councils and the instruction given by the itinerant lecturers and teachers revived the industry as far as the skill in manufacture was concerned, but carried the de-development no further. The same methods of commerce were pursued. The farmers' wives and daughters were supposed to be the people who ought to superintend and work in the dairy, and the whole conduct and management of the business was left in their hands.

Now the old-fashioned method of selling dairy produce was to exhibit it in the market-place on the market-day. The farmer's wife drove with her husband to the town, having filled her basket with eggs, poultry, butter, and so forth. On their arrival at the town the good man put up his horse and cart and went to sell his corn, and she sat at the market-cross and offered her wares to the passers-by. This is the system beloved by the sentimentalist and described by the story-teller. It is difficult to conceive any more wasteful method, and as given above in all its crudeness never perhaps really existed. A farmer's wife who had nothing better to do than to sit in the market-place all day must have been a very bad manager. But undoubtedly there were plenty of women so employed, and a large part of the butter that was prepared was sold in that way. Even when they did sell their produce they did not always do so to the best advantage. Individual enterprise, without combination of any sort, is apt to be worsted in the contest with organised bodies unless the individual has exceptional skill and energy, and it cannot be said that stallholders in a market are distinguished for those two qualities. The market-women frequently knew little of values or what prices were fetching in other places. So recently as November, 1903, it was stated at a public meeting, reported by the *Western Times* on the 27th of that month, that in one town in Devonshire the dealers bought eggs in the market in the morning, but nothing was said about price till late in the day, when an old man would write up the prices on a blackboard, and the farmers' wives would have to accept that price from the dealers whatever the stock was like. It is improbable that the vendors of butter fared much better.

The market-places at which these wares are exhibited are frequently out of doors, or if they are held under cover the hall is invaded in the wet weather by other dealers, and the stallholders are crowded out, to the detriment of their business.

Attempts were made in various parts of England to build covered markets, for it frequently happened that the stallholders sat out in the wind and rain all day, or in the heat and dust, with the result that even if the constitutions of the country folk were thereby hardened, as has been claimed by an enthusiastic supporter of the old ways, the quality of the farm produce was not improved. But in most cases the stallholders would have none of it. They found that the advantages of the open street were greater than the covered market, that customers would not come to the new building, or went to other stalls, and one by one they went back to the market-cross. Meanwhile the agricultural revolution was going on its course ; arable land was being turned to pasture, and the farmer turned his attention more and more to his cattle, with the result that dairying became recognised as an important branch of husbandry.

The change in the commercial methods that came followed two directions. In a certain number of cases enterprising persons, not necessarily farmers, seeing the importance of a constant and uniform supply, started proprietary butter factories. At these institutions the milk, or sometimes the butter, of the farmers was bought at a fixed scale, and then by means of machinery worked up again to the required standard, so that the manufacturer was able to sell to the wholesale dealer or the large shopkeeper a butter which was uniform throughout the year. Even then his supplies often failed him, and he was forced to supplement them with French or Danish butter, bought in the market, in order to fulfil his contract. It may be supposed that he took every advantage of the farmer, who often found no other outlet for his goods, and was forced to sell at the price the manufacturer chose to offer, which was not often a highly profitable one. Many of these butter factories are in existence, but the co-operative movement has now taken firm hold of this branch of farming, and the proprietary butter factories are not likely to develop much further.

The other change that has come over the trade is due to the influence of the shopkeeper. The grocers and provision dealers were at all times extremely jealous of the stallholders in the market, and complained that their business, in connection with which they had to pay heavy rates, was seriously interfered with by the country people who came into the town on the busy days, and sold in competition with the legitimate traders without paying any rates and only a small market toll. As the markets, however, were there before the shopkeepers, it was impossible to put a stop to the competition. They had therefore to adopt the methods of the most formidable of their rivals. There are in all markets perhaps, certainly in all markets at which small goods are sold, a class of men known as higglers or hucksters. These men may, or may not, be producers of the class of goods they sell, very often they are not. They attend, however, at markets, and sell minor agricultural produce which they have collected from farmers, allotment holders, or small market-gardeners. They will usually visit the growers at their own homes and make their bargains there; but in times of competition and activity they will go along the road away from the market, and meeting the incomers, bargain with them for their wares. The small owner, very often pressed for time, anxious to get his money at once, and without further trouble, sells his produce to a higgler and returns home. This forestalling is extensively practised in some markets, the speculators sometimes being able to rule the market, and settle the prices according to their fancy. This plan was adopted occasionally by the tradesmen, and they were thus able to secure the custom for their shops. The system of course is capable of further development, and when applied to large farmers is a serious improvement in method. The growth of some of these trading establishments has brought wealthier competitors into the field, and the large grocers are able to buy up supplies from numbers of farmers direct. The great shops combine the wholesale and retail trade under one roof. The tradesman is wealthy enough to venture on large transactions, and yet his premises are extensive enough to sell in very small quantities. The elimination of the middleman is carried to the greatest extent possible, considering that the convenience of the buying public and the range of articles offered them are the first considerations of the trader.

This system has been applied yet more completely to the sale of milk, the part of farming which is now the most profitable, and in which the home producer has only a very small foreign competition to contend with. Some years ago the supply of milk for large towns was drawn from cows kept in sheds within the district itself. The number of cows kept in London at present is about 4,500, but in 1865 it is believed there were as many as 40,000, while one large owner in the north of London is known to have had as many as 1,000 in his possession. The advantages of this system were obvious. There was little or no carriage to pay for, milk was supplied to the customer within a short time of its being given by the cows, and any surplus not disposed of would not cost the milk-seller more than the value of the milk. Unfortunately the appearance first of cattle-plague, and then contagious pleuropneumonia among the cowsheds of London, seriously affected the trade, and did an immense injury to the owners. The tendency of modern sanitation to require greater precautions in the keeping of cows in towns, to prevent tuberculosis, was a further blow, and the natural reluctance of the public to buy milk from urban sheds when milk was offered from country farms had a grave effect also. It thus happened that the sale of milk became profitable, and many farmers, unable to stand against foreign competition in the butter trade, took to sending their milk to towns.

The former state of affairs has, therefore, been almost completely reversed, and instead of being supplied from the sheds in the towns and the farms in the suburbs, the greater part of the milk is brought daily from great distances, and only a small part is produced in the towns. An excellent description of the present condition of the milk trade as carried on in a typical industrial district of London is to be found in the report on the milk trade of Finsbury, which has recently (1903) been prepared by Dr. Newman, the medical officer of health for that borough, and a well-known writer on bacteriology. The investigation has been complete, as a register is kept of the source of the milk of every milk-seller, whether it be town or country, as well as a register of all the milk-shops in the borough, containing particulars of each in respect to sanitation, and the management of their trade.

Finsbury has a population slightly over 100,000, neither the richest nor the poorest in London. There are 261 milk-sellers in the district, some of whom are traders in a very small way, combining the sale of milk with other kinds of food and small stores. These vendors have three ways of obtaining their milk. First, they may obtain their supply through a milk contractor (and it is said there are no less than fourteen such contractors trading in the borough); secondly, they may obtain their milk through other milk-sellers from country farms; and thirdly, they may procure the milk from cowsheds situated in the borough itself. Of the first class there are 185, the second class numbers about 50, and the remainder, some 25, get all or part of their supplies from the locality, and so fall within the third category. In a more prosperous district we should probably find a large number of traders who get their milk direct from a farmer without the intervention of a middleman, and the shops of the big dairy companies who keep their own cows on their own farms in Hertfordshire and Buckinghamshire.

The 14 contractors who supply milk to Finsbury

deal with about 1,200 farms at varying distances from London, and in widely different districts. Thus we learn that one contractor deals with 13 farmers in Derbyshire and Essex, another with 43 farmers in Wilts, Derbyshire, Berkshire, Somerset, Norfolk, Hampshire, Worcestershire, Dorset, Oxfordshire, Gloucestershire, and Cambridgeshire, and a third with no less than 400 farmers in Berkshire, Wiltshire, and Buckinghamshire; while others deal with 70, 100, or 200, as the case may be. It is not easy to judge of the extent of the trade in any case, for while there are two contractors who deal with 60 farmers and supply only two shopkeepers, another who deals with 58 supplies 16, only two less than the contractor who draws his milk from 400 farms.

The great complexity of the business of bringing milk from these country centres to the consumers is admirably illustrated by an instance related by Dr. Newman. A certain contractor deals with farms situated in thirty-eight towns or villages,[1] from whom he receives, we will say, between 1,000 and 1,500 gallons of milk daily. This milk is in some

[1] The farms are situated in the following counties :—

Bedfordshire	. 2	...	Cambridgeshire	. 1	...	Notts	. 1
Worcestershire	. 1	...	Warwickshire	. 2	...	Bucks	. 2
Norfolk .	. 2	...	Staffordshire	. 2	...	Rutland	. 2
Derbyshire	. 12	...	Essex .	. 1	...	Northants	. 2
Leicestershire	. 7	...	Hertfordshire	. 1			

cases not sent direct from the farmer to the contractor, but is collected from two or three farmers by
an agent, and forwarded by rail to London. It is
met in the early morning by the contractor, who
loads up his churns and distributes them to his
customers as rapidly as possible. In the case quoted
above there are thirty-two of such milk-sellers, nine
of whom sell part of their store to smaller traders,
some of whom perhaps sell part of it again to the
proprietors of those curious little shops where lamp
oil, soap, pickles, candles, bacon, boot blacking, and
Dutch herrings are offered for sale. And yet there
is probably no article of daily food which passes
through the hands of fewer middlemen and agents
on its way from the producer to the consumer.

It is remarkable what a great distance the contractors go for their supplies. The great milk-
producing counties of Derbyshire, Staffordshire,
Leicestershire, Warwickshire, and Wiltshire furnish
the greater part, in spite of the great markets that are
open to the farmers of those counties in the great
towns of Lancashire, Warwickshire, and Staffordshire.
In order to illustrate the length of the journey that
the milk consumed in Finsbury has to travel, Dr.
Newman has prepared a table showing the number
of farms that lie within the zones drawn at a radius
of 25, 50, 100, 150, 200 miles from London. There

K

are 281 towns and villages from which the supplies are daily drawn: only 2, or less than 1 per cent., lie in the innermost zone; 13, or 4·6 per cent., are situated in the next; 111, or 39·5 per cent., are in the zone stretching from 50 to 100 miles from the metropolis; 145, or 51·9 per cent., are to be found in the next zone extending from 100 to 150 miles from the consumers; and 10 places, or 3·5 per cent., are more than 150 miles. In every case, of course, the distance by train must be still greater. And yet, in spite of the difficulties and expense of this traffic, it competes successfully with the urban producer. The number of cowsheds in Finsbury is scarcely half what it was ten years ago, and even these are not full. In one respect, at any rate, the country seems to hold its own as against the towns.

The sale of cheese is far more in the hands of the dealer than the sale of milk. It is an article of food in which there is far greater variety than in butter, which, nominally at least, should be of one standard only. Cheeses are made in so many different ways and with such varying proportions of cream, whole milk, and skim milk, that the producer has great opportunity to exhibit his skill or ingenuity. Moreover, it is an article which takes longer to make, is usually made in large quantities, and which keeps good for a longer period than butter. When we add

to this that few consumers buy cheeses in large quantities, we have practically summed up the difficulties
in the way of establishing direct communication
between the producer and the consumer. In such
cases the dealer invariably makes his appearance.
There are certain towns in the West of England,
like Shrewsbury, where the cheese markets are held
with a circumstance resembling a cattle market.
The sellers take their stands in the square with the
great cheeses piled up round them, and patiently
wait for bids.   The persons who frequent these
markets, however, are able to wait their time, and
unless the demand is unusually brisk and the supply
short they can secure the goods pretty much at their
own prices.   But even in a trade so unprofitable to a
farmer there are compensations.   The anxiety of
dealers to get their supplies fresh and undamaged by
weather leads them to anticipate the markets and
visit the farmers in their own homes. This is
especially the case where the towns are not big
enough to provide suitable markets, and in the
counties lying towards the south-west of England the
greater part of the business is done through cheese
factors, as they are called.   These are no small
hucksters, but generally men in a fairly large way of
business, occasionally grocers or tradesmen.   As a
rule, however, they merely buy to sell to a cheese

merchant in Birmingham or London. The cheeses are bought outright and not sold on commission, and the factor is of considerable assistance in guiding the maker as to the trend of popular taste. But though there is no reason to suppose that the factors do not deal honourably by their customers, it is clear that the advantage in bargaining must generally lie with the one who is most conversant with the prices that are being paid elsewhere. The dealer, then, who knows at what price he can sell his wares to the merchant or shopkeeper, and where he can get other cheeses in case one particular farmer fails to supply his wants, is generally able to fix his price.

Before leaving the subject of selling farm produce through an itinerant dealer, it may be as well to notice a curious development of the business that has taken place in Sussex. That district is famous for the production of what are called Surrey fowls; that is to say, the poultry that are sold in the London markets and shops. The trade is an old one, and was in full swing before the railways were built, but it has very greatly increased in the last few years. The chickens are occasionally imported from Ireland to be fattened, but the greater number of the birds, and those of the best, are bred on the spot. The breeding and the fattening, however, are two distinct branches; that is to say, the chickens are reared by

one man and fattened by another.   The first operation is carried on by nearly every inhabitant of the
Heathfield district, from farmer to labourer, from
breeders of many thousands a year to breeders
of a few dozen.   The finishing business, however,
is in the hands of a few men, who are seldom, if
ever, breeders.   They visit the breeders from time
to time—daily if in a large way of business, twice or
thrice a week if in a smaller way—and buy the
chickens from their clients.   Each man has, it seems,
his special circle of customers, and it is held to be
a point of honour not to trespass on another man's
preserves.   The birds are taken when three or four
months old, and the prices vary according to the
season; but though the breeders declare it does not
pay them to fatten, the higglers seem so anxious
to procure chicken that they are willing to pay full
prices.   A curious result—that one set of men are so
anxious to buy (a transaction on which presumably
they expect to make a profit) that it "does not pay"
another set of men to enter into competition with
them.   The fatteners kill and prepare the fowls for
market, but they are again collected by carriers, who
take the packages to the station, whence they are
consigned to the Leadenhall or central markets of
London.   What the origin of this curious dual
system was it is difficult to say.   Possibly the

higglers were at one time merely petty traders, who, finding that the breeders did not supply the chicken in the condition that the London consumer required, kept their purchases and attempted to bring them to a higher state of perfection. This being found profitable, led to a development of the fattening business, and at the same time induced the breeders to give up any attempt at putting a finished article on the market. As the matter stands, it appears to be a system by which the birds pass through the hands of a multitude of middlemen on their way to the consumer, and yet the business appears to pay. Perhaps it would be more easily understood if we call it by the magic title, "division of labour."

There is one article of farm produce to which scanty reference has as yet been made, and that is wool. Although it has now sunk from the proud position of pre-eminence that it occupied in the fourteenth and fifteenth centuries, or even from the favoured place held in the eighteenth, it is still of no little importance. Some 20 million pounds of British and Irish wool, of the value of half a million pounds, are yearly exported, besides what is used in the home manufacture, though, of course, this sinks into insignificance when compared with the amount, some 375 to 400 million pounds, imported for use in this country. This competition has materially reduced the price of native wools of all classes, and they are worth less than half what they fetched some twenty or thirty years ago. It is to be regretted that the result seems to have produced a feeling of carelessness in the flock masters, for complaints have been made that less care is taken over the fleeces of the sheep than formerly, and that they are consigned to market in such a condition as to interfere with the process of manufacture. Instead of endeavouring, by improving the article, to secure a better price, too many farmers are content to let the advantage which might be obtained that way fall into the hands of dealers or hucksters, who visit the farms and buy up all the fleeces they may find. Such traders are common in some parts of the kingdom. But there is no end to the ways in which the wool trade is carried on. We have already noticed the way in which it is dealt with in the Inverness Character Fairs. Further south, however, a different mode prevails. A great deal is consigned to auctioneers and salesmen in the large towns in Scotland and sold publicly, but a great deal is sent direct to brokers or merchants for private bargains. It is possible some is sold without the intervention of any third party.

In estimating the value of his wool the farmer is,

of course, dependent upon the published tables of prices. In the case of auction sales the exact prices that are realised are published by the auctioneer or the trade newspaper; but as the sales of wool are held only at certain seasons of the year, the producer cannot tell the value till after the transaction is completed. In the case of wool consigned to a broker, he is able to form some estimate by examining the published circulars which these gentlemen issue, and it is satisfactory to notice that no complaint was made before the Departmental Committee on Scottish Agricultural Prices as to the accuracy or fairness of these lists, though the reports of the prices fetched by fat cattle in the auctioneers' saleyards were frequently the subject of unfavourable comment.

CHAPTER IV

CONCLUSION: RECENT DEVELOPMENTS IN THE PROCESSES OF DISTRIBUTION

THE methods we have examined in the two preceding chapters are those which have grown up naturally and almost unconsciously. They represent the result of a slow growth over hundreds of years, and the product, it must be admitted, is what has arisen from the inclinations and peculiarities of the persons most immediately concerned. Systems such as these have one distinct advantage over all others—we know that they will work. Whatever disadvantages there are connected with them, it stands to reason that business can be done efficiently under them, and, it is possible, more efficiently than under any other plan, when the economic difficulties of the situation, the local peculiarities, or the social circumstances are taken into consideration.

This is not, however, as much as saying that it is the best, certainly not the ideal, and there are obvious disadvantages attending the customary methods of marketing which are the stock complaints of every seller, and which are continually in the mouth of the reformer. Markets are continually subject to "rigging," prices are driven down by unscrupulous speculators, and even in small markets advantage is taken by smart buyers to make purchases at prices far below the real value of the article. Thus wheat, we are continually being told, is lowered in price, to the ruin of the British farmer, by the system of options and futures. It is constantly asserted that in certain auction markets the butchers form a ring and agree not to bid against each other, with the result that unless a reserve price is fixed, which is seldom the case, beasts are sold to members of the "knock-out" gang, as it is called, at rates quite unremunerative and ruinous to the farmers. Fruit, potatoes, and vegetables of all sorts consigned to fruit salesmen in the large towns are sold at prices which, when the cost of carriage and the salesman's commission are deducted, leave the unhappy owner next to nothing, and even on some occasions less than nothing at all.

Nor does the general public gain by such transactions. It is asserted that on occasions when beasts are knocked down at quarter their real value, or a potato grower finds his return on a ton of potatoes to be eighteenpence, that beef and potatoes are no cheaper in the shops than before. This is probably true. But it only takes into account the cases in which one trader has made a better bargain than his neighbours, when he has, of course, every right to make a better profit, and altogether omits those cases in which a trader may find he has over-bought himself, and cannot dispose of all his supplies in the market, in which circumstances he runs a great risk of losing far more than he gained by some sharp transaction on another occasion.

Be that as it may, human nature is equally strong in buyer and seller, and either would be prepared to make full use of any disadvantage in which he found the other placed. There seems no reason, therefore, why sympathy should be extended to one party more than to the other, were it not for one circumstance which materially affects the situation. The function of the middleman in trade is to act as the governor of a steam engine, and regulate the amount of produce which flows in and out of the market. He is expected to know the probable demand of the consumer as well as the probable supply of the producer, and both parties are prepared to allow him to take his profit, provided that he is able to take from them or supply them with a day's requirements every day. The immense improvement effected in recent years in the means of communication and transit have enabled the salesman and the trader to do this efficiently in most cases, especially when the article is one which is not rapidly perishable, and when, therefore, the surplus of one day can be kept till the next, or he is able to calculate with some exactness what the demand is likely to be. Thus we do not hear of sudden failures on the part of bakers to supply bread, or of butchers to have meat on sale.

There are, however, many articles which come within the category referred to and are offered only in seasons, such as many kinds of fruit, or which will not keep longer than a few hours, such as milk, or the freshness and goodness of which it is difficult to ensure in the ordinary market. The sale of these is often very erratic. Fruit is of so uncertain a nature that a few days' brilliant weather will yield vast quantities of ripe strawberries or plums, which the grower cannot store and is obliged to send to market, only to find, perhaps, an unremunerative price. And all the while there are perhaps hundreds of persons anxious to buy who are quite unaware of the opportunity offered them. Or it may be that the farmer is quite unable to find a market for his milk or any reasonable price for his butter, while the housewife complains she is unable to get pure milk or good butter. Each party blames the dealer, and wishes he or she could get in touch with each other. The extinction of the middleman is raised as a cry for the revival of agriculture, and the farmer is advised to turn shopkeeper himself. A good many schemes have been started in the last two decades with this avowed object, and no examination of the methods of a farmer's business would be complete without an account of some of them.

The first and simplest of these is the system inaugurated and carried to its highest development by the Great Eastern Railway, a company which serves the eastern counties, and can claim to be, above all others, the agricultural railway company, though the system has now been adopted by most, if not all, other lines. A list is printed in pamphlet form of producers in the district through which the Great Eastern Railway Company passes who undertake to supply purchasers with simple farm produce. No charge is made for the insertion of the names, and the list is issued free to the public, who are invited to communicate with the producers. The company, on their part, undertake to carry the produce from any one of their stations to London or to stations in the Great Eastern suburban districts at the reduced charge of 4*d.* for 20 lbs. and 1*d.* additional for every 5 lbs. or part thereof up to 60 lbs. The consignment is carried by passenger train, and no charge is made for delivery within the usual limits of the company's area, which is about three miles of Charing Cross. But these rates will only be admitted on four conditions : that the produce shall be packed in the specially constructed boxes made and sold by the railway company ; that the boxes shall be nailed, and not secured by cord or rope ; that the parcels shall be prepaid and conveyed at owner's risk ; and that no box shall weigh more than 60 lbs. The success of this plan is shown by the fact that it has been copied by most other railway companies, and that the list, which has now reached its twelfth edition, contains some 1,050 names. The producers are invited to state what they are prepared to supply, and whether they can offer large or small quantities. Some describe themselves as able to sell farm produce generally, or mangels and potatoes in large quantities. There are, of course, farmers in the ordinary way of business who take advantage—very properly no doubt—of the facilities offered by the railway company to extend their business. But they are not of the class that figures most prominently in the list. A very large number of others undertake to supply eggs, butter, fruit, and vegetables or poultry in large or small quantities, but there are also many who can only offer one or two of these articles, and that in small amounts.

It is interesting to note the names of several clergymen in the list, as well as the large number of "glass" farmers, who are now engaged in the development of Essex as a high-class fruit-growing district.

An organisation such as this, however, is of the very simplest kind, and depends for its success on the energy, good faith, and business-like ways of both buyer and seller. The Great Eastern Railway Company take no steps beyond publishing the names of the producers willing to sell, and the rates at which they will carry the goods. There is no guarantee of the quality of the produce or any attempt to organise the producers or the consumers in such a way as to further business. That is left entirely to the two interested parties. There are, however, a number of bodies devoted to the development of agriculture who carry their energies further in that direction, and announce their readiness to guide and instruct the producer in the most scientific method of preparing his goods for the market. Most of these societies or organisations concern themselves mainly with the productive side of a farmer's business. They offer to teach him how to cultivate his fields to the best advantage, what is the most profitable class of animal or vegetable to rear, having regard to the climate, soil, or district in which the owner may be; but they generally leave him to find his customer for himself, or at most tell him how to procure the best prices in the ordinary markets.

Such societies, however useful, are not those that we are proposing to discuss in this book ; but there are some who go beyond this narrow limit, and are prepared to render services in the direction of teaching the farmer how to dispose of his stock, or even of assisting him to do so. A very good example of the simpler kind of organisation conducted on these lines is the National Poultry Organisation Society, which has its offices at present at 12, Hanover Square, London, W. The objects of this society, as set out in one of their leaflets, are as follows :—

The National Poultry Organisation Committee has been formed for the purpose of encouraging and developing the production of the best qualities of poultry and eggs in the United Kingdom, and of bringing producers into more direct communication with retailers, thus organising the system of marketing which at the present time, in respect of many parts of the country, compares so unfavourably with the methods adopted by foreigners, who have perfected their organisations, and practically captured the British market. So far as eggs are concerned, the chief requirements are more regular supplies, especially in winter, greater rapidity in marketing, and improved packing. It is hoped that a better state of things will be obtained by the establishment of branches for the collection of eggs and poultry and by arranging with the trade for the sale of produce.

The National Poultry Organisation Society endeavours to make more widely known the facts to which reference has here been briefly made; is establishing branches with the object of developing the poultry industry and forming collecting centres for eggs and poultry in each district connected with the central organisation; affords practical information as to the class of poultry-keeping most suited to each district, having regard to the soil and the market available; indicates the breeds which give the best results; renders assistance in obtaining on the best terms appliances of a right kind; disseminates leaflets providing reliable information bearing upon the various aspects of poultry culture; registers and supplies names of traders willing to take the produce; keeps a register of poultrymen and women desiring situations, and generally assists the branches, and through them the individual breeders, in every manner possible.

A further leaflet describes in detail the approved method of forming a branch, and states that when it has been formed and registered by the executive committee of the society, arrangements can be made for the services of an officer of the society, whose business it will be to give information with regard to the breeds most suitable to the district, the best markets, and the methods of packing eggs and

L

preparing table poultry. The plan most favoured, evidently, is to form a collecting depôt, to which each member should send *all* his eggs for at least twelve months, care being taken that they are absolutely fresh, and if possible over a certain weight and size. The society has a special trade mark, which members and depôts are allowed to use under these conditions, and which, of course, is a guarantee of high quality. The society has published a number of valuable leaflets on the subject of production of eggs, and of preparation for the market, but there is little information given as to the best means of disposing of them, except a few scattered sentences, such as : "No pains on the part of the society will be spared to try and obtain the best prices for eggs, but to be able to secure these good prices the constant energy and loyalty of every member is essential"; or, "When sufficient supplies of eggs and poultry are produced in a district a collecting depôt may be established. But careful inquiry should be made before this step is taken. In some districts it is unnecessary by reason of large local demand."

These sentences, coupled with the absence of any scheme for sale of eggs, suggest that the promoters hope to effect a market rather by push and the high quality of their goods than by the discovery or development of any fresh market. A society of this

kind naturally finds its chief supporters animated by
that spirit of union which usually finds expression in
the formation of co-operative societies. But it is no
essential part of the National Poultry Organisation
Society's projects to urge on their clients the formation of such bodies, and their leaflets contemplate
the organisation of the industry on usual commercial
lines. The method of the society appears to be
rather to further improved organisation of the trade
than definite co-operative societies, and to aim at
bringing the producer and the consumer into closer
communication. But there have been other societies
which have set out from the beginning to create
co-operative bodies, believing that the only hope for
the farmer is to induce him to conduct his industry
on the lines of those foreign societies which have
entered into such severe competition with him. The
best known and the most enterprising of these was
the British Produce Supply Association, Limited,
started by the late Earl of Winchelsea, and fostered
and maintained, so long as its author lived, by his
splendid enthusiasm and energy. The objects of the
society, as set out in their handbook, are described in
the following manner :—

The object of the Association is to assist the producer
in the disposal of his produce at every stage from the farm to
the market. This it proposes to do in the following ways :—

1. By establishing depôts for the direct sale of agricultural produce and by selling also on commission, through salesmen of its own stationed in London and in the principal provincial markets. By this means the farmer, instead of being obliged to consign his produce to salesmen of whom he often knows little, and whose returns he has no means of checking, can send it to an association established in his own interest, and thus have a satisfactory guarantee that it makes all it is worth.

2. By establishing from time to time depôts at convenient centres in country districts, where produce can be collected and consigned to whatever market furnishes the best demand at the moment.

3. By establishing in connection with one or more of the depôts, according to the nature of the district, an abattoir or butter factory, which will answer the double purpose of effecting a further and important economy in the treatment of meat or butter produced in the locality ; and of serving as models for the imitation of associations of farmers in other parts of the country which might desire to follow in the footsteps of the parent society, and while erecting their own abattoir or butter factory, as the case might be, to avail themselves of its services for the ultimate disposal of their produce in the market.

4. It aims at gradually organising a better system for the collection of produce in rural districts surrounding the depôt, a system which may of course be made available as an outlet for many rural industries not immediately connected with agriculture, but scarcely less valuable as a means of providing occupation for labourers and their families during the winter.

The scheme was full of great promise, and was an immense improvement on any organisation that was in existence before. It suffered, however, from the great defect of being dependent on the energy of one man, even before whose death it began to languish. It was eventually taken over by another organisation, which, profiting by experience, is apparently on the road to success. Whether the British Produce Supply Association would ever have been a commercial success it is impossible to say, but it appears to have suffered from two grave defects. In the first place it proposed to substitute—somewhat in the manner of a beneficent despot—one middleman for another, the only difference being that the new middleman was to give the farmer better terms than the trader it was proposed to displace. In order to do this, therefore, it was thought necessary to start a large store, somewhat like the Civil Service Stores, so well known in London, at which good patriots were invited to make their purchases. So large a venture must have crippled the society's resources. In the second place, there was no inducement for the housewife to deal at this store, since the ordinary Englishman does not in the least care where his food is produced provided that it is what he wants, and of the appearance, colour, flavour, and consistency that he has been taught to believe in. It is probable, too, that a vague suggestion of philanthropy attached to the scheme, which made business men fight shy of it.

The mistakes inherent to the nature of the British Produce Supply Association have been very carefully avoided by the Agricultural Organisation Society, which describes itself as existing for the purpose of showing farmers how to form throughout the country co-operative societies, registered under the Industrial and Provident Societies Act, so as to secure limited liability. It is supported by voluntary contributions, and is in no way a company trading for profit, so that its success does not depend on the turn of the market, or the volume of business passing through its books. The justification of its propaganda is contained in the following sentence, taken from one of the leaflets it publishes: "The daily life of a farmer is so full of harassing details that he has not the time or sufficient knowledge of outside affairs necessary to avail himself of the means of combating traders who are constantly imposing on him." In the same publication its principal objects are attractively, though somewhat vaguely and unmethodically, described as :—

1. To aid the farmer in securing the best market for purchase and sale.

2. To improve the quality and increase the quantity of farm products.

3. To direct agricultural trade into profitable channels.

4. To stop the "cornering" of the produce by middlemen.

5. To secure the reduction of railway rates.

6. To educate the farmer in self-help.

7. To secure purity of feeding stuff, seeds, and manures.

8. To provide up-to-date machinery for farmers.

9. To improve live-stock by the co-operative ownership of pedigree bulls, boars, etc.

10. To point out to the farmer that he cannot afford to "buy retail and sell wholesale."

The strange assortment of aims is elucidated by an extract from the society's formal rules, which states that it seeks "to secure the co-operation of all connected with the land, whether as owners, occupiers, or labourers, and to promote the formation of agricultural co-operative societies for the purchase of requisites for the sale of produce for agricultural credit, banking, and insurance, and for all other forms of co-operation for the benefit of agriculture." Any examination of the greater part of these aims would lie outside the scope of this inquiry. It is clear, however, from a perusal of the other publications of the society, that co-operation for the purchase of farming requisites is more attractive and more feasible in the eyes of most of the adherents and advocates of the association than co-operation for the sale of produce. The advantages of the former policy are obvious, and lend themselves readily to exposition, while the profit of the latter is often overlooked. But some of the best work of co-operators has been done in this direction.

The second annual report of the society gives a most interesting account of the trading operations of the Bewdley Agricultural Supply Association, Limited. This energetic society went boldly into the fruit and vegetable trade, and bought orchards after the manner of the dealers in that part of England. A gang of trained pickers moved from farm to farm gathering the fruit, which, when properly graded and packed in a large warehouse, was sold at a satisfactory profit, while it is also pleasant to learn the prices given to the farmers by the society met with approval. The same business was undertaken with like results in the case of plums, damsons, and blackberries, though the crops being poor, there was not much to be done. Large quantities of potatoes were bought, and an excellent market for them was found in London, after they had been carefully graded. A contract was made to supply the Great Western Railway refreshment-rooms with vegetables, fruit, poultry, eggs, etc., from the beginning of the year 1903. But the most interesting experiment took place in connection with the green pea and cherry markets. Very large quantities of green peas of a good quality had been produced, the season having been favourable for the growth of large crops even on poor land. The price in Birmingham and the Black Country towns was extremely low, and as it was suspected that the dealers would endeavour to form a "knock-out" ring, and drive the price down to a yet lower figure, the society, with a rare enterprise, bought up something like a hundred acres of peas, in lots varying from two to nine acres each, with the result, as the report states, that farmers were enabled to obtain a reasonable price for their peas. The same policy was adopted when an attempt was made to make the low price of strawberries an excuse for cutting down the price of cherries.

Results such as these amply justify the existence of the Bewdley Society, and must further the cause of co-operation both in that and other districts.

The Agricultural Organisation Society is still in its infancy, and as time goes on, and if the society receives adequate support, we may expect to see many other co-operative societies started, and the sphere of usefulness of that body greatly extended. An especially fertile field for its efforts appears to exist in Wales, where the conditions are at present very favourable to its enterprise. But, of course, there were many co-operative agricultural societies in existence before this organisation existed, and its promoters would probably admit that it is modelled as far as circumstances permit on the lines of the more famous society in Ireland, with which the name of Sir Horace Plunkett is so honourably associated. The great success of this body, and the valuable work it has done, are known all over the world. The labours of its founder, for so many years fruitless and regarded with suspicion, have had the most surprising results. The circumstances were in some respects favourable, for the Irish have been trained for long years in forming associations, while the English farmer has been taught to depend on individual effort. The peculiar adaptability of the soil and climate for the manufacture of dairy produce, an article which experience has shown lends itself to co-operative effort, the almost total absence of home markets, and the difficulty experienced by the small farmer in procuring modern appliances and producing marketable articles, were at once an advantage and a hindrance. Once guided in the right direction, the forces that impeded progress would assist the movement on its way, but it needed years of toil to achieve that result.

The benefits gained by the co-operation have been manifest and substantial. Apart from the growing numbers of new members and new societies, the interest shown in the movement in distant countries, and the organisations that have arisen in its imitation, are clear signs of its prosperity. The reports of the society show that on all sides better prices have been paid to the producers who bring their eggs and milk to the collecting depôt than were offered by the dealers in the old days. The different local societies have been obliged to pay higher prices in recent years than they gave when they began business, while the farmers have been relieved of the trouble of finding a market for their goods. But the process has been carried a step further, and a body has been created for the purpose of selling the produce of these societies. This body, in the words of the reports of the Irish Agricultural Organisation Society for 1899 and 1901, was established in 1893 by a number of the dairy societies, which found it necessary to form a federation for the purpose of jointly selling their produce in the large English markets, and of establishing a distinct reputation and, if possible, a national brand for unadulterated Irish creamery butter. Repeated difficulties, incidental to a totally novel and extensive class of business undertaken by farmers hitherto inexperienced in large commercial transactions, beset the earlier years of this enterprise. But it has succeeded in overcoming all difficulties, and now stands in a secure financial position. Shipping depôts have been established at Dublin and Belfast, and new premises have been built at Limerick out of the society's accumulated profit; and if the constituent bodies can be induced to sell all their produce through this agency instead of sending to it only what they are unable to sell elsewhere, it would appear to have a great future before it. The success of all co-operative societies depends on the loyalty with which their members observe the rule that the whole of the produce of each member shall be sent to the depôt, and not merely the balance that he is unable to dispose of through the ordinary trade channels.

The Irish Agricultural Wholesale Society is a kindred body formed for the purpose of doing for agricultural societies in Ireland what the Co-operative Agency has done for the creameries. To a great extent the business transactions of this union consist in the purchase of farm requirements and their sale to co-operators, but a great deal has been done in the direction of the sale of produce. A number of societies in the south and west have sold their barley and oats at the Dublin Corn Exchange through the Irish Agricultural Wholesale Society, and by this means not only has a better price been secured, but it is claimed that the price in the local markets has been raised. A like result was achieved in the sale of pigs, which were sold direct to the curers instead of at the local fairs. Emboldened by the success of these two associations, the Irish Agricultural Organisation Society have boldly undertaken to promote the formation of bee-keepers' societies on co-operative principles. These societies, it announces in its leaflet, are to be affiliated to the Irish Bee-keepers' Federation, which will undertake all the business of marketing honey for its members and federated societies, distributing the profits among the members in proportion to the amount of their purchases and sales.

With the record of so brilliant a success in so short a space of time confronting the critic, it is difficult to say what the confines of this great development will be. With the knowledge of the benefit it has been to Ireland, of the salvation it has been to many small farmers struggling with adversity in isolation and ignorance, it seems ungracious to find fault with its ideals or to suggest that the great hopes cherished by its advocates may be blighted. It is true it has done more than help the farmer to buy his requisites cheaper or sell his produce dearer : it has roused a spirit of energy, independence, and thrift, stimulated a feeling of loyalty and trust, and may bring goodwill into many a home formerly swayed by class hatred, jealousy, and superstition. But in itself co-operation is not a virtue, it is a method of doing business, and like all other such methods, is subject to its limitations. It is beyond all cavil admirably suited to the production and sale of certain classes of farm produce, among which butter and cream are the most conspicuous. It is probably equally well suited to bee-keeping, fruit and vegetable growing, and perhaps to some forms of stock-rearing. But it is not easy to see how it can be applied to such extensive operations as wheat-growing, sheep-feeding, or any of the styles of farming which are usually practised by large farmers, with anything like the same amount of success. At all events, when it encroaches on these domains it will have to meet with an opposition combined, intelligent, and resourceful beyond all present experience. It is not to be supposed that the men who through so many difficulties have fought their way alone and have established themselves in their businesses or their occupation will be driven out of it without a desperate struggle.

Be that as it may, there are two points in which the English farmer may perhaps learn a valuable lesson from the Irish co-operators. The Irish Agricultural Organisation Society has shown conclusively that in the modern world of trade there exists a superfluity of intermediaries between the producer and the consumer, who live, or at any rate make their profits out of the labour of the farmer, driving down the prices he is given for his commodities below their true value. Such men serve no useful purpose in the present rapid system of commercial transactions, and are better eliminated. They have shown that one of the secrets of profitable marketing consists in the careful sampling, grading, and packing of goods for the salesmen, whereby agricultural produce can pass from hand to hand unexamined and untested, in the same way as a bale of textile goods bearing the stamp of some honourable manufacturer. And, finally, they have demonstrated that it is the duty of the farmer to produce, and that the business of trading in his product should not be carried out by him in person, but should be delegated to some agent, whether on the co-operative or the individual system, who should be skilled in disposing of his wares to the best advantage not of himself, but of the farmer. Who knows but that a great fortune may still lie before the English farmer, if he will but learn the lesson?

INDEX

A CATALOGUE OF

MESSRS. METHUEN'S
PUBLICATIONS

Colonial Editions are published of all Messrs. METHUEN's Novels issued at a price above 2s. 6d., and similar editions are published of some works of General Literature. These are marked in the Catalogue. Colonial editions are only for circulation in the British Colonies and India.

An asterisk denotes that a book is in the Press.

PART I.—GENERAL LITERATURE

THE MOTOR YEAR BOOK FOR 1905. With many Illustrations and Diagrams. *Crown 8vo. 5s. net.*

HEALTH, WEALTH AND WISDOM. *Crown 8vo. 1s. net.*

FELISSA; OR, THE LIFE AND OPINIONS OF A KITTEN OF SENTIMENT. With 12 Coloured Plates. *Post 16mo. 2s. 6d. net*

Abbot (Jacob). See Little Blue Books.
*Abbott (J. H. M.), Author of 'Tommy Cornstalk.' THE OLD COUNTRY : IMPRESSIONS OF AN AUSTRALIAN IN ENGLAND. *Crown 8vo. 6s.*
Acatos (M. J.). See Junior School Books.
Adams (Frank). JACK SPRATT. With 24 Coloured Pictures. *Super Royal 16mo. 2s.*
Adeney (W. F.), M.A. See Bennett and Adeney.
Æschylus. See Classical Translations.
Æsop. See Illustrated Pocket Library.
Ainsworth (W. Harrison). See Illustrated Pocket Library.
*Aldis (Janet). MADAME GEOFFRIN, HER SALON, AND HER TIMES. With many Portraits and Illustrations. *Demy 8vo. 10s. 6d. net.*
A Colonial Edition is also published.
Alderson (J. P.). MR. ASQUITH. With Portraits and Illustrations. *Demy 8vo. 7s. 6d. net.*
Alexander (William), D.D., Archbishop of Armagh. THOUGHTS AND COUNSELS OF MANY YEARS. Selected by J. H. BURN, B.D. *Demy 16mo. 2s. 6d.*
Aiken (Henry). THE NATIONAL SPORTS OF GREAT BRITAIN. With descriptions in English and French. With 51 Coloured Plates. *Royal Folio. Five Guineas net.*
See also Illustrated Pocket Library.

Allen (Jessie). See Little Books on Art.
Allen (J. Romilly), F.S.A. See Antiquary's Books.
Almack (E.). See Little Books on Art.
Amherst (Lady). A SKETCH OF EGYPTIAN HISTORY FROM THE EARLIEST TIMES TO THE PRESENT DAY. With many Illustrations, some of which are in Colour. *Demy 8vo. 10s. 6d. net.*
Anderson (F. M.). THE STORY OF THE BRITISH EMPIRE FOR CHILDREN. With many Illustrations. *Crown 8vo. 2s.*
*Anderson (J. G.), B.A., Examiner to London University, the College of Preceptors, and the Welsh Intermediate Board. NOUVELLE GRAMMAIRE FRANÇAISE. *Crown 8vo. 2s.*
*EXERCISES ON NOUVELLE GRAMMAIRE FRANÇAISE. *Crown 8vo. 1s. 6d.*
Andrewes (Bishop). PRECES PRIVATAE. Edited, with Notes, by F. E. BRIGHTMAN, M.A., of Pusey House, Oxford. *Crown 8vo. 6s.*
Anglo-Australian. AFTER-GLOW MEMORIES. *Crown 8vo. 6s.*
Aristophanes. THE FROGS. Translated into English by E. W. HUNTINGFORD, M.A., Professor of Classics in Trinity College, Toronto. *Crown 8vo. 2s. 6d.*
Aristotle. THE NICOMACHEAN ETHICS. Edited, with an Introduction and Notes, by JOHN BURNET, M.A., Professor of Greek at St. Andrews. *Demy 8vo. 10s. 6d. net.*
Ashton (R.). See Little Blue Books.
*Askham (Richard). THE LIFE OF WALT WHITMAN. With Portraits and Illustrations. *Demy 8vo. 10s. 6d. net.*
A Colonial Edition is also published.
Atkins (H. G.). See Oxford Biographies.
Atkinson (C. M.). JEREMY BENTHAM. *Demy 8vo. 5s. net.*

Atkinson (T. D.). A SHORT HISTORY OF ENGLISH ARCHITECTURE. With over 200 Illustrations by the Author and others. *Second Edition. Fcap. 8vo. 3s. 6d. net.*

*A GLOSSARY OF TERMS USED IN ENGLISH ARCHITECTURE. *Fcap. 8vo. 3s. 6d. net.*

Auden (T.), M.A., F.S.A. See Ancient Cities.

Aurelius (Marcus). See Methuen's Standard Library.

Austen (Jane). See Little Library and Methuen's Standard Library.

Aves (Ernest). See Books on Business.

Bacon (Francis). See Little Library and Methuen's Standard Library.

Baden-Powell (R. S. S.), Major-General. THE DOWNFALL OF PREMPEH. A Diary of Life in Ashanti, 1895. With 21 Illustrations and a Map. *Third Edition. Large Crown 8vo. 6s.*
A Colonial Edition is also published.

THE MATABELE CAMPAIGN, 1896. With nearly 100 Illustrations. *Fourth and Cheaper Edition. Large Crown 8vo. 6s.*
A Colonial Edition is also published.

Bailey (J. C.), M.A. See Cowper.

Baker (W. G.), M.A. See Junior Examination Series.

Baker (Julian L.), F.I.C., F.C.S. See Books on Business.

Balfour (Graham). THE LIFE OF ROBERT LOUIS STEVENSON. *Second Edition. Two Volumes. Demy 8vo. 25s. net.*
A Colonial Edition is also published.

Bally (S. E.) See Commercial Series.

Banks (Elizabeth L.). THE AUTO-BIOGRAPHY OF A 'NEWSPAPER GIRL.' With a Portrait of the Author and her Dog. *Second Edition. Crown 8vo. 6s.*
A Colonial Edition is also published.

Barham (R. H.). See Little Library.

Baring (The Hon. Maurice). WITH THE RUSSIANS IN MANCHURIA. *Second Edition. Demy 8vo. 7s. 6d. net.*
A Colonial Edition is also published.

Baring-Gould (S.). THE LIFE OF NAPOLEON BONAPARTE. With over 450 Illustrations in the Text, and 12 Photogravure Plates. *Gilt top. Large quarto. 36s.*

THE TRAGEDY OF THE CÆSARS. With numerous Illustrations from Busts, Gems, Cameos, etc. *Fifth Edition. Royal 8vo. 10s. 6d. net.*

A BOOK OF FAIRY TALES. With numerous Illustrations and Initial Letters by ARTHUR J. GASKIN. *Second Edition. Crown 8vo. Buckram. 6s.*

A BOOK OF BRITTANY. With numerous Illustrations. *Crown 8vo. 6s.*

OLD ENGLISH FAIRY TALES. With numerous Illustrations by F. D. BEDFORD. *Second Edition. Crown 8vo. Buckram. 6s.*
A Colonial Edition is also published.

THE VICAR OF MORWENSTOW: A Biography. A new and Revised Edition. With a Portrait. *Crown 8vo. 3s. 6d.*

DARTMOOR: A Descriptive and Historical Sketch. With Plans and numerous Illustrations. *Crown 8vo. 6s.*

THE BOOK OF THE WEST. With numerous Illustrations. *Two volumes.* Vol. I. Devon. *Second Edition.* Vol. II. Cornwall. *Second Edition. Crown 8vo. 6s. each.*

A BOOK OF NORTH WALES. With numerous Illustrations. *Crown 8vo. 6s.*

A BOOK OF SOUTH WALES. With many Illustrations. *Crown 8vo. 6s.*

*THE RIVIERA. With many Illustrations. *Crown 8vo. 6s.*
A Colonial Edition is also published.

A BOOK OF GHOSTS. With 8 Illustrations by D. Murray Smith. *Second Edition. Crown 8vo. 6s.*
A Colonial Edition is also published.

OLD COUNTRY LIFE. With 67 Illustrations. *Fifth Edition. Large Crown 8vo. 6s.*

A GARLAND OF COUNTRY SONG: English Folk Songs with their Traditional Melodies. Collected and arranged by S. BARING-GOULD and H. F. SHEPPARD. *Demy 4to. 6s.*

SONGS OF THE WEST: Traditional Ballads and Songs of the West of England, with their Melodies. Collected by S. BARING-GOULD, M.A., and H. F. SHEPPARD, M.A. In 4 Parts. *Parts I., II., III., 2s. 6d. each. Part IV., 4s. In One Volume, Paper Sides, Cloth Back, 10s. net.; Roan, 15s.*
See also The Little Guides and Methuen's Half-Crown Library.

Barker (Aldred F.). See Textbooks of Technology.

Barnes (W. E.), D.D. See Churchman's Bible.

Barnett (Mrs. P. A.). See Little Library.

Baron (R. R. N.), M.A. FRENCH PROSE COMPOSITION. *Second Edition. Cr. 8vo. 2s. 6d. Key, 3s. net.* See also Junior School Books.

Barron (H. M.), M.A., Wadham College, Oxford. TEXTS FOR SERMONS. With a Preface by Canon SCOTT HOLLAND. *Crown 8vo. 3s. 6d.*

Bastable (C. F.), M.A. See Social Questions Series.

Batson (Mrs. Stephen). A BOOK OF THE COUNTRY AND THE GARDEN. Illustrated by F. CARRUTHERS GOULD and A. C. GOULD. *Demy 8vo. 10s. 6d.*

A CONCISE HANDBOOK OF GARDEN FLOWERS. *Fcap. 8vo. 3s. 6d.*

Batten (Loring W.), Ph.D., S.T.D., Some time Professor in the Philadelphia Divinity School. THE HEBREW PROPHET. *Crown 8vo. 6s.*

Beaman (A. Hulme). PONS ASINORUM; OR, A GUIDE TO BRIDGE. *Second Edition. Fcap. 8vo. 2s.*

Beard (W. S.). See Junior Examination Series and the Beginner's Books.

Beckford (Peter). THOUGHTS ON HUNTING. Edited by J. OTHO PAGET, and Illustrated by G. H. JALLAND. *Second and Cheaper Edition. Demy 8vo. 6s.*

Beckford (William). See Little Library.

Beeching (H. C.), M.A., Canon of Westminster. See Library of Devotion.

*****Begbie (Harold).** MASTER WORKERS. With Illustrations. *Demy 8vo. 7s. 6d. net.*

Behmen (Jacob). DIALOGUES ON THE SUPERSENSUAL LIFE. Edited by BERNARD HOLLAND. *Fcap. 8vo. 3s. 6d.*

Belloc (Hilaire). PARIS. With Maps and Illustrations. *Crown 8vo. 6s.*

Bellot (H. H. L.), M.A. THE INNER AND MIDDLE TEMPLE. With numerous Illustrations. *Crown 8vo. 6s. net.*
See also **L. A. A. Jones.**

Bennett (W. H.), M.A. A PRIMER OF THE BIBLE. *Second Edition. Cr. 8vo. 2s. 6d.*

Bennett (W. H.) and Adeney (W. F.). A BIBLICAL INTRODUCTION. *Second Edition. Crown 8vo. 7s. 6d.*

Benson (Archbishop). GOD'S BOARD: Communion Addresses. *Fcap. 8vo. 3s. 6d. net.*

Benson (A. C.), M.A. See Oxford Biographies.

Benson (R. M.). THE WAY OF HOLINESS: a Devotional Commentary on the 119th Psalm. *Crown 8vo. 5s.*

Bernard (E. R.), M.A., Canon of Salisbury. THE ENGLISH SUNDAY. *Fcap. 8vo. 1s. 6d.*

Bertouch (Baroness de). THE LIFE OF FATHER IGNATIUS, O.S.B., THE MONK OF LLANTHONY. With Illustrations. *Demy 8vo. 10s. 6d. net.*
A Colonial Edition is also published.

Betham-Edwards (M.). HOME LIFE IN FRANCE. With many Illustrations. *Second Edition. Demy 8vo. 7s. 6d. net.*

Bethune-Baker (J. F.), M.A., Fellow of Pembroke College, Cambridge. See Handbooks of Theology.

Bidez (M.). See Byzantine Texts.

Biggs (C. R. D.), D.D. See Churchman's Bible.

Bindley (T. Herbert), B.D. THE OECUMENICAL DOCUMENTS OF THE FAITH. With Introductions and Notes. *Crown 8vo. 6s.*

Binyon (Laurence). THE DEATH OF ADAM, AND OTHER POEMS. *Crown 8vo. 3s. 6d. net.*

*****WILLIAM BLAKE.** In 2 volumes. *Quarto. £1, 1s. each. Vol. I.*

Birnstingl (Ethel). See Little Books on Art.

Blair (Robert). See Illustrated Pocket Library.

Blake (William). See Illustrated Pocket Library and Little Library.

Blaxland (B.), M.A. See Library of Devotion.

Bloom (T. Harvey), M.A. SHAKESPEARE'S GARDEN. With Illustrations. *Fcap. 8vo. 3s. 6d. ; leather, 4s. 6d. net.*

Blouet (Henri). See The Beginner's Books.

Boardman (T. H.), M.A. See Text Books of Technology.

Bodley (J. E. C.). Author of 'France.' THE CORONATION OF EDWARD VII. *Demy 8vo. 21s. net.* By Command of the King.

Body (George), D.D. THE SOUL'S PILGRIMAGE : Devotional Readings from his published and unpublished writings. Selected and arranged by J. H. BURN, B.D. F.R.S.E. *Pott 8vo. 2s. 6d.*

Bona (Cardinal). See Library of Devotion.

Boon (F. C.). See Commercial Series.

Borrow (George). See Little Library.

Bos (J. Ritzema). AGRICULTURAL ZOOLOGY. Translated by J. R. AINSWORTH DAVIS, M.A. With an Introduction by ELEANOR A. ORMEROD, F.E.S. With 155 Illustrations. *Crown 8vo. Third Edition. 3s. 6d.*

Botting (C. G.), B.A. EASY GREEK EXERCISES. *Crown 8vo. 2s.* See also Junior Examination Series.

Boulton (E. S.), M.A. GEOMETRY ON MODERN LINES. *Crown 8vo. 2s.*

*****Boulton (William B.).** THOMAS GAINSBOROUGH : His Life, Times, Work, Sitters, and Friends. With 40 Illustrations. *Demy 8vo. 7s. 6d. net.*

SIR JOSHUA REYNOLDS. With 49 Illustrations. *Demy 8vo. 7s. 6d. net.*

Bowden (E. M.). THE IMITATION OF BUDDHA : Being Quotations from Buddhist Literature for each Day in the Year. *Fifth Edition. Crown 16mo. 2s. 6d.*

Boyle (W.). CHRISTMAS AT THE ZOO. With Verses by W. BOYLE and 24 Coloured Pictures by H. B. NEILSON. *Super Royal 16mo. 2s.*

Brabant (F. G.), M.A. See The Little Guides.

Brodrick (Mary) and Morton (Anderson). A CONCISE HANDBOOK OF EGYPTIAN ARCHÆOLOGY. With many Illustrations. *Crown 8vo. 3s. 6d.*

Brooke (A. S.), M.A. SLINGSBY AND SLINGSBY CASTLE. With many Illustrations. *Crown 8vo. 7s. 6d.*

Brooks (E. W.). See Byzantine Tests.

Brown (P. H.), Fraser Professor of Ancient (Scottish) History at the University of Edinburgh. SCOTLAND IN THE TIME OF QUEEN MARY. *Demy 8vo. 7s. 6d. net.*

Browne (Sir Thomas). See Methuen's Standard Library.

Brownell (C. L.). THE HEART OF JAPAN. Illustrated. *Third Edition. Crown 8vo. 6s. ; also Demy 8vo. 6d.*
A Colonial Edition is also published.

Browning (Robert). See Little Library.

Buckland (Francis T.). CURIOSITIES OF NATURAL HISTORY. With Illustrations by HARRY B. NEILSON. *Crown 8vo. 3s. 6d.*

Buckton (A. M.). THE BURDEN OF ENGELA: a Ballad-Epic. *Second Edition. Crown 8vo. 3s. 6d. net.*

EAGER HEART: A Mystery Play. *Third Edition. Crown 8vo. 1s. net.*

Budge (E. A. Wallis). THE GODS OF THE EGYPTIANS. With over 100 Coloured Plates and many Illustrations. *Two Volumes. Royal 8vo. £3, 3s. net.*

Bull (Paul), Army Chaplain. GOD AND OUR SOLDIERS. *Crown 8vo. 6s.*
A Colonial Edition is also published.

Bulley (Miss). See Social Questions Series.

Bunyan (John). THE PILGRIM'S PROGRESS. Edited, with an Introduction, by C. H. FIRTH, M.A. With 39 Illustrations by R. ANNING BELL. *Cr. 8vo. 6s.*
See also Library of Devotion and Methuen's Standard Library.

Burch (G. J.), M.A., F.R.S. A MANUAL OF ELECTRICAL SCIENCE. With numerous Illustrations. *Crown 8vo. 3s.*

Burgess (Gelett). GOOPS AND HOW TO BE THEM. With numerous Illustrations. *Small 4to. 6s.*

Burke (Edmund). See Methuen's Standard Library.

Burn (A. E.), D.D., Prebendary of Lichfield. See Handbooks of Theology.

Burn (J. H.), B.D. See Library of Devotion.

Burnand (Sir F. C.). RECORDS AND REMINISCENCES, PERSONAL AND GENERAL. With a Portrait by H. v. HERKOMER. *Crown 8vo. Fourth and Cheaper Edition. 6s.*
A Colonial Edition is also published.

Burns (Robert), THE POEMS OF. Edited by ANDREW LANG and W. A. CRAIGIE. With Portrait. *Third Edition. Demy 8vo, gilt top. 6s.*

Burnside (W. F.), M.A. OLD TESTAMENT HISTORY FOR USE IN SCHOOLS. *Crown 8vo. 3s. 6d.*

Burton (Alfred). See Illustrated Pocket Library.

*****Bussell (F. W.),** D.D., Fellow and Vice-President of Brasenose College, Oxford. CHRISTIAN THEOLOGY AND SOCIAL PROGRESS: The Bampton Lectures for 1905. *Demy 8vo. 12s. 6d. net.*

Butler (Joseph). See Methuen's Standard Library.

Caldecott (Alfred), D.D. See Handbooks of Theology.

Calderwood (D. S.), Headmaster of the Normal School, Edinburgh. TEST CARDS IN EUCLID AND ALGEBRA. In three packets of 40, with Answers. *1s. each.* Or in three Books, price *2d., 2d.,* and *3d.*

Cambridge (Ada) [Mrs. Cross]. THIRTY YEARS IN AUSTRALIA. *Demy 8vo 7s. 6d.*
A Colonial Edition is also published.

Canning (George). See Little Library.

Capey (E. F. H.). See Oxford Biographies.

Careless (John). See Illustrated Pocket Library.

Carlyle (Thomas). THE FRENCH REVOLUTION. Edited by C. R. L. FLETCHER, Fellow of Magdalen College, Oxford. *Three Volumes. Crown 8vo. 18s.*
THE LIFE AND LETTERS OF OLIVER CROMWELL. With an Introduction by C. H. FIRTH, M.A., and Notes and Appendices by Mrs. S. C. LOMAS. *Three Volumes. Demy 8vo. 18s. net.*

Carlyle (R. M. and A. J.), M.A. See Leaders of Religion.

*****Carpenter (Margaret).** THE CHILD IN ART. With numerous Illustrations. *Crown 8vo. 6s.*

Chamberlin (Wilbur B.). ORDERED TO CHINA. *Crown 8vo. 6s.*
A Colonial Edition is also published.

Channer (C. C.) and Roberts (M. E.). LACE-MAKING IN THE MIDLANDS, PAST AND PRESENT. With 16 full-page Illustrations. *Crown 8vo. 2s. 6d.*

Chatterton (Thomas). See Methuen's Standard Library.

Chesterfield (Lord), THE LETTERS OF, TO HIS SON. Edited, with an Introduction by C. STRACHEY, and Notes by A. CALTHROP. *Two Volumes. Cr. 8vo. 12s.*

*****Chesterton (G. K.).** DICKENS. With Portraits and Illustrations. *Demy 8vo. 7s. 6d. net.*
A Colonial Edition is also published.

Christian (F. W.) THE CAROLINE ISLANDS. With many Illustrations and Maps. *Demy 8vo. 12s. 6d. net.*

Cicero. See Classical Translations.

Clarke (F. A.), M.A. See Leaders of Religion.

Cleather (A. L.) and Crump (B.). RICHARD WAGNERS MUSIC DRAMAS: Interpretations, embodying Wagner's own explanations. *In Four Volumes. Fcap 8vo. 2s. 6d. each.*
VOL. I.—THE RING OF THE NIBELUNG.
VOL. II.—PARSIFAL, LOHENGRIN, and THE HOLY GRAIL.
VOL. III.—TRISTAN AND ISOLDE.

Clinch (G.) See The Little Guides.

Clough (W. T.), See Junior School Books.

Coast (W. G), B.A. EXAMINATION PAPERS IN VERGIL. *Crown 8vo. 2s.*

Cobb (T.). See Little Blue Books.

*****Cobb (W. F.),** M.A. THE BOOK OF PSALMS: with a Commentary. *Demy 8vo. 10s. 6d. net.*

Coleridge (S. T.), SELECTIONS FROM. Edited by ARTHUR SYMONS. *Fcap. 8vo. 2s. 6d. net.*

Collins (W. E.), M.A. See Churchman's Library.

Colonna. HYPNEROTOMACHIA POLIPHILI UBI HUMANA OMNIA NON NISI SOMNIUM ESSE DOCET ATQUE OBITER PLURIMA SCITU SANE QUAM DIGNA COMMEMORAT. An edition limited to 350 copies on handmade paper. *Folio. Three Guineas net.*

Combe (William). See Illustrated Pocket Library.

Cook (A. M.), M.A. See E. C. Marchant.

Cooke-Taylor (R. W.). See Social Questions Series.

Corelli (Marie). THE PASSING OF THE GREAT QUEEN: A Tribute to the Noble Life of Victoria Regina. *Small 4to. 1s.*

A CHRISTMAS GREETING. *Sm. 4to. 1s.*

Corkran (Alice). See Little Books on Art.

Cotes (Rosemary). DANTE'S GARDEN. With a Frontispiece. *Second Edition. Fcap. 8vo. 2s. 6d.; leather, 3s. 6d. net.*

BIBLE FLOWERS. With a Frontispiece and Plan. *Fcap. 8vo. 2s. 6d. net.*

Cowley (Abraham). See Little Library.

***Cowper (William)**, THE POEMS OF. Edited with an Introduction and Notes by J. C. BAILEY, M.A. With Illustrations, including two unpublished designs by WILLIAM BLAKE. *Two Volumes. Demy 8vo. 10s. 6d. net.*

Cox (J. Charles), LL.D., F.S.A. See Little Guides, The Antiquary's Books, and Ancient Cities.

Cox (Harold), B.A. See Social Questions Series.

Crabbe (George). See Little Library.

Craigie (W. A.). A PRIMER OF BURNS. *Crown 8vo. 2s. 6d.*

Craik (Mrs.). See Little Library.

Crashaw (Richard). See Little Library.

Crawford (F. G.). See Mary C. Danson.

Crouch (W.). BRYAN KING. With a Portrait. *Crown 8vo. 3s. 6d. net.*

Cruikshank (G.) THE LOVING BALLAD OF LORD BATEMAN. With 11 Plates. *Crown 16mo. 1s. 6d. net.* From the edition published by C. Tilt, 1811.

Crump (B.). See A. L. Cleather.

Cunliffe (F. H. E.), Fellow of All Souls' College, Oxford. THE HISTORY OF THE BOER WAR. With many Illustrations, Plans, and Portraits. *In 2 vols. Quarto. 15s. each.*

Cutts (E. L.), D.D. See Leaders of Religion.

Daniell (G. W.), M.A. See Leaders of Religion.

Danson (Mary C.) and Crawford (F. G.). FATHERS IN THE FAITH. *Small 8vo. 1s. 6d.*

Dante. LA COMMEDIA DI DANTE. The Italian Text edited by PAGET TOYNBEE, M.A., D.Litt. *Crown 8vo. 6s.*

***THE PURGATORIO OF DANTE.** Translated into Spenserian Prose by C. GORDON WRIGHT. With the Italian text. *Fcap. 8vo. 2s. 6d. net.* See also Paget Toynbee and Little Library.

Darley (George). See Little Library.

***D'Arcy (R. F.)**, M.A. A NEW TRIGONOMETRY FOR BEGINNERS. *Crown 8vo. 2s. 6d.*

Davenport (Cyril). See Connoisseur's Library and Little Books on Art.

***Davis (H. W. C.)**, M.A., Fellow and Tutor of Balliol College, Author of 'Charlemagne.' ENGLAND UNDER THE NORMANS AND ANGEVINS: 1066-1072. With Maps and Illustrations. *Demy 8vo. 10s. 6d. net.*

Dawson (A. J.). MOROCCO. Being a bundle of jottings, notes, impressions, tales, and tributes. With many Illustrations. *Demy 8vo. 10s. 6d. net.*

Deane (A. C.). See Little Library.

Delbos (Leon). THE METRIC SYSTEM. *Crown 8vo. 2s.*

Demosthenes. THE OLYNTHIACS AND PHILIPPICS. Translated upon a new principle by OTHO HOLLAND. *Crown 8vo. 2s. 6d.*

Demosthenes. AGAINST CONON AND CALLICLES. Edited with Notes and Vocabulary, by F. DARWIN SWIFT, M.A. *Fcap. 8vo. 2s.*

Dickens (Charles). See Little Library and Illustrated Pocket Library.

Dickinson (Emily). POEMS. First Series. *Crown 8vo. 4s. 6d. net.*

Dickinson (G. L.), M.A., Fellow of King's College, Cambridge. THE GREEK VIEW OF LIFE. *Third Edition. Crown 8vo. 2s. 6d.*

Dickson (H. N.), F.R.S.E., F.R.Met. Soc. METEOROLOGY. Illustrated. *Crown 8vo. 2s. 6d.*

Dilke (Lady). See Social Questions Series.

Dillon (Edward). See Connoisseur's Library.

Ditchfield (P. H.), M.A., F.S.A. THE STORY OF OUR ENGLISH TOWNS. With an Introduction by AUGUSTUS JESSOPP, D.D. *Second Edition. Crown 8vo. 6s.*

OLD ENGLISH CUSTOMS: Extant at the Present Time. *Crown 8vo. 6s.* See also Methuen's Half-crown Library.

Dixon (W. M.), M.A. A PRIMER OF TENNYSON. *Second Edition. Crown 8vo. 2s. 6d.*

ENGLISH POETRY FROM BLAKE TO BROWNING. *Second Edition. Crown 8vo. 2s. 6d.*

Dole (N. H.). FAMOUS COMPOSERS. With Portraits. *Two Volumes. Demy 8vo. 12s. net.*

Doney (May). SONGS OF THE REAL. *Crown 8vo. 3s. 6d. net.* A volume of poems.

Douglas (James). THE MAN IN THE PULPIT. *Crown 8vo. 2s. 6d. net.*

Dowden (J.), D.D., Lord Bishop of Edinburgh. See Churchman's Library.

Drage (G.) See Books on Business.

Driver (S. R.), D.D., D.C.L., Canon of Christ Church, Regius Professor of Hebrew in the University of Oxford. SERMONS ON SUBJECTS CONNECTED WITH THE OLD TESTAMENT. *Crown 8vo. 6s.* See also Westminster Commentaries.

Dryhurst (A. R.). See Little Books on Art.

Duguid (Charles). See Books on Business.

Duncan (S. J.) (Mrs. COTES), Author of 'A Voyage of Consolation.' ON THE OTHER SIDE OF THE LATCH. *Second Edition. Crown 8vo. 6s.*

Dunn (J. T.), D.Sc., **and Mundella (V. A.).** GENERAL ELEMENTARY SCIENCE. With 114 Illustrations. *Second Edition. Crown 8vo. 3s. 6d.*

Dunstan (A. E.), B.Sc. See Junior School Books.

Durham (The Earl of). A REPORT ON CANADA. With an Introductory Note. *Demy 8vo. 4s. 6d. net.*

Dutt (W. A.). A POPULAR GUIDE TO NORFOLK. *Medium 8vo. 6d. net.* THE NORFOLK BROADS. With coloured and other Illustrations by FRANK SOUTHGATE. *Large Demy 8vo. 6s.* See also The Little Guides.

Earle (John), Bishop of Salisbury. MICRO-COSMOGRAPHIE, OR A PIECE OF THE WORLD DISCOVERED; IN ESSAYES AND CHARACTERS. *Post 16mo. 2s net.*

Edmonds (Major J. E.), R.E. ; D.A.Q.-M.G. See W. Birkbeck Wood.

Edwards (Clement). See Social Questions Series.

Edwards (W. Douglas). See Commercial Series.

Egan (Pierce). See Illustrated Pocket Library.

*Egerton (H. E.), M.A. A HISTORY OF BRITISH COLONIAL POLICY. New and Cheaper Issue. *Demy 8vo. 7s. 6d. net.* A Colonial Edition is also published.

Ellaby (C. G.). See The Little Guides.

Ellerton (F. G.). See S. J. Stone.

Ellwood (Thomas), THE HISTORY OF THE LIFE OF. Edited by C. G. CRUMP, M.A. *Crown 8vo. 6s.*

Engel (E.). A HISTORY OF ENGLISH LITERATURE: From its Beginning to Tennyson. Translated from the German. *Demy 8vo. 7s. 6d. net.*

Erasmus. A Book called in Latin EN-CHIRIDION MILITIS CHRISTIANI, and in English the Manual of the Christian Knight, replenished with most wholesome precepts, made by the famous clerk Erasmus of Roterdame, to the which is added a new and marvellous profitable preface.

From the edition printed by Wynken de Worde for John Byddell, 1533. *Fcap. 8vo. 3s. 6d. net.*

Fairbrother (W. H.), M.A. THE PHILO-SOPHY OF T. H. GREEN. *Second Edition. Crown 8vo. 3s. 6d.*

Farrer (Reginald). THE GARDEN OF ASIA. *Second Edition. Crown 8vo. 6s.* A Colonial Edition is also published.

Ferrier (Susan). See Little Library.

Fidler (T. Claxton), M.Inst. C.E. See Books on Business.

Fielding (Henry). See Methuen's Standard Library.

Finn (S. W.), M.A. See Junior Examination Series.

Firth (C. H.), M.A. CROMWELL'S ARMY: A History of the English Soldier during the Civil Wars, the Commonwealth, and the Protectorate. *Crown 8vo. 6s.*

Fisher (G. W.), M.A. ANNALS OF SHREWSBURY SCHOOL. With numerous Illustrations. *Demy 8vo. 10s. 6d.*

FitzGerald (Edward). THE RUBÁIYÁT OF OMAR KHAYYÁM. Printed from the Fifth and last Edition. With a Commentary by Mrs. STEPHEN BATSON, and a Biography of Omar by E. D. ROSS. *Crown 8vo. 6s.* See also Miniature Library.

Flecker (W. H.), M.A., D.C.L., Headmaster of the Dean Close School, Cheltenham. THE STUDENT'S PRAYER BOOK. Part I. MORNING AND EVENING PRAYER AND LITANY. With an Introduction and Notes. *Crown 8vo. 2s. 6d.*

Flux (A. W.), M.A., William Dow Professor of Political Economy in M'Gill University, Montreal. ECONOMIC PRINCIPLES. *Demy 8vo. 7s. 6d. net.*

Fortescue (Mrs. G.) See Little Books on Art.

Fraser (David). A MODERN CAM-PAIGN ; OR, WAR AND WIRELESS TELEGRAPHY IN THE FAR EAST. Illustrated. *Crown 8vo. 6s.* A Colonial Edition is also published.

Fraser (J. F.). ROUND THE WORLD ON A WHEEL. With 100 Illustrations. *Fourth Edition Crown 8vo. 6s.* A Colonial Edition is also published.

French (W.), M.A. See Textbooks of Technology.

Freudenreich (Ed. von). DAIRY BAC-TERIOLOGY. A Short Manual for the Use of Students. Translated by J. R. AINSWORTH DAVIS, M.A. *Second Edition Revised. Crown 8vo. 2s. 6d.*

Fulford (H. W.), M.A. See Churchman's Bible.

C. G., and F. C. G. JOHN BULL'S AD-VENTURES IN THE FISCAL WON-DERLAND. By CHARLES GEAKE. With 46 Illustrations by F. CARRUTHERS GOULD. *Second Edition. Crown 8vo. 1s. net.*

Gallichan (W. M.). See The Little Guides.

Gambado (Geoffrey, Esq.). See Illustrated Pocket Library.

Gaskell (Mrs.). See Little Library.

Gasquet, the Right Rev. Abbot, O.S.B. See Antiquary's Books.

George (H. B.), M.A., Fellow of New College, Oxford. BATTLES OF ENGLISH HISTORY. With numerous Plans. *Fourth Edition.* Revised, with a new Chapter including the South African War. *Crown 8vo. 3s. 6d.*

A HISTORICAL GEOGRAPHY OF THE BRITISH EMPIRE. *Crown 8vo. 3s. 6d.*

Gibbins (H. de B.), Litt.D., M.A. INDUSTRY IN ENGLAND : HISTORICAL OUTLINES. With 5 Maps. *Third Edition. Demy 8vo. 10s. 6d.*

A COMPANION GERMAN GRAMMAR. *Crown 8vo. 1s. 6d.*

THE INDUSTRIAL HISTORY OF ENGLAND. *Tenth Edition.* Revised. With Maps and Plans. *Crown 8vo. 3s.*

ENGLISH SOCIAL REFORMERS. *Second Edition. Crown 8vo. 2s. 6d.* See also Commercial Series and Social Questions Series.

Gibbon (Edward). THE DECLINE AND FALL OF THE ROMAN EMPIRE. A New Edition, edited with Notes, Appendices, and Maps, by J. B. BURY, M.A., Litt.D., Regius Professor of Greek at Cambridge. *In Seven Volumes. Demy 8vo. Gilt top, 8s. 6d. each. Also, Crown 8vo. 6s. each.*

MEMOIRS OF MY LIFE AND WRITINGS. Edited, with an Introduction and Notes, by G. BIRKBECK HILL, LL.D. *Crown 8vo. 6s.*

See also Methuen's Standard Library.

Gibson (E. C. S.), D.D., Lord Bishop of Gloucester. See Westminster Commentaries, Handbooks of Theology, and Oxford Biographies.

Gilbert (A. R.). See Little Books on Art.

Godfrey (Elizabeth). A BOOK OF REMEMBRANCE. *Second Edition. Fcap. 8vo. 2s. 6d. net.*

Godley (A. D.), M.A., Fellow of Magdalen College, Oxford. LYRA FRIVOLA. *Third Edition. Fcap. 8vo. 2s. 6d.*

VERSES TO ORDER. *Second Edition. Fcap. 8vo. 2s. 6d.*

SECOND STRINGS. *Fcap. 8vo. 2s. 6d.*

Goldsmith (Oliver). THE VICAR OF WAKEFIELD. With 24 Coloured Plates by T. ROWLANDSON. *Royal 8vo. One Guinea net.*

Reprinted from the edition of 1817. Also *Fcap. 32mo.* With 10 Plates in Photogravure by Tony Johannot. *Leather, 2s. 6d. net.* See also Illustrated Pocket Library and Methuen's Standard Library.

Goodrich-Freer (A.). IN A SYRIAN SADDLE. *Demy 8vo. 7s. 6d. net.*

Goudge (H. L.), M.A., Principal of Wells

Theological College. See Westminster Commentaries.

Graham (P. Anderson). See Social Questions Series.

Granger (F. S.), M.A., Litt.D. PSYCHOLOGY. *Second Edition. Crown 8vo. 2s. 6d.*

THE SOUL OF A CHRISTIAN. *Crown 8vo. 6s.*

Gray (E. M'Queen). GERMAN PASSAGES FOR UNSEEN TRANSLATION. *Crown 8vo, 2s. 6d.*

Gray (P. L.), B.Sc. THE PRINCIPLES OF MAGNETISM AND ELECTRICITY: an Elementary Text-Book. With 181 Diagrams. *Crown 8vo. 3s. 6d.*

Green (G. Buckland), M.A., Assistant Master at Edinburgh Academy, late Fellow of St. John's College, Oxon. NOTES ON GREEK AND LATIN SYNTAX. *Crown 8vo. 3s. 6d.*

Green (E. T.), M.A. See Churchman's Library.

Greenidge (A. H. J.), M.A. A HISTORY OF ROME: During the Later Republic and the Early Principate. *In Six Volumes. Demy 8vo.* Vol. I. (133-104 B.C.). *10s. 6d. net.*

Greenwell (Dora). See Miniature Library.

Gregory (R. A.) THE VAULT OF HEAVEN. A Popular Introduction to Astronomy. With numerous Illustrations. *Crown 8vo. 2s. 6d.*

Gregory (Miss E. C.). See Library of Devotion.

Greville Minor. A MODERN JOURNAL. Edited by J. A. SPENDER. *Crown 8vo. 3s. 6d. net.*

Grinling (C. H.). A HISTORY OF THE GREAT NORTHERN RAILWAY, 1845-95. With Illustrations. Revised, with an additional chapter. *Demy 8vo. 10s. 6d.*

Grubb (H. C.). See Textbooks of Technology.

Guiney (Louisa I.). HURRELL FROUDE: Memoranda and Comments. Illustrated. *Demy 8vo. 10s. 6d. net.*

*****Gwynn (M. L.).** A BIRTHDAY BOOK. New and cheaper issue. *Royal 8vo. 5s. net.*

Hackett (John), B.D. A HISTORY OF THE ORTHODOX CHURCH OF CYPRUS. With Maps and Illustrations. *Demy 8vo. 15s. net.*

Haddon (A. C.), Sc.D., F.R.S. HEADHUNTERS, BLACK, WHITE, AND BROWN. With many Illustrations and a Map. *Demy 8vo. 15s.*

Hadfield (R. A.). See Social Questions Series.

Hall (R. N.) and Neal (W. G.). THE ANCIENT RUINS OF RHODESIA. With numerous Illustrations. *Second Edition, revised. Demy 8vo. 10s. 6d. net.*

Hall (R. N.). GREAT ZIMBABWE. With numerous Plans and Illustrations. *Royal 8vo. 21s. net.*

Hamilton (F. J.), D.D. See Byzantine Texts.

Hammond (J. L.). CHARLES JAMES FOX : A Biographical Study. *Demy 8vo.* 10s. 6d.

Hannay (D.). A SHORT HISTORY OF THE ROYAL NAVY, FROM EARLY TIMES TO THE PRESENT DAY. Illustrated. *Two Volumes. Demy 8vo.* 7s. 6d. each. Vol. I. 1200-1688.

Hannay (James O.), M.A. THE SPIRIT AND ORIGIN OF CHRISTIAN MONASTICISM. *Crown 8vo.* 6s. THE WISDOM OF THE DESERT. *Crown 8vo.* 3s. 6d. net.

Hare, (A. T.), M.A. THE CONSTRUCTION OF LARGE INDUCTION COILS. With numerous Diagrams. *Demy 8vo.* 6s.

Harrison (Clifford). READING AND READERS. *Fcap. 8vo.* 2s. 6d.

Hawthorne (Nathaniel). See Little Library.

Heath (Frank R.). See The Little Guides.

Heath (Dudley). See Connoisseur's Library.

Hello (Ernest). STUDIES IN SAINTSHIP. Translated from the French by V. M. CRAWFORD. *Fcap 8vo.* 3s. 6d.

***Henderson (B. W.),** Fellow of Exeter College, Oxford. THE LIFE AND PRINCIPATE OF THE EMPEROR NERO. With Illustrations. *New and cheaper issue. Demy 8vo.* 7s. 6d. net.

Henderson (T. F.). See Little Library and Oxford Biographies.

Henley (W. E.). See Methuen's Half-Crown Library.

Henley (W. E.) and Whibley (C.). See Methuen's Half-Crown Library.

Henson (H. H.), B.D., Canon of Westminster. APOSTOLIC CHRISTIANITY: As Illustrated by the Epistles of St. Paul to the Corinthians. *Crown 8vo.* 6s. LIGHT AND LEAVEN : HISTORICAL AND SOCIAL SERMONS. *Crown 8vo.* 6s. DISCIPLINE AND LAW. *Fcap. 8vo.* 2s. 6d.

Herbert (George). See Library of Devotion.

Herbert of Cherbury (Lord). See Miniature Library.

Hewins (W. A. S.), B.A. ENGLISH TRADE AND FINANCE IN THE SEVENTEENTH CENTURY. *Crown 8vo.* 2s. 6d.

Hewitt (Ethel M.) A GOLDEN DIAL. *Fcap. 8vo.* 2s. 6d. net.

Heywood (W.). PALIO AND PONTE : A Book of Tuscan Games. Illustrated. *Royal 8vo.* 21s. net.

Hilbert (T.). See Little Blue Books.

Hill (Clare). See Textbooks of Technology.

Hill (Henry), B.A., Headmaster of the Boy's High School, Worcester, Cape Colony. A SOUTH AFRICAN ARITHMETIC. *Crown 8vo.* 3s. 6d.

Hillegas (Howard C.). WITH THE BOER FORCES. With 24 Illustrations. *Second Edition. Crown 8vo.* 6s. A Colonial Edition is also published.

Hobhouse (Emily). THE BRUNT OF THE WAR. With Map and Illustrations. *Crown 8vo.* 6s. A Colonial Edition is also published.

Hobhouse (L. T.), Fellow of C.C.C., Oxford. THE THEORY OF KNOWLEDGE. *Demy 8vo.* 10s. 6d. net.

Hobson (J. A.), M.A. INTERNATIONAL TRADE : A Study of Economic Principles. *Crown 8vo.* 2s. 6d. net. See also Social Questions Series.

Hodgkin (T.), D.C.L. See Leaders of Religion.

Hodgson (Mrs. A. W.). HOW TO IDENTIFY OLD CHINESE PORCELAIN. *Post 8vo.* 6s.

Hogg (Thomas Jefferson). SHELLEY AT OXFORD. With an Introduction by R. A. STREATFEILD. *Fcap. 8vo.* 2s. net.

Holden-Stone (G. de). See Books on Business.

Holdich (Sir T. H.), K.C.I.E. THE INDIAN BORDERLAND : being a Personal Record of Twenty Years. Illustrated. *Demy 8vo.* 10s. 6d. net.

Holdsworth (W. S.), M.A. A HISTORY OF ENGLISH LAW. *In Two Volumes.* Vol. I. *Demy 8vo.* 10s. 6d. net.

***Holt (Emily).** THE SECRET OF POPULARITY. *Crown 8vo.* 3s. 6d. net. A Colonial Edition is also published.

Holyoake (G. J.). See Social Questions Series.

Hone (Nathaniel J.). See Antiquary's Books.

Hoppner. See Little Galleries.

Horace. See Classical Translations.

Horsburgh (E. L. S.), M.A. WATERLOO : A Narrative and Criticism. With Plans. *Second Edition. Crown 8vo.* 5s. See also Oxford Biographies.

Horth (A.C.). See Textbooks of Technology.

Horton (R. F.), D.D. See Leaders of Religion.

Hosie (Alexander). MANCHURIA. With Illustrations and a Map. *Second Edition. Demy 8vo.* 7s. 6d. net. A Colonial Edition is also published.

How (F. D.). SIX GREAT SCHOOLMASTERS. With Portraits and Illustrations. *Second Edition. Demy 8vo.* 7s. 6d.

Howell (G.). See Social Questions Series.

Hudson (Robert). MEMORIALS OF A WARWICKSHIRE VILLAGE. With many Illustrations. *Demy 8vo.* 15s. net.

Hughes (C. E.). THE PRAISE OF SHAKESPEARE. An English Anthology. With a Preface by SIDNEY LEE. *Demy 8vo.* 3s. 6d. net.

Hughes (Thomas). TOM BROWN'S SCHOOLDAYS. With an Introduction and Notes by VERNON RENDALL. *Leather. Royal 32mo.* 2s. 6d. net.

Hutchinson (Horace G.). THE NEW FOREST. Illustrated in colour with 50 Pictures by WALTER TYNDALE and 4 by Miss LUCY KEMP WELCH. *Large Demy 8vo.* 21s. *net.*

Hutton (A. W.), M.A. See Leaders of Religion.

Hutton (Edward), THE CITIES OF UMBRIA. With many Illustrations, of which 20 are in Colour, by A. PISA. *Crown 8vo.* 6s.

ENGLISH LOVE POEMS. Edited with an Introduction. *Fcap. 8vo.* 3s. 6d. *net.*

Hutton (R. H.). See Leaders of Religion.

Hutton (W. H.), M.A. THE LIFE OF SIR THOMAS MORE. With Portraits. *Second Edition. Crown 8vo.* 5s. See also Leaders of Religion.

Hyett (F. A.). A SHORT HISTORY OF FLORENCE. *Demy 8vo.* 7s. 6d. *net.*

Ibsen (Henrik). BRAND. A Drama. Translated by WILLIAM WILSON. *Third Edition. Crown 8vo.* 3s. 6d.

Inge (W. R.), M.A., Fellow and Tutor of Hertford College, Oxford. CHRISTIAN MYSTICISM. The Bampton Lectures for 1899. *Demy 8vo.* 12s. 6d. *net.* See also Library of Devotion.

Innes (A. D.), M.A. A HISTORY OF THE BRITISH IN INDIA. With Maps and Plans. *Crown 8vo.* 6s.

*ENGLAND UNDER THE TUDORS. With Maps. *Demy 8vo.* 10s. 6d. *net.*

*Jackson (C. E.),** B.A., Science Master at Bradford Grammar School. EXAMPLES IN PHYSICS. *Crown 8vo.* 2s. 6d.

Jackson (S.), M.A. See Commercial Series.

Jackson (F. Hamilton). See The Little Guides.

Jacob (F.), M.A. See Junior Examination Series.

Jeans (J. Stephen). See Social Questions Series and Business Books.

Jeffreys (D. Gwyn). DOLLY'S THEATRICALS. Described and Illustrated with 24 Coloured Pictures. *Super Royal 16mo.* 2s. 6d.

Jenks (E.), M.A., Reader in Law in the University of Oxford. ENGLISH LOCAL GOVERNMENT. *Crown 8vo.* 2s. 6d.

Jenner (Mrs. H.). See Little Books on Art.

Jessopp (Augustus), D.D. See Leaders of Religion.

Jevons (F. B.), M.A., Litt.D., Principal of Hatfield Hall, Durham. See Churchman's Library and Handbooks of Theology.

Johnson (Mrs. Barham). WILLIAM BODHAM DONNE AND HIS FRIENDS. With Illustrations. *Demy 8vo.* 10s. 6d. *net.*

Johnston (Sir H. H.), K.C.B. BRITISH CENTRAL AFRICA. With nearly 200 Illustrations and Six Maps. *Second Edition. Crown 4to.* 18s. *net.*

*Jones (E. Crompton).** POEMS OF THE INNER LIFE. Selected by. *Eleventh Edition. Fcap. 8vo.* 2s. 6d. *net.*

Jonés (H.). See Commercial Series.

Jones (L. A. Atherley), K.C., M.P., and **Bellot (Hugh H. L.).** THE MINERS' GUIDE TO THE COAL MINES' REGULATION ACTS. *Crown 8vo.* 2s. 6d. *net.*

Jonson (Ben). See Methuen's Standard Library.

Julian (Lady) of Norwich. REVELATIONS OF DIVINE LOVE. Edited by GRACE WARRACK. *Crown 8vo.* 3s. 6d.

Juvenal. See Classical Translations.

Kaufmann (M.). See Social Questions Series.

Keating (J. F.), D.D. THE AGAPE AND THE EUCHARIST. *Crown 8vo.* 3s. 6d.

Keats (John). THE POEMS OF. Edited with Introduction and Notes by E. de Selincourt, M.A. *Demy 8vo.* 7s. 6d. *net.* See also Little Library and Methuen's Universal Library.

Keble (John). THE CHRISTIAN YEAR. With an Introduction and Notes by W. LOCK, D.D., Warden of Keble College. Illustrated by R. ANNING BELL. *Third Edition. Fcap. 8vo.* 3s. 6d. ; *padded morocco,* 5s. See also Library of Devotion.

Kempis (Thomas A). THE IMITATION OF CHRIST. With an Introduction by DEAN FARRAR. Illustrated by C. M. GERE. *Third Edition. Fcap. 8vo.* 3s. 6d.; *padded morocco,* 5s. See also Library of Devotion and Methuen's Standard Library.

Also Translated by C. BIGG, D.D. *Crown 8vo.* 3s. 6d.

Kennedy (Bart.). THE GREEN SPHINX. *Crown 8vo.* 3s. 6d. *net.*

Kennedy (James Houghton), D.D., Assistant Lecturer in Divinity in the University of Dublin. ST. PAUL'S SECOND AND THIRD EPISTLES TO THE CORINTHIANS. With Introduction, Dissertations and Notes. *Crown 8vo.* 6s.

Kestell (J. D.). THROUGH SHOT AND FLAME : Being the Adventures and Experiences of J. D. KESTELL, Chaplain to General Christian de Wet. *Crown 8vo.* 6s.

A Colonial Edition is also published.

Kimmins (C. W.), M.A. THE CHEMISTRY OF LIFE AND HEALTH. Illustrated. *Crown 8vo.* 2s. 6d.

Kinglake (A. W.). See Little Library.

Kipling (Rudyard). BARRACK-ROOM BALLADS. *73rd Thousand. Crown 8vo. Twenty-first Edition.* 6s.

A Colonial Edition is also published.

THE SEVEN SEAS. *62nd Thousand. Tenth Edition. Crown 8vo, gilt top,* 6s.

A Colonial Edition is also published.

THE FIVE NATIONS. *41st Thousand. Second Edition. Crown 8vo.* 6s.

A Colonial Edition is also published.

DEPARTMENTAL DITTIES. *Sixteenth Edition. Crown 8vo. Buckram.* 6s.

A Colonial Edition is also published.

Knowling (R. J.), M.A., Professor of New Testament Exegesis at King's College, London. See Westminster Commentaries.

Lamb (Charles and Mary), THE WORKS OF. Edited by E. V. LUCAS. With Numerous Illustrations. *In Seven Volumes. Demy 8vo. 7s. 6d. each.*

THE LIFE OF. See E. V. Lucas.

THE ESSAYS OF ELIA. With over 100 Illustrations by A. GARTH JONES, and an Introduction by E. V. LUCAS. *Demy 8vo. 10s. 6d.*

THE KING AND QUEEN OF HEARTS: An 1805 Book for Children. Illustrated by WILLIAM MULREADY. A new edition, in facsimile, edited by E. V. LUCAS. 1s. 6d. See also Little Library.

Lambert (F. A. H.). See The Little Guides.

Lambros (Professor). See Byzantine Texts.

Lane-Poole (Stanley). A HISTORY OF EGYPT IN THE MIDDLE AGES. Fully Illustrated. *Crown 8vo. 6s.*

Langbridge (F.) M.A. BALLADS OF THE BRAVE: Poems of Chivalry, Enterprise, Courage, and Constancy. *Second Edition. Crown 8vo. 2s. 6d.*

Law (William). See Library of Devotion.

Leach (Henry). THE DUKE OF DEVON-SHIRE. A Biography. With 12 Illustrations. *Demy 8vo. 12s. 6d. net.*
A Colonial Edition is also published.

Lee (Captain L. Melville). A HISTORY OF POLICE IN ENGLAND. *Crown 8vo. 3s. 6d. net.*

Leigh (Percival). THE COMIC ENGLISH GRAMMAR. Embellished with upwards of 50 characteristic Illustrations by JOHN LEECH. *Post 16mo. 2s. 6d. net.*

Lewes (V. B.), M.A. AIR AND WATER. Illustrated. *Crown 8vo. 2s. 6d.*

Lisle (Fortunée de). See Little Books on Art.

Littlehales (H.). See Antiquary's Books.

Lock (Walter), D.D., Warden of Keble College. ST. PAUL, THE MASTER-BUILDER. *Second Edition. Crown 8vo. 3s. 6d.*

*THE BIBLE AND CHRISTIAN LIFE: BEING ADDRESSES AND SERMONS. *Crown 8vo. 6s.*
See also Leaders of Religion and Library of Devotion.

Locke (John). See Methuen's Standard Library.

Locker (F.). See Little Library.

Longfellow (H. W.) See Little Library.

Lorimer (George Horace). LETTERS FROM A SELF-MADE MERCHANT TO HIS SON. *Thirteenth Edition. Crown 8vo. 6s.*
A Colonial Edition is also published.

OLD GORGON GRAHAM. *Second Edition. Crown 8vo. 6s.*
A Colonial Edition is also published.

Lover (Samuel). See Illustrated Pocket Library.

E. V. L. and C. L. G. ENGLAND DAY BY DAY: Or, The Englishman's Handbook to Efficiency. Illustrated by GEORGE MORROW. *Fourth Edition. Fcap. 4to 1s. net.*
A burlesque Year-Book and Almanac.

Lucas (E. V.). THE LIFE OF CHARLES LAMB. With numerous Portraits and Illustrations. *Two Vols. Demy 8vo. 21s. net.*

A WANDERER IN HOLLAND. With many Illustrations, of which 20 are in Colour by HERBERT MARSHALL. *Crown 8vo. 6s.*
A Colonial Edition is also published.

Lucian. See Classical Translations.

Lyde (L. W.), M.A. See Commercial Series.

Lydon (Noel S.). See Junior School Books.

Lyttelton (Hon. Mrs. A.). WOMEN AND THEIR WORK. *Crown 8vo. 2s. 6d.*

M. M. HOW TO DRESS AND WHAT TO WEAR. *Crown 8vo. 1s. net.*

Macaulay (Lord). CRITICAL AND HIS-TORICAL ESSAYS. Edited by F. C. MONTAGUE, M.A. *Three Volumes. Crown 8vo. 18s.*
The only edition of this book completely annotated.

M'Allen (J. E. B.), M.A. See Commercial Series.

MacCulloch (J. A.). See Churchman's Library.

***MacCunn (Florence).** MARY STUART. With over 60 Illustrations, including a Frontispiece in Photogravure. *Demy 8vo. 10s. 6d. net.*
A Colonial Edition is also published. See also Leaders of Religion.

McDermott (E. R.). See Books on Business.

M'Dowall (A. S.). See Oxford Biographies.

Mackay (A. M.). See Churchman's Library.

Magnus (Laurie), M.A. A PRIMER OF WORDSWORTH. *Crown 8vo. 2s. 6d.*

Mahaffy (J. P.), Litt.D. A HISTORY OF THE EGYPT OF THE PTOLEMIES. Fully Illustrated. *Crown 8vo. 6s.*

Maitland (F. W.), LL.D., Downing Professor of the Laws of England in the University of Cambridge. CANON LAW IN ENG-LAND. *Royal 8vo. 7s. 6d.*

Malden (H. E.), M.A. ENGLISH RE-CORDS. A Companion to the History of England. *Crown 8vo. 3s. 6d.*

THE ENGLISH CITIZEN: HIS RIGHTS AND DUTIES. *Second Edition. Crown 8vo. 1s. 6d.*

*A SCHOOL HISTORY OF SURREY. With many Illustrations. *Crown 8vo. 1s. 6d.*

Marchant (E. C.), M.A., Fellow of Peterhouse, Cambridge. A GREEK ANTHO-LOGY. *Second Edition. Crown 8vo. 3s. 6d.*

Marchant (C. E.), M.A., and **Cook (A. M.)**, M.A. PASSAGES FOR UNSEEN TRANSLATION. *Second Edition. Crown 8vo. 3s. 6d.*

Marlowe (Christopher). See Methuen's Standard Library.

Marr (J. E.), F.R.S., Fellow of St John's College, Cambridge. THE SCIENTIFIC STUDY OF SCENERY. *Second Edition.* Illustrated. *Crown 8vo.* 6s.
AGRICULTURAL GEOLOGY. With numerous Illustrations. *Crown 8vo.* 6s.

Marvell (Andrew). See Little Library.

Masefield (J. E.) SEA LIFE IN NELSON'S TIME. With many Illustrations. *Crown 8vo.* 3s. 6d. net.

Maskell (A.) See Connoisseur's Library.

Mason (A. J.), D.D. See Leaders of Religion.

Massee (George). THE EVOLUTION OF PLANT LIFE: Lower Forms. With Illustrations. *Crown 8vo.* 2s. 6d.

Masterman (C. F. G.), M.A. TENNYSON AS A RELIGIOUS TEACHER. *Crown 8vo.* 6s.

*****Matheson (Hon. E. F.).** COUNSELS OF LIFE. *Fcap. 8vo.* 2s. 6d. net.
A volume of Selections in Prose and Verse.

May (Phil). THE PHIL MAY ALBUM. *Second Edition.* 4to. 1s. net.

Mellows (Emma S.) A SHORT STORY OF ENGLISH LITERATURE. *Crown 8vo.* 3s. 6d.

*****Methuen (A. M. S.).** THE TRAGEDY OF SOUTH AFRICA. *Cr. 8vo.* 2s. net.
A revised and enlarged edition of the author's 'Peace or War in South Africa.'

ENGLAND'S RUIN: DISCUSSED IN SIXTEEN LETTERS TO THE RIGHT HON. JOSEPH CHAMBERLAIN, M.P. *Crown 8vo.* 3d. net.

Michell (E. B.). THE ART AND PRACTICE OF HAWKING. With 3 Photogravures by G. E. LODGE, and other Illustrations. *Demy 8vo.* 10s. 6d.

Millais (J. G.). THE LIFE AND LETTERS OF SIR JOHN EVERETT MILLAIS, President of the Royal Academy. With many Illustrations, of which 2 are in Photogravure. *New Edition.* *Demy 8vo.* 7s. 6d. net.

Millais (Sir John Everett). See Little Galleries.

Millis (C. T.), M.I.M.E. See Textbooks of Technology.

Milne (J. G.), M.A. A HISTORY OF ROMAN EGYPT. Fully Illustrated. *Crown 8vo.* 6s.

*****Milton, John,** THE POEMS OF, BOTH ENGLISH AND LATIN, Compos'd at several times. Printed by his true Copies.
The Songs were set in Musick by Mr. HENRY LAWES, Gentleman of the Kings Chappel, and one of His Majesties Private Musick.
Printed and publish'd according to Order. Printed by RUTH RAWORTH for HUMPHREY MOSELEY, and are to be sold at the signe of the Princes Armes in Pauls Churchyard, 1645.

*****A MILTON DAY BOOK.** Edited by R. F. TOWNDROW. *Fcap. 8vo.* 2s. 6d. net.
See also Little Library and Methuen's Standard Library.

Mitchell (P. Chalmers), M.A. OUTLINES OF BIOLOGY. Illustrated. *Second Edition.* *Crown 8vo.* 6s.

*****Mitton (G. E.).** JANE AUSTEN AND HER ENGLAND. With many Portraits and Illustrations. *Demy 8vo.* 10s. 6d. net.
A Colonial Edition is also published.

'Moil (A.).' See Books on Business.

Moir (D. M.). See Little Library.

*****Money (L. G. Chiozza).** WEALTH AND POVERTY. *Demy 8vo.* 5s. net.

Moore (H. E.). See Social Questions Series.

Moran (Clarence G.). See Books on Business.

More (Sir Thomas). See Methuen's Standard Library.

Morfill (W. R.), Oriel College, Oxford. A HISTORY OF RUSSIA FROM PETER THE GREAT TO ALEXANDER II. With Maps and Plans. *Crown 8vo.* 3s. 6d.

Morich (R. J.), late of Clifton College. See School Examination Series.

*****Morris (J.)** THE MAKERS OF JAPAN. With many portraits and Illustrations. *Demy 8vo.* 12s. 6d. net.
A Colonial Edition is also published.

Morris (J. E.). See The Little Guides.

Morton (Miss Anderson). See Miss Brodrick.

Moule (H. C. G.), D.D., Lord Bishop of Durham. See Leaders of Religion.

Muir (M. M. Pattison), M.A. THE CHEMISTRY OF FIRE. The Elementary Principles of Chemistry. Illustrated. *Crown 8vo.* 2s. 6d.

Mundella (V. A.), M.A. See J. T. Dunn.

Munro (R.), LL.D. See Antiquary's Books.

Naval Officer (A.). See Illustrated Pocket Library.

Neal (W. G.). See R. N. Hall.

Newman (J. H.) and others. See Library of Devotion.

Nichols (J. B. B.). See Little Library.

Nicklin (T.), M.A. EXAMINATION PAPERS IN THUCYDIDES. *Crown 8vo.* 2s.

Nimrod. See Illustrated Pocket Library.

Northcote (James), R.A. THE CONVERSATIONS OF JAMES NORTHCOTE, R.A., AND JAMES WARD. Edited by ERNEST FLETCHER. With many Portraits. *Demy 8vo.* 10s. 6d.

Norway (A. H.), Author of 'Highways and Byways in Devon and Cornwall.' NAPLES. With 25 Coloured Illustrations by MAURICE GREIFFENHAGEN. A New Edition. *Crown 8vo.* 6s.

Novalis. THE DISCIPLES AT SAÏS AND OTHER FRAGMENTS. Edited by Miss UNA BIRCH. *Fcap. 8vo.* 3s. 6d.

Oliphant (Mrs.). See Leaders of Religion.

Oman (C. W. C.), M.A., Fellow of All Souls', Oxford. A HISTORY OF THE ART OF WAR. Vol. II.: The Middle Ages, from the Fourth to the Fourteenth Century. Illustrated. *Demy 8vo.* 10s. 6d. net.

Ottley (R. L.), D.D. See Handbooks of Theology and Leaders of Religion.

Owen (Douglas). See Books on Business.

Oxford (M. N.), of Guy's Hospital. A HANDBOOK OF NURSING. *Second Edition. Crown 8vo.* 3s. 6d.

Pakes (W. C. C.). THE SCIENCE OF HYGIENE. With numerous Illustrations. *Demy 8vo.* 15s.

Palmer (Frederick). WITH KUROKI IN MANCHURIA. With many Illustrations. *Third Edition. Demy 8vo.* 7s. 6d. net. A Colonial Edition is also published.

Parker (Gilbert). A LOVER'S DIARY : SONGS IN SEQUENCE. *Fcap. 8vo.* 5s.

Parkinson (John). PARADISI IN SOLE PARADISUS TERRISTRIS, OR A GARDEN OF ALL SORTS OF PLEASANT FLOWERS. *Folio.* £4, 4s. net.

Parmenter (John). HELIO-TROPES, OR NEW POSIES FOR SUNDIALS, 1625. Edited by PERCIVAL LANDON. *Quarto.* 3s. 6d. net.

Parmentier (Prof. Léon). See Byzantine Texts.

Pascal. See Library of Devotion.

*Paston (George). SOCIAL CARICATURES OF THE EIGHTEENTH CENTURY. *Imperial Quarto.* £2, 12s. 6d. net. See also Little Books on Art and Illustrated Pocket Library.

Paterson (W. R.) (Benjamin Swift). LIFE'S QUESTIONINGS. *Crown 8vo.* 3s. 6d. net.

Patterson (A. H.). NOTES OF AN EAST COAST NATURALIST. Illustrated in Colour by F. SOUTHGATE. *Second Edition. Crown 8vo.* 6s.

*NATURE NOTES IN EASTERN NORFOLK. A series of observations on the Birds, Fishes, Mammals, Reptiles, and stalk-eyed Crustaceans found in that neighbourhood, with a list of the species. With 12 Illustrations in colour, by FRANK SOUTHGATE. *Crown 8vo.* 6s.

Peacock (N.). See Little Books on Art.

Pearce (E. H.), M.A. ANNALS OF CHRIST'S HOSPITAL. With many Illustrations. *Demy 8vo.* 7s. 6d.

Peel (Sidney), late Fellow of Trinity College, Oxford, and Secretary to the Royal Commission on the Licensing Laws. PRACTICAL LICENSING REFORM. *Second Edition. Crown 8vo.* 1s. 6d.

Peters (J. P.), D.D. See Churchman's Library.

Petrie (W. M. Flinders), D.C.L., LL.D., Professor of Egyptology at University College. A HISTORY OF EGYPT, FROM THE EARLIEST TIMES TO THE PRESENT DAY. Fully Illustrated. *In six volumes. Crown 8vo.* 6s. each.

VOL. I. PREHISTORIC TIMES TO XVITH DYNASTY. *Fifth Edition.*

VOL. II. THE XVIITH AND XVIIITH DYNASTIES. *Fourth Edition.*

VOL. III. XIXTH TO XXXTH DYNASTIES.

VOL. IV. THE EGYPT OF THE PTOLEMIES. J. P. MAHAFFY, Litt.D.

VOL. V. ROMAN EGYPT. J. G. MILNE, M.A.

VOL. VI. EGYPT IN THE MIDDLE AGES. STANLEY LANE-POOLE, M.A.

RELIGION AND CONSCIENCE IN ANCIENT EGYPT. Fully Illustrated. *Crown 8vo.* 2s. 6d.

SYRIA AND EGYPT, FROM THE TELL EL AMARNA TABLETS. *Crown 8vo.* 2s. 6d.

EGYPTIAN TALES. Illustrated by TRISTRAM ELLIS. *In Two Volumes. Crown 8vo.* 3s. 6d. each.

EGYPTIAN DECORATIVE ART. With 120 Illustrations. *Crown 8vo.* 3s. 6d.

Phillips (W. A.). See Oxford Biographies.

Phillpotts (Eden). MY DEVON YEAR. With 38 Illustrations by J. LEY PETHYBRIDGE. *Second and Cheaper Edition. Large Crown 8vo.* 6s.

*UP ALONG AND DOWN ALONG. Illustrated by CLAUDE SHEPPERSON. *Crown 8vo.* 5s. net. A volume of poems.

Pienaar (Philip). WITH STEYN AND DE WET. *Second Edition. Crown 8vo.* 3s. 6d. A Colonial Edition is also published.

*Plarr (Victor) and Walton (F. W.). A SCHOOL HISTORY OF MIDDLESEX. With many Illustrations. *Crown 8vo.* 1s. 6d.

Plautus. THE CAPTIVI. Edited, with an Introduction, Textual Notes, and a Commentary, by W. M. LINDSAY, Fellow of Jesus College, Oxford. *Demy 8vo.* 10s. 6d. net.

Plowden-Wardlaw (J. T.), B.A., King's College, Cambridge. See School Examination Series.

Pocock (Roger). A FRONTIERSMAN. *Third Edition. Crown 8vo.* 6s. A Colonial Edition is also published.

Podmore (Frank). MODERN SPIRITUALISM. *Two Volumes. Demy 8vo.* 21s. net. A History and a Criticism.

Poer (J. Patrick Le). A MODERN LEGIONARY. *Crown 8vo.* 6s. A Colonial Edition is also published.

Pollard (Alice). See Little Books on Art.

Pollard (A. W.). OLD PICTURE BOOKS. With many Illustrations. *Demy 8vo.* 7s. 6d. net.

Pollard (Eliza F.). See Little Books on Art.

Pollock (David), M.I.N.A. See Books on Business.

*Pond (0. F.) A MONTAIGNE DAY-BOOK. Edited by. *Fcap. 8vo. 2s. 6d. net.*

Potter (M. C.), M.A., F.L.S. A TEXT-BOOK OF AGRICULTURAL BOTANY. Illustrated. *Second Edition. Crown 8vo. 4s. 6d.*

Potter Boy (An Old). WHEN I WAS A CHILD. *Crown 8vo. 6s.*

Pradeau (G.). A KEY TO THE TIME ALLUSIONS IN THE DIVINE COMEDY. With a Dial. *Small quarto. 3s. 6d.*

Prance (G.). See R. Wyon.

Prescott (O. L.). ABOUT MUSIC, AND WHAT IT IS MADE OF. *Crown 8vo. 3s. 6d. net.*

Price (L. L.), M.A., Fellow of Oriel College, Oxon. A HISTORY OF ENGLISH POLITICAL ECONOMY. *Fourth Edition. Crown 8vo. 2s. 6d.*

Primrose (Deborah). A MODERN BŒOTIA. *Crown 8vo. 6s.*

Pugin and **Rowlandson.** THE MICRO-COSM OF LONDON, OR LONDON IN MINIATURE. With 104 Illustrations in colour. *In Three Volumes. Small 4to. £3, 3s. net.*

'**Q**'(**A. T. Quiller Couch**). See Methuen's Half-Crown Library.

Quevedo Villegas. See Miniature Library.

G.R. and E. S. THE WOODHOUSE CORRESPONDENCE. *Crown 8vo. 6s.*
A Colonial Edition is also published.

Rackham (R. B.), M.A. See Westminster Commentaries.

Randolph (B. W.), D.D. See Library of Devotion.

Rannie (D. W.), M.A. A STUDENT'S HISTORY OF SCOTLAND. *Cr. 8vo. 3s. 6d.*

Rashdall (Hastings), M.A., Fellow and Tutor of New College, Oxford. DOCTRINE AND DEVELOPMENT. *Crown 8vo. 6s.*

Rawstorne (Lawrence, Esq.). See Illustrated Pocket Library.

A Real Paddy. See Illustrated Pocket Library.

Reason (W.), M.A. See Social Questions Series.

Redfern (W. B.), Author of ' Ancient Wood and Iron Work in Cambridge,' etc. ROYAL AND HISTORIC GLOVES AND ANCIENT SHOES. Profusely Illustrated in colour and half-tone. *Quarto, £2, 2s. net.*

Reynolds. See Little Galleries.

Roberts (M. E.). See C. C. Channer.

Robertson, (A.), D.D., Lord Bishop of Exeter. REGNUM DEI. The Bampton Lectures of 1901. *Demy 8vo. 12s. 6d. net.*

Robertson (C. Grant), M.A., Fellow of All Souls' College, Oxford, Examiner in the Honours School of Modern History, Oxford, 1901-1904. SELECT STATUTES, CASES, AND CONSTITUTIONAL DOCUMENTS, 1660-1832. *Demy 8vo. 10s. 6d. net.*

*Robertson (C. Grant) and **Bartholomew (J. G.),** F.R.S.E., F.R.G.S. THE STUDENT'S HISTORICAL ¦ATLAS OF THE BRITISH EMPIRE. *Quarto 3s. 6d. net.*

Robertson (Sir G. S.) K.C.S.I. See Methuen's Half-Crown Library.

Robinson (A. W.), M.A. See Churchman's Bible.

Robinson (Cecilia). THE MINISTRY OF DEACONESSES. With an Introduction by the late Archbishop of Canterbury. *Crown 8vo. 3s. 6d.*

Robinson (F. S.) See Connoisseur's Library.

Rochefoucauld (La). See Little Library.

Rodwell (G.), B.A. NEW TESTAMENT GREEK. A Course for Beginners. With a Preface by WALTER LOCK, D.D., Warden of Keble College. *Fcap. 8vo. 3s. 6d.*

Roe (Fred). ANCIENT COFFERS AND CUPBOARDS: Their History and Description. With many Illustrations. *Quarto. £3, 3s. net.*

*OLD OAK FURNITURE. With many Illustrations by the Author, including a frontispiece in colour. *Demy 8vo. 10s. 6d. net.*

Rogers (A. G. L.), M.A. See Books on Business.

*Romney. A GALLERY OF ROMNEY. By ARTHUR B. CHAMBERLAIN. With 66 Plates in Photogravure. *Imperial Quarto. £3, 3s. net.* See Little Galleries.

Roscoe (E. S.). ROBERT HARLEY, EARL OF OXFORD. Illustrated. *Demy 8vo. 7s. 6d.*
This is the only life of Harley in existence. See also The Little Guides.

Rose (Edward). THE ROSE READER. With numerous Illustrations. *Crown 8vo. 2s. 6d. Also in 4 Parts. Parts I. and II. 6d. each ; Part III. 8d. ; Part IV. 10d.*

Rowntree (Joshua). THE IMPERIAL DRUG TRADE. *Crown 8vo. 5s. net.*

Rubie (A. E.), D.D. See Junior School Books.

Russell (W. Clark). THE LIFE OF ADMIRAL LORD COLLINGWOOD. With Illustrations by F. BRANGWYN. *Fourth Edition. Crown 8vo. 6s.*
A Colonial Edition is also published.

St. Anselm. See Library of Devotion.

St. Augustine. See Library of Devotion.

St. Cyres (Viscount). See Oxford Biographies.

'**Saki**'(**H. Munro**). REGINALD. *Second Edition. Fcap. 8vo. 2s. 6d. net.*

Sales (St. Francis de). See Library of Devotion.

Salmon (A. L.). A POPULAR GUIDE TO DEVON. *Medium 8vo. 6d. net.* See also The Little Guides.

Sargeaunt (J.), M.A. ANNALS OF WESTMINSTER SCHOOL. With numerous Illustrations. *Demy 8vo.* 7s. 6d.

Sathas (C.). See Byzantine Texts.

Schmitt (John). See Byzantine Texts.

Scott, (A. M.). WINSTON SPENCER CHURCHILL. With Portraits and Illustrations. *Crown 8vo.* 3s. 6d.

Seeley (H. G.) F.R.S. DRAGONS OF THE AIR. With many Illustrations. *Cr. 8vo.* 6s.

Sells (V. P.), M.A. THE MECHANICS OF DAILY LIFE. Illustrated. *Cr. 8vo.* 2s. 6d.

Selous (Edmund). TOMMY SMITH'S ANIMALS. Illustrated by G. W. ORD. *Third Edition. Fcap. 8vo.* 2s. 6d.

Settle (J. H.). ANECDOTES OF SOLDIERS, in Peace and War. *Crown 8vo.* 3s. 6d. net.
A Colonial Edition is also published.

Shakespeare (William).
THE FOUR FOLIOS, 1623; 1632; 1664; 1685. Each *Four Guineas net*, or a complete set, *Twelve Guineas net.*

The Arden Shakespeare.
Demy 8vo. 2s. 6d. *net each volume.*
General Editor, W. J. CRAIG. An Edition of Shakespeare in single Plays. Edited with a full Introduction, Textual Notes, and a Commentary at the foot of the page.

HAMLET. Edited by EDWARD DOWDEN, Litt.D.

ROMEO AND JULIET. Edited by EDWARD DOWDEN, Litt.D.

KING LEAR. Edited by W. J. CRAIG.

JULIUS CAESAR. Edited by M. MAC-MILLAN, M.A.

THE TEMPEST. Edited by MORETON LUCE.

OTHELLO. Edited by H. C. HART.

TITUS ANDRONICUS. Edited by H. B. BAILDON.

CYMBELINE. Edited by EDWARD DOWDEN.

THE MERRY WIVES OF WINDSOR. Edited by H. C. HART.

A MIDSUMMER NIGHT'S DREAM. Edited by H. CUNINGHAM.

KING HENRY V. Edited by H. A. EVANS.

ALL'S WELL THAT ENDS WELL. Edited by W. O. BRIGSTOCKE.

THE TAMING OF THE SHREW. Edited by R. WARWICK BOND.

TIMON OF ATHENS. Edited by K. DEIGHTON.

MEASURE FOR MEASURE. Edited by H. C. HART.

TWELFTH NIGHT. Edited by MORETON LUCE.

THE MERCHANT OF VENICE. Edited by C. KNOX POOLER.

The Little Quarto Shakespeare. Edited by W. J. CRAIG. With Introductions and Notes. *Pott 16mo. In 40 Volumes.* Leather, *price* 1s. net each volume.
See also Methuen's Standard Library.

Sharp (A.). VICTORIAN POETS. *Crown 8vo.* 2s. 6d.

Sharp (Mrs. E. A.). See Little Books on Art.

Shedlock (J. S.), THE PIANOFORTE SONATA: Its Origin and Development. *Crown 8vo.* 5s.

Shelley (Percy B.). ADONAIS; an Elegy on the death of John Keats, Author of 'Endymion,' etc. Pisa. From the types of Didot, 1821. 2s. net.
See also Methuen's Standard Library.

Sherwell (Arthur), M.A. See Social Questions Series.

Shipley (Mary E.). AN ENGLISH CHURCH HISTORY FOR CHILDREN. With a Preface by the Bishop of Gibraltar. With Maps and Illustrations. Part I. *Crown 8vo.* 2s. 6d. net.

Sichel (Walter). DISRAELI: A Study in Personality and Ideas. With 3 Portraits. *Demy 8vo.* 12s. 6d. net.
A Colonial Edition is also published.
See also Oxford Biographies.

Sime (J.). See Little Books on Art.

Simonson (G. A.). FRANCESCO GUARDI. With 41 Plates. *Royal folio.* £2, 2s. net.

Sketchley (R. E. D.). See Little Books on Art.

Skipton (H. P. K.). See Little Books on Art.

Sladen (Douglas). SICILY: The New Winter Resort. With over 200 Illustrations. *Second Edition. Crown 8vo.* 5s. net.

Small (Evan), M.A. THE EARTH. An Introduction to Physiography. Illustrated. *Crown 8vo.* 2s. 6d.

Smallwood, (M. G.). See Little Books on Art.

Smedley (F. E.). See Illustrated Pocket Library.

Smith (Adam). THE WEALTH OF NATIONS. Edited with an Introduction and numerous Notes by EDWIN CANNAN, M.A. *Two volumes. Demy 8vo.* 21s. net.
See also Methuen's Standard Library.

Smith (Horace and James). See Little Library.

*Smith (H. Bompas), M.A.** A NEW JUNIOR ARITHMETIC. *Crown 8vo.* 2s. 6d.

*Smith (John Thomas).** A BOOK FOR A RAINY DAY. Edited by WILFRID WHITTEN. Illustrated. *Demy 8vo.* 15s. net.

Snell (F. J.). A BOOK OF EXMOOR. Illustrated. *Crown 8vo.* 6s.

Snowden (C. E.). A BRIEF SURVEY OF BRITISH HISTORY. *Demy 8vo.* 4s. 6d.

Sophocles. See Classical Translations.

Sornet (L. A.). See Junior School Books.

South (Wilton E.), M.A. See Junior School Books.

Southey (R.) ENGLISH SEAMEN. Edited, with an Introduction, by DAVID HANNAY.

Vol. I. (Howard, Clifford, Hawkins, Drake, Cavendish). *Second Edition. Crown 8vo. 6s.*

Vol. II. (Richard Hawkins, Grenville, Essex, and Raleigh). *Crown 8vo. 6s.*

Spence (C. H.), M.A. See School Examination Series.

Spooner (W. A.), M.A. See Leaders of Religion.

Stanbridge (J. W.), B.D. See Library of Devotion.

'Stancliffe.' GOLF DO'S AND DONT'S. *Second Edition. Fcap. 8vo. 1s.*

Stedman (A. M. M.), M.A.

INITIA LATINA: Easy Lessons on Elementary Accidence. *Eighth Edition. Fcap. 8vo. 1s.*

FIRST LATIN LESSONS. *Ninth Edition. Crown 8vo. 2s.*

FIRST LATIN READER. With Notes adapted to the Shorter Latin Primer and Vocabulary. *Sixth Edition revised. 18mo. 1s. 6d.*

EASY SELECTIONS FROM CÆSAR. The Helvetian War. *Second Edition. 18mo. 1s.*

EASY SELECTIONS FROM LIVY. Part I. The Kings of Rome. *18mo. Second Edition. 1s. 6d.*

EASY LATIN PASSAGES FOR UNSEEN TRANSLATION. *Ninth Edition Fcap. 8vo. 1s. 6d.*

EXEMPLA LATINA. First Exercises in Latin Accidence. With Vocabulary. *Third Edition. Crown 8vo. 1s.*

EASY LATIN EXERCISES ON THE SYNTAX OF THE SHORTER AND REVISED LATIN PRIMER. With Vocabulary. *Tenth and Cheaper Edition, re-written. Crown 8vo. 1s. 6d. Original Edition. 2s. 6d.* KEY, *3s. net.*

THE LATIN COMPOUND SENTENCE: Rules and Exercises. *Second Edition. Crown 8vo. 1s. 6d.* With Vocabulary. *2s.*

NOTANDA QUAEDAM: Miscellaneous Latin Exercises on Common Rules and Idioms. *Fourth Edition. Fcap. 8vo. 1s. 6d.* With Vocabulary. *2s.* Key, *2s. net.*

LATIN VOCABULARIES FOR REPETITION: Arranged according to Subjects. *Thirteenth Edition. Fcap. 8vo. 1s. 6d.*

A VOCABULARY OF LATIN IDIOMS. *18mo. Second Edition. 1s.*

STEPS TO GREEK. *Second Edition, revised. 18mo. 1s.*

A SHORTER GREEK PRIMER. *Crown 8vo. 1s. 6d.*

EASY GREEK PASSAGES FOR UNSEEN TRANSLATION. *Third Edition, revised. Fcap. 8vo. 1s. 6d.*

GREEK VOCABULARIES FOR REPETITION. Arranged according to Subjects. *Fourth Edition. Fcap. 8vo. 1s. 6d.*

GREEK TESTAMENT SELECTIONS. For the use of Schools. With Introduction, Notes, and Vocabulary. *Fourth Edition. Fcap. 8vo. 2s. 6d.*

STEPS TO FRENCH. *Sixth Edition. 18mo. 8d.*

FIRST FRENCH LESSONS. *Sixth Edition, revised. Crown 8vo. 1s.*

EASY FRENCH PASSAGES FOR UNSEEN TRANSLATION. *Fifth Edition. revised. Fcap. 8vo. 1s. 6d.*

EASY FRENCH EXERCISES ON ELEMENTARY SYNTAX. With Vocabulary. *Fourth Edition. Crown 8vo. 2s. 6d.* KEY. *3s. net.*

FRENCH VOCABULARIES FOR REPETITION: Arranged according to Subjects. *Twelfth Edition. Fcap. 8vo. 1s.*

See also School Examination Series.

Steel (R. Elliott), M.A., F.C.S. THE WORLD OF SCIENCE. With 147 Illustrations. *Second Edition. Crown 8vo. 2s. 6d.*

See also School Examination Series.

Stephenson (C.), of the Technical College, Bradford, and **Suddards (F.)** of the Yorkshire College, Leeds. ORNAMENTAL DESIGN FOR WOVEN FABRICS. Illustrated. *Demy 8vo. Second Edition. 7s. 6d.*

Stephenson (J.), M.A. THE CHIEF TRUTHS OF THE CHRISTIAN FAITH. *Crown 8vo. 3s. 6d.*

Sterne (Laurence). See Little Library.

Sterry (W.), M.A. ANNALS OF ETON COLLEGE. With numerous Illustrations. *Demy 8vo. 7s. 6d.*

Steuart (Katherine). BY ALLAN WATER. *Second Edition. Crown 8vo. 6s.*

Stevenson (R. L.). THE LETTERS OF ROBERT LOUIS STEVENSON TO HIS FAMILY AND FRIENDS. Selected and Edited, with Notes and Introductions, by SIDNEY COLVIN. *Sixth and Cheaper Edition. Crown 8vo. 12s.* LIBRARY EDITION. *Demy 8vo. 2 vols. 25s. net.*

A Colonial Edition is also published.

VAILIMA LETTERS. With an Etched Portrait by WILLIAM STRANG. *Fourth Edition. Crown 8vo. Buckram. 6s.*

A Colonial Edition is also published.

THE LIFE OF R. L. STEVENSON. See G. Balfour.

Stevenson (M. I.). FROM SARANAC TO THE MARQUESAS. Being Letters written by Mrs. M. I. STEVENSON during 1887-8 to her sister, Miss JANE WHYTE BALFOUR. With an Introduction by GEORGE W. BALFOUR, M.D., LL.D., F.R.S.S. *Crown 8vo. 6s. net.*

A Colonial Edition is also published.

Stoddart (Anna M.). See Oxford Biographies.

Stone (E. D.), M.A. SELECTIONS FROM THE ODYSSEY. *Fcap. 8vo.* 1s. 6d.

Stone (S. J.). POEMS AND HYMNS. With a Memoir by F. G. ELLERTON, M.A. With Portrait. *Crown 8vo.* 6s.

Straker (F.). See Books on Business.

Streane (A. W.), D.D. See Churchman's Bible.

Stroud (H.), D.Sc., M.A. See Textbooks of Technology.

Strutt (Joseph). THE SPORTS AND PASTIMES OF THE PEOPLE OF ENGLAND. Illustrated by many engravings. Revised by J. CHARLES COX, LL.D., F.S.A. *Quarto.* 21s. net.

Stuart (Capt. Donald). THE STRUGGLE FOR PERSIA. With a Map. *Crown 8vo.* 6s.

*Sturch (F.), Staff Instructor to the Surrey County Council. SOLUTIONS TO THE CITY AND GUILDS QUESTIONS IN MANUAL INSTRUCTION DRAWING. *Imp. 4to.*

*Suckling (Sir John). FRAGMENTA AUREA: a Collection of all the Incomparable Peeces, written by. And published by a friend to perpetuate his memory. Printed by his own copies.
Printed for HUMPHREY MOSELEY, and are to be sold at his shop, at the sign of the Princes Arms in St. Paul's Churchyard, 1646.

Suddards (F.). See C. Stephenson.

Surtees (R. S.). See Illustrated Pocket Library.

Swift (Jonathan). THE JOURNAL TO STELLA. Edited by G. A. AITKEN. *Cr. 8vo.* 6s.

Symes (J. E.), M.A. THE FRENCH REVOLUTION. *Second Edition. Crown 8vo.* 2s. 6d.

Syrett (Netta). See Little Blue Books.

Tacitus. AGRICOLA. With Introduction, Notes, Map, etc. by R. F. DAVIS, M.A. *Fcap. 8vo.* 2s.
GERMANIA. By the same Editor. *Fcap. 8vo.* 2s. See also Classical Translations.

Tallack (W.) HOWARD LETTERS AND MEMORIES. *Demy 8vo.* 10s. 6d. net.

Tauler (J.). See Library of Devotion.

Taunton (E. L.). A HISTORY OF THE JESUITS IN ENGLAND. With Illustrations. *Demy 8vo.* 21s. net.

Taylor (A. E.). THE ELEMENTS OF METAPHYSICS. *Demy 8vo.* 10s. 6d. net.

Taylor (F. G.), M.A. See Commercial Series.

Taylor (I. A.). See Oxford Biographies.

Taylor (T. M.), M.A., Fellow of Gonville and Caius College, Cambridge. A CONSTITUTIONAL AND POLITICAL

HISTORY OF ROME. *Crown 8vo.* 7s. 6d.

Tennyson (Alfred, Lord). THE EARLY POEMS OF. Edited, with Notes and an Introduction, by J. CHURTON COLLINS, M.A. *Crown 8vo.* 6s.
IN MEMORIAM, MAUD, AND THE PRINCESS. Edited by J. CHURTON COLLINS, M.A. *Crown 8vo.* 6s. See also Little Library.

Terry (C. S.). See Oxford Biographies.

Terton (Alice). LIGHTS AND SHADOWS IN A HOSPITAL. *Crown 8vo.* 3s. 6d.

Thackeray (W. M.). See Little Library.

Theobald (F. W.), M.A. INSECT LIFE. Illustrated. *Second Ed. Revised. Cr. 8vo.* 2s. 6d.

Thompson (A. H.). See The Little Guides.

Tileston (Mary W.). DAILY STRENGTH FOR DAILY NEEDS. *Eleventh Edition. Fcap. 8vo.* 2s. 6d. net. Also an edition in superior binding 6s.

Tompkins (H. W.), F.R.H.S. See The Little Guides.

Townley (Lady Susan). MY CHINESE NOTE-BOOK With 16 Illustrations and 2 Maps. *Third Edition. Demy 8vo.* 10s. 6d. net.
A Colonial Edition is also published.

Toynbee (Paget), M.A., D.Litt. DANTE STUDIES AND RESEARCHES. *Demy 8vo.* 10s. 6d. net. See also Oxford Biographies.

Trench (Herbert). DEIRDRE WED: and Other Poems. *Crown 8vo.* 5s.

Trevelyan (G. M.), Fellow of Trinity College, Cambridge. ENGLAND UNDER THE STUARTS. With Maps and Plans. *Second Edition. Demy 8vo.* 10s. 6d. net.

Troutbeck (G. E.). See The Little Guides.

Tuckwell (Gertrude). See Social Questions Series.

Twining (Louisa). See Social Questions Series.

Tyler (E. A.), B.A., F.C.S. See Junior School Books.

Tyrell-Gill (Frances). See Little Books on Art.

Vardon (Harry). THE COMPLETE GOLFER. With numerous Illustrations. *Fourth Edition. Demy 8vo.* 10s. 6d. net.
A Colonial Edition is also published.

Vaughan (Henry). See Little Library.

Voegelin (A.), M.A. See Junior Examination Series.

Wade (G. W.), D.D. OLD TESTAMENT HISTORY. With Maps. *Third Edition. Crown 8vo.* 6s.

Wagner (Richard). See A. L. Cleather.

Wall (J. C.). DEVILS. Illustrated by the Author and from photographs. *Demy 8vo.* 4s. 6d. net. See also Antiquary's Books.

Walters (H. B.). See Little Books on Art.

Walton (F. W.). See Victor Plarr.

A 3

Walton (Izaac) and **Cotton (Charles).**
See Illustrated Pocket Library, Methuen's
Standard Library, and Little Library.
Warmelo (D. S. Van). ON COMMANDO.
With Portrait. *Crown 8vo.* 3s. 6d.
A Colonial Edition is also published.
Waterhouse (Mrs. Alfred). WITH THE
SIMPLE-HEARTED: Little Homilies to
Women in Country Places. *Second Edition.*
Small Pott 8vo. 2s. net. See also Little
Library.
Weatherhead (T. C.), M.A. EXAMINA-
TION PAPERS IN HORACE. *Cr. 8vo.*
2s. See also Junior Examination Series.
Webb (W. T.). See Little Blue Books.
Webber (F. C.). See Textbooks of Techno-
logy.
Wells (Sidney H.). See Textbooks of
Technology.
Wells (J.), M.A., Fellow and Tutor of Wadham
College. OXFORD AND OXFORD
LIFE. By Members of the University.
Third Edition. Crown 8vo. 3s. 6d.
A SHORT HISTORY OF ROME. *Sixth
Edition.* With 3 Maps. *Crown 8vo.*
3s. 6d.
This book is intended for the Middle and
Upper Forms of Public Schools and for Pass
Students at the Universities. It contains
copious Tables, etc. See also The Little
Guides.
Wetmore (Helen C.). THE LAST OF
THE GREAT SCOUTS ('Buffalo Bill').
With Illustrations. *Second Edition. Demy
8vo.* 6s.
A Colonial Edition is also published.
Whibley (C.). See Henley and Whibley.
Whibley (L.), M.A., Fellow of Pembroke
College, Cambridge. GREEK OLIGAR-
CHIES: THEIR ORGANISATION
AND CHARACTER. *Crown 8vo.* 6s.
Whitaker (G. H.), M.A. See Churchman's
Bible.
White (Gilbert). THE NATURAL
HISTORY OF SELBORNE. Edited by
L. C. MIALL, F.R.S., assisted by W. WARDE
FOWLER, M.A. *Crown 8vo.* 6s. See also
Methuen's Standard Library.
Whitfield (E. E.). See Commercial Series.
Whitehead (A. W.). GASPARD DE
COLIGNY. With many Illustrations.
Demy 8vo. 12s. 6d. net.
Whiteley (R. Lloyd), F.I.C., Principal of
the Technical Institute, West Bromwich.
AN ELEMENTARY TEXT-BOOK OF
INORGANIC CHEMISTRY. *Crown
8vo.* 2s. 6d.
Whitley (Miss). See Social Questions Series.
Whitten (W.). See Thomas Smith.
Whyte (A. G.), B.Sc. See Books on Business.
Wilberforce (Wilfrid). See Little Books
on Art.
Wilde (Oscar). DE PROFUNDIS. *Fifth
Edition. Crown 8vo.* 5s. net.
A Colonial Edition is also published.

Wilkins (W. H.), B.A. See Social Questions
Series.
Wilkinson (J. Frome). See Social Ques-
tions Series.
Williamson (W.). THE BRITISH
GARDENER. Illustrated. *Demy 8vo.*
10s. 6d.
Williamson (W.), B.A. See Junior Ex-
amination Series, Junior School Books, and
The Beginner's Books.
Wilmot-Buxton (E. M.). MAKERS OF
EUROPE. *Crown 8vo.* Third Edition.
3s. 6d.
A Text-book of European History for
Middle Forms.
THE ANCIENT WORLD. With Maps and
Illustrations. *Crown 8vo.* 3s. 6d.
See also The Beginner's Books.
Wilson (Bishop). See Library of Devotion.
Willson (Beckles). LORD STRATH-
CONA: the Story of his Life. Illustrated.
Demy 8vo. 7s. 6d.
A Colonial Edition is also published.
Wilson (A. J.). See Books on Business.
Wilson (H. A.). See Books on Business.
Wilton (Richard), M.A. LYRA PAS-
TORALIS: Songs of Nature, Church, and
Home. *Pott 8vo.* 2s. 6d.
Winbolt (S. E.), M.A. EXERCISES IN
LATIN ACCIDENCE. *Cr. 8vo.* 1s. 6d.
LATIN HEXAMETER VERSE: An Aid
to Composition. *Crown 8vo.* 3s. 6d. KEY,
5s. net.
Windle (B. C. A.), D.Sc., F.R.S. See Anti-
quary's Books and The Little Guides.
Winterbotham (Canon), M.A., B.Sc.,
LL.B. See Churchman's Library.
Wood (J. A. E.). See Textbooks of Technology.
***Wood (J. Hickory).** DAN LENO: HIS
LIFE AND ACHIEVEMENTS, With many
Illustrations. *Crown 8vo.* 6s.
A Colonial Edition is also published.
Wood (W. Birkbeck), M.A., late Scholar of
Worcester College, Oxford, and **Edmonds
(Major J. E.),** R.E., D.A.Q.-M.G. A
HISTORY OF THE AMERICAN
CIVIL WAR. With an Introduction by
H. SPENSER WILKINSON. With 24 Maps
and Plans. *Demy 8vo.* 12s 6d. net.
Wordsworth (Christopher). See Anti-
quary's Books.
Wordsworth (W.). See Little Library.
Wordsworth (W.) and **Coleridge (S. T.).**
See Little Library.
Wright (Arthur), M.A., Fellow of Queen's
College, Cambridge. See Churchman's
Library.
Wright (C. Gordon). See Dante.
Wright (Sophie). GERMAN VOCABU-
LARIES FOR REPETITION. *Fcap. 8vo.*
1s. 6d.
Wrong, (George M.), Professor of History
in the University of Toronto. THE
EARL OF ELGIN. With Illustrations.
Demy 8vo. 7s. 6d. net.

Wylde (A. B.). MODERN ABYSSINIA. With a Map and a Portrait. *Demy 8vo. 15s. net.*

Wyndham (G.). THE POEMS OF WILLIAM SHAKESPEARE. With an Introduction and Notes. *Demy 8vo. Buckram, gilt top.* 10s. 6d.

Wyon (R.) and Prance (G.). THE LAND OF THE BLACK MOUNTAIN. Being a description of Montenegro. With 40 Illustrations. *Crown 8vo.* 6s.

A Colonial Edition is also published.

Yeats (W. B.). AN ANTHOLOGY OF IRISH VERSE. *Revised and Enlarged Edition. Crown 8vo.* 3s. 6d.

Yendis (M.). THE GREAT RED FROG.

A Story told in 40 Coloured Pictures. *Fcap. 8vo.* 1s. net.

Young (Filson). THE COMPLETE MOTORIST. With 138 Illustrations. *Fourth Edition. Demy 8vo.* 12s. 6d. net.

Young (T. M.). THE AMERICAN COTTON INDUSTRY: A Study of Work and Workers. With an Introduction by ELIJAH HELM, Secretary to the Manchester Chamber of Commerce. *Crown 8vo. Cloth, 2s. 6d. ; paper boards, 1s. 6d.*

Zenker (E. V.). ANARCHISM. *Demy 8vo.* 7s. 6d.

Zimmern (Antonia). WHAT DO WE KNOW CONCERNING ELECTRICITY? *Crown 8vo.* 1s. 6d. net.

Ancient Cities

Crown 8vo. 4s. 6d. net.

CHESTER. Illustrated by E. H. New. *Crown 8vo.* 4s. 6d. net.

SHREWSBURY. By T. Auden, M.A., F.S.A.

Illustrated. *Crown 8vo.* 4s. 6d. net.

*CANTERBURY. By J. C. Cox, LL.D., F.S.A. Illustrated. *Crown 8vo.* 4s. 6d. net.

Antiquary's Books, The

General Editor, J. CHARLES COX, LL.D., F.S.A.

A series of volumes dealing with various branches of English Antiquities ; comprehensive and popular, as well as accurate and scholarly.

Demy 8vo. 7s. 6d. net.

ENGLISH MONASTIC LIFE. By the Right Rev. Abbot Gasquet, O.S.B. Illustrated. *Third Edition.*

REMAINS OF THE PREHISTORIC AGE IN ENGLAND. By B. C. A. Windle, D.Sc., F.R.S. With numerous Illustrations and Plans.

OLD SERVICE BOOKS OF THE ENGLISH CHURCH. By Christopher Wordsworth, M.A., and Henry Littlehales. With Coloured and other Illustrations.

CELTIC ART. By J. Romilly Allen, F.S.A. With numerous Illustrations and Plans.

ARCHÆOLOGY AND FALSE ANTIQUITIES. By R. Munro, LL.D. With numerous Illustrations.

SHRINES OF BRITISH SAINTS. By J. C. Wall. With numerous Illustrations and Plans.

*THE ROYAL FORESTS OF ENGLAND. By J. C. Cox, LL.D., F.S.A. With many Illustrations.

*THE MANOR AND MANORIAL RECORDS. By Nathaniel J. Hone. With many Illustrations.

Beginner's Books, The

EASY FRENCH RHYMES. By Henri Blouet. Illustrated. *Fcap. 8vo.* 1s.

EASY STORIES FROM ENGLISH HISTORY. By E. M. Wilmot-Buxton, Author of 'Makers of Europe.' *Crown 8vo.* 1s.

EASY EXERCISES IN ARITHMETIC. Arranged by W. S. Beard. *Fcap. 8vo.* Without Answers, 1s. With Answers, 1s. 3d.

EASY DICTATION AND SPELLING. By W. Williamson, B.A. *Fourth Edition. Fcap. 8vo.* 1s.

Business, Books on

Crown 8vo.   2s. 6d. net.

A series of volumes dealing with all the most important aspects of commercial and financial activity. The volumes are intended to treat separately all the considerable industries and forms of business, and to explain accurately and clearly what they do and how they do it. Some are Illustrated. The first volumes are—

PORTS AND DOCKS. By Douglas Owen.

RAILWAYS. By E. R. McDermott.

THE STOCK EXCHANGE. By Chas. Duguid. *Second Edition.*

THE BUSINESS OF INSURANCE. By A. J. Wilson.

THE ELECTRICAL INDUSTRY : LIGHTING, TRACTION, AND POWER. By A. G. Whyte, B.Sc.

THE SHIPBUILDING INDUSTRY : Its History, Science, Practice, and Finance. By David Pollock, M.I.N.A.

THE MONEY MARKET. By F. Straker.

THE BUSINESS SIDE OF AGRICULTURE. By A. G. L. Rogers, M.A.

LAW IN BUSINESS. By H. A. Wilson.

THE BREWING INDUSTRY. By Julian L. Baker, F.I.C., F.C.S.

THE AUTOMOBILE INDUSTRY. By G. de H. Stone.

MINING AND MINING INVESTMENTS. By ' A. Moil.'

THE BUSINESS OF ADVERTISING. By Clarence G. Moran, Barrister-at-Law. Illustrated.

TRADE UNIONS. By G. Drage.

CIVIL ENGINEERING. By T. Claxton Fidler, M.Inst. C.E. Illustrated.

*THE COAL INDUSTRY. By Ernest Aves. Illustrated.

*THE IRON TRADE. By J. Stephen Jeans. Illus.

MONOPOLIES, TRUSTS, AND KARTELLS. By F. W. Hirst.

*THE COTTON INDUSTRY AND TRADE. By Prof. S. J. Chapman, Dean of the Faculty of Commerce in the University of Manchester. Illustrated.

Byzantine Texts

Edited by J. B. BURY, M.A., Litt.D.

A series of texts of Byzantine Historians, edited by English and foreign scholars.

ZACHARIAH OF MITYLENE. Translated by F. J. Hamilton, D.D., and E. W. Brooks. *Demy 8vo.   12s. 6d. net.*

EVAGRIUS. Edited by Léon Parmentier and M. Bidez. *Demy 8vo.   10s. 6d. net.*

THE HISTORY OF PSELLUS. Edited by C. Sathas. *Demy 8vo.   15s. net.*

ECTHESIS CHRONICA. Edited by Professor Lambros. *Demy 8vo.   7s. 6d. net.*

THE CHRONICLE OF MOREA. Edited by John Schmitt. *Demy 8vo.   15s. net.*

Churchman's Bible, The

General Editor, J. H. BURN, B.D., F.R.S.E.

A series of Expositions on the Books of the Bible, which will be of service to the general reader in the practical and devotional study of the Sacred Text.

Each Book is provided with a full and clear Introductory Section, in which is stated what is known or conjectured respecting the date and occasion of the composition of the Book, and any other particulars that may help to elucidate its meaning as a whole. The Exposition is divided into sections of a convenient length, corresponding as far as possible with the divisions of the Church Lectionary. The Translation of the Authorised Version is printed in full, such corrections as are deemed necessary being placed in footnotes.

THE EPISTLE OF ST. PAUL THE APOSTLE TO THE GALATIANS. Edited by A. W. Robinson, M.A. *Second Edition. Fcap. 8vo. 1s. 6d. net.*

ECCLESIASTES. Edited by A. W. Streane, D.D. *Fcap. 8vo. 1s. 6d. net.*

THE EPISTLE OF ST. PAUL THE APOSTLE TO THE PHILIPPIANS. Edited by C. R. D. Biggs, D.D. *Second Edition. Fcap 8vo. 1s. 6d. net.*

THE EPISTLE OF ST. JAMES. Edited by H. W. Fulford, M.A. *Fcap. 8vo. 1s. 6d. net.*

ISAIAH. Edited by W. E. Barnes, D.D. *Two Volumes. Fcap. 8vo. 2s. net each.* With Map.

THE EPISTLE OF ST. PAUL THE APOSTLE TO THE EPHESIANS. Edited by G. H. Whitaker, M.A. *Fcap. 8vo. 1s. 6d. net.*

Churchman's Library, The

General Editor, J. H. BURN, B.D., F.R.S.E.

A series of volumes upon such questions as are occupying the attention of Church people at the present time. The Editor has enlisted the services of a band of scholars, who, having made a special study of their respective subjects, are in a position to furnish the best results of modern research accurately and attractively.

THE BEGINNINGS OF ENGLISH CHRISTIANITY. By W. E. Collins, M.A. With Map. *Crown 8vo.* 3s. 6d.

SOME NEW TESTAMENT PROBLEMS. By Arthur Wright, M.A. *Crown 8vo.* 6s.

THE KINGDOM OF HEAVEN HERE AND HERE-AFTER. By Canon Winterbotham, M.A., B.Sc., LL.B. *Crown 8vo.* 3s. 6d.

THE WORKMANSHIP OF THE PRAYER BOOK: Its Literary and Liturgical Aspects. By J. Dowden, D.D. *Second Edition. Crown 8vo.* 3s. 6d.

EVOLUTION. By F. B. Jevons, M.A., Litt.D. *Crown 8vo.* 3s. 6d.

THE OLD TESTAMENT AND THE NEW SCHOLAR-SHIP. By J. W. Peters, D.D. *Crown 8vo.* 6s.

THE CHURCHMAN'S INTRODUCTION TO THE OLD TESTAMENT. By A. M. Mackay, B.A. *Crown 8vo.* 3s. 6d.

THE CHURCH OF CHRIST. By E. T. Green, M.A. *Crown 8vo.* 6s.

COMPARATIVE THEOLOGY. By J. A. Mac-Culloch. *Crown 8vo.* 6s.

Classical Translations

Edited by H. F. FOX, M.A., Fellow and Tutor of Brasenose College, Oxford.

Crown 8vo.

A series of Translations from the Greek and Latin Classics, distinguished by literary excellence as well as by scholarly accuracy.

ÆSCHYLUS—Agamemnon, Choephoroe, Eumenides. Translated by Lewis Campbell, LL.D. 5s.

CICERO—De Oratore I. Translated by E. N. P. Moor, M.A. 3s. 6d.

CICERO—Select Orations (Pro Milone, Pro Mureno, Philippic II., in Catilinam). Translated by H. E. D. Blakiston, M.A. 5s.

CICERO—De Natura Deorum. Translated by F. Brooks, M.A. 3s. 6d.

CICERO—De Officiis. Translated by G. B. Gardiner, M.A. 2s. 6d.

HORACE—The Odes and Epodes. Translated by A. D. Godley, M.A. 2s.

LUCIAN—Six Dialogues (Nigrinus, Icaro-Menippus, The Cock, The Ship, The Parasite, The Lover of Falsehood). Translated by S. T. Irwin, M.A. 3s. 6d.

SOPHOCLES—Electra and Ajax. Translated by E. D. A. Morshead, M.A. 2s. 6d.

TACITUS—Agricola and Germania. Translated by R. B. Townshend. 2s. 6d.

THE SATIRES OF JUVENAL. Translated by S. G. Owen. 2s. 6d.

Commercial Series, Methuen's

Edited by H. DE B. GIBBINS, Litt.D., M.A.

Crown 8vo.

A series intended to assist students and young men preparing for a commercial career, by supplying useful handbooks of a clear and practical character, dealing with those subjects which are absolutely essential in the business life.

COMMERCIAL EDUCATION IN THEORY AND PRACTICE. By E. E. Whitfield, M.A. 5s.
An introduction to Methuen's Commercial Series treating the question of Commercial Education fully from both the point of view of the teacher and of the parent.

BRITISH COMMERCE AND COLONIES FROM ELIZABETH TO VICTORIA. By H. de B. Gibbins, Litt.D., M.A. *Third Edition.* 2s.

COMMERCIAL EXAMINATION PAPERS. By H. de B. Gibbins, Litt.D., M.A. 1s. 6d.

THE ECONOMICS OF COMMERCE. By H. de B. Gibbins, Litt.D., M.A. *Second Edition.* 1s. 6d.

A GERMAN COMMERCIAL READER. By S. E. Bally. With Vocabulary. 2s.

A COMMERCIAL GEOGRAPHY OF THE BRITISH EMPIRE. By L. W. Lyde, M.A. *Fourth Edition.* 2s.

A COMMERCIAL GEOGRAPHY OF FOREIGN NATIONS. By F. C. Boon, B.A. 2s.

A PRIMER OF BUSINESS. By S. Jackson, M.A. *Third Edition.* 1s. 6d.

COMMERCIAL ARITHMETIC. By F. G. Taylor, M.A. *Fourth Edition.* 1s. 6d.

FRENCH COMMERCIAL CORRESPONDENCE. By S. E. Bally. With Vocabulary. *Third Edition.* 2s.

[Continued.

METHUEN'S COMMERCIAL SERIES—*continued.*

GERMAN COMMERCIAL CORRESPONDENCE. By S. E. Bally. With Vocabulary. *2s. 6d.*

A FRENCH COMMERCIAL READER. By S. E. Bally. With Vocabulary. *Second Edition. 2s.*

PRECIS WRITING AND OFFICE CORRESPONDENCE. By E. E. Whitfield, M.A. *Second Edition. 2s.*

A GUIDE TO PROFESSIONS AND BUSINESS. By H. Jones. *1s. 6d.*

THE PRINCIPLES OF BOOK-KEEPING BY DOUBLE ENTRY. By J. E. B. M'Allen, M.A. *2s.*

COMMERCIAL LAW. By W. Douglas Edwards. *Second Edition. 2s.*

Connoisseur's Library, The
Wide Royal 8vo.   25s. net.

A sumptuous series of 20 books on art, written by experts for collectors, superbly illustrated in photogravure, collotype, and colour. The technical side of the art is duly treated. The first volumes are—

MEZZOTINTS. By Cyril Davenport. With 40 Plates in Photogravure.

PORCELAIN. By Edward Dillon. With 19 Plates in Colour, 20 in Collotype, and 5 in Photogravure.

MINIATURES. By Dudley Heath. With 9

Plates in Colour, 15 in Collotype, and 15 in Photogravure.

IVORIES. By A. Maskell. With 80 Plates in Collotype and Photogravure.

*ENGLISH FURNITURE. By F. S. Robinson. With 160 Plates in Collotype and one in Photogravure.

Devotion, The Library of
With Introductions and (where necessary) Notes.
Small Pott 8vo, cloth, 2s. ; leather, 2s. 6d. net.

These masterpieces of devotional literature are furnished with such Introductions and Notes as may be necessary to explain the standpoint of the author and the obvious difficulties of the text, without unnecessary intrusion between the author and the devout mind.

THE CONFESSIONS OF ST. AUGUSTINE. Edited by C. Bigg, D.D. *Third Edition.*

THE CHRISTIAN YEAR. Edited by Walter Lock, D.D. *Second Edition.*

THE IMITATION OF CHRIST. Edited by C. Bigg, D.D. *Fourth Edition.*

A BOOK OF DEVOTIONS. Edited by J. W. Stanbridge. B.D. *Second Edition.*

LYRA INNOCENTIUM. Edited by Walter Lock, D.D.

A SERIOUS CALL TO A DEVOUT AND HOLY LIFE. Edited by C. Bigg, D.D. *Second Edition.*

THE TEMPLE. Edited by E. C. S. Gibson, D.D. *Second Edition.*

A GUIDE TO ETERNITY. Edited by J. W. Stanbridge, B.D.

THE PSALMS OF DAVID. Edited by B. W. Randolph, D.D.

LYRA APOSTOLICA. Edited by Canon Scott Holland and Canon H. C. Beeching, M.A.

THE INNER WAY. By J. Tauler. Edited by A. W. Hutton, M.A.

THE THOUGHTS OF PASCAL. Edited by C. S. Jerram, M.A.

ON THE LOVE OF GOD. By St. Francis de Sales. Edited by W. J. Knox-Little, M.A.

A MANUAL OF CONSOLATION FROM THE SAINTS AND FATHERS. Edited by J. H. Burn, B.D.

THE SONG OF SONGS. Edited by B. Blaxland, M.A.

THE DEVOTIONS OF ST. ANSELM. Edited by C. C. J. Webb, M.A.

GRACE ABOUNDING. By John Bunyan. Edited by S. C. Freer, M A.

BISHOP WILSON'S SACRA PRIVATA. Edited by A. E. Burn, B.D.

LYRA SACRA : A Book of Sacred Verse. Edited by H. C. Beeching, M.A., Canon of Westminster.

A DAY BOOK FROM THE SAINTS AND FATHERS. Edited by J. H. Burn, B.D.

HEAVENLY WISDOM. A Selection from the English Mystics. Edited by E. C. Gregory.

LIGHT, LIFE, and LOVE. A Selection from the German Mystics. Edited by W. R. Inge, M.A.

*THE DEVOUT LIFE OF ST. FRANCIS DE SALES. Translated and Edited by T. Barns, M.A.

Methuen's Half-Crown Library

Crown 8vo. 2s. 6d. net.

THE LIFE OF JOHN RUSKIN. By W. G. Collingwood, M.A. With Portraits. *Fourth Edition.*

ENGLISH LYRICS. By W. E. Henley. *Second Edition.*

THE GOLDEN POMP. A Procession of English Lyrics. Arranged by A. T. Quiller Couch. *Second Edition.*

CHITRAL: The Story of a Minor Siege. By Sir G. S. Robertson, K.C.S.I. *Third Edition.* With numerous Illustrations, Map, and Plan.

STRANGE SURVIVALS AND SUPERSTITIONS. By S. Baring-Gould. *Third Edition.*

*YORKSHIRE ODDITIES AND STRANGE EVENTS. By S. Baring-Gould. *Fourth Edition.*

ENGLISH VILLAGES. By P. H. Ditchfield, M.A., F.S.A. With many Illustrations.

*A BOOK OF ENGLISH PROSE. By W. E. Henley and C. Whibley.

*THE LAND OF THE BLACK MOUNTAIN. Being a Description of Montenegro. By R. Wyon and G. Prance. With 40 Illustrations.

Illustrated Pocket Library of Plain and Coloured Books, The

Fcap 8vo. 3s. 6d. net each volume.

A series, in small form, of some of the famous illustrated books of fiction and general literature. These are faithfully reprinted from the first or best editions without introduction or notes. The Illustrations are chiefly in colour.

COLOURED BOOKS

OLD COLOURED BOOKS. By George Paston. With 16 Coloured Plates. *Fcap. 8vo. 2s. net.*

THE LIFE AND DEATH OF JOHN MYTTON, ESQ. By Nimrod. With 18 Coloured Plates by Henry Alken and T. J. Rawlins. *Third Edition.*

THE LIFE OF A SPORTSMAN. By Nimrod. With 35 Coloured Plates by Henry Alken.

HANDLEY CROSS. By R. S. Surtees. With 17 Coloured Plates and 100 Woodcuts in the Text by John Leech.

MR. SPONGE'S SPORTING TOUR. By R. S. Surtees. With 13 Coloured Plates and 90 Woodcuts in the Text by John Leech.

JORROCKS' JAUNTS AND JOLLITIES. By R. S. Surtees. With 15 Coloured Plates by H. Alken.

This volume is reprinted from the extremely rare and costly edition of 1843, which contains Alken's very fine illustrations instead of the usual ones by Phiz.

ASK MAMMA. By R. S. Surtees. With 13 Coloured Plates and 70 Woodcuts in the Text by John Leech.

THE ANALYSIS OF THE HUNTING FIELD. By R. S. Surtees. With 7 Coloured Plates by Henry Alken, and 43 Illustrations on Wood.

THE TOUR OF DR. SYNTAX IN SEARCH OF THE PICTURESQUE. By William Combe. With 30 Coloured Plates by T. Rowlandson.

THE TOUR OF DOCTOR SYNTAX IN SEARCH OF CONSOLATION. By William Combe. With 24 Coloured Plates by T. Rowlandson.

THE THIRD TOUR OF DOCTOR SYNTAX IN SEARCH OF A WIFE. By William Combe. With 24 Coloured Plates by T. Rowlandson.

THE HISTORY OF JOHNNY QUAE GENUS: the Little Foundling of the late Dr. Syntax. By the Author of 'The Three Tours.' With 24 Coloured Plates by Rowlandson.

THE ENGLISH DANCE OF DEATH, from the Designs of T. Rowlandson, with Metrical Illustrations by the Author of 'Doctor Syntax.' *Two Volumes.*

This book contains 76 Coloured Plates.

THE DANCE OF LIFE: A Poem. By the Author of 'Doctor Syntax.' Illustrated with 26 Coloured Engravings by T. Rowlandson.

LIFE IN LONDON: or, the Day and Night Scenes of Jerry Hawthorn, Esq., and his Elegant Friend, Corinthian Tom. By Pierce Egan. With 36 Coloured Plates by I. R. and G. Cruikshank. With numerous Designs on Wood.

REAL LIFE IN LONDON: or, the Rambles and Adventures of Bob Tallyho, Esq., and his Cousin, The Hon. Tom Dashall. By an Amateur (Pierce Egan). With 31 Coloured Plates by Alken and Rowlandson, etc. *Two Volumes.*

THE LIFE OF AN ACTOR. By Pierce Egan. With 27 Coloured Plates by Theodore Lane, and several Designs on Wood.

THE VICAR OF WAKEFIELD. By Oliver Goldsmith. With 24 Coloured Plates by T. Rowlandson.

A reproduction of a very rare book.

THE MILITARY ADVENTURES OF JOHNNY NEWCOME. By an Officer. With 15 Coloured Plates by T. Rowlandson.

THE NATIONAL SPORTS OF GREAT BRITAIN. With Descriptions and 51 Coloured Plates by Henry Alken.

This book is completely different from the large folio edition of 'National Sports' by the same artist, and none of the plates are similar.

THE ADVENTURES OF A POST CAPTAIN. By A Naval Officer. With 24 Coloured Plates by Mr. Williams.

[Continued.

THE ILLUSTRATED POCKET LIBRARY—*continued.*

GAMONIA : or, the Art of Preserving Game ; and an Improved Method of making Plantations and Covers, explained and illustrated by Lawrence Rawstorne, Esq.   With 15 Coloured Plates by T. Rawlins.

AN ACADEMY FOR GROWN HORSEMEN : Containing the completest Instructions for Walking, Trotting, Cantering, Galloping, Stumbling, and Tumbling. Illustrated with a 27 Coloured Plates, and adorned with a Portrait of the Author.   By Geoffrey Gambado, Esq.

REAL LIFE IN IRELAND, or, the Day and Night Scenes of Brian Boru, Esq., and his Elegant Friend, Sir Shawn O'Dogherty. By a Real Paddy.   With 19 Coloured Plates by Heath, Marks, etc.

THE ADVENTURES OF JOHNNY NEWCOME IN THE NAVY.   By Alfred Burton.   With 16 Coloured Plates by T. Rowlandson.

THE OLD ENGLISH SQUIRE: A Poem   By John Careless, Esq.   With 20 Coloured Plates after the style of T. Rowlandson.

*THE ENGLISH SPY.   By Bernard Blackmantle.   With 72 Coloured Plates by R. Cruikshank, and many Illustrations on wood.   *Two Volumes.*

PLAIN BOOKS

THE GRAVE : A Poem.   By Robert Blair. Illustrated by 12 Etchings executed by Louis Schiavonetti from the original Inventions of William Blake. With an Engraved Title Page and a Portrait of Blake by T. Phillips, R.A.
The illustrations are reproduced in photogravure.

ILLUSTRATIONS OF THE BOOK OF JOB.   Invented and engraved by William Blake. These famous Illustrations—21 in number —are reproduced in photogravure.

ÆSOP'S FABLES.   With 380 Woodcuts by Thomas Bewick.

WINDSOR CASTLE. By W. Harrison Ainsworth. With 22 Plates and 87 Woodcuts in the Text by George Cruikshank.

THE TOWER OF LONDON.   By W. Harrison Ainsworth. With 40 Plates and 58 Woodcuts in the Text by George Cruikshank.

FRANK FAIRLEGH. By F. E. Smedley. With 30 Plates by George Cruikshank.

HANDY ANDY.   By Samuel Lover.   With 24 Illustrations by the Author.

THE COMPLEAT ANGLER.   By Izaak Walton and Charles Cotton.   With 14 Plates and 77 Woodcuts in the Text.
This volume is reproduced from the beautiful edition of John Major of 1824.

THE PICKWICK PAPERS.   By Charles Dickens. With the 43 Illustrations by Seymour and Phiz, the two Buss Plates, and the 32 Contemporary Onwhyn Plates.

Junior Examination Series

Edited by A. M. M. STEDMAN, M.A.   *Fcap.* 8vo.   1s.

This series is intended to lead up to the School Examination Series, and is intended for the use of teachers and students, to supply material for the former and practice for the latter.   The papers are carefully graduated, cover the whole of the subject usually taught, and are intended to form part of the ordinary class work.   They may be used *vivâ voce* or as a written examination.

JUNIOR FRENCH EXAMINATION PAPERS.   By F. Jacob, M.A.

JUNIOR LATIN EXAMINATION PAPERS.   By C. G. Botting, M.A.   *Third Edition.*

JUNIOR ENGLISH EXAMINATION PAPERS.   By W. Williamson, M.A.

JUNIOR ARITHMETIC EXAMINATION PAPERS.   By W. S. Beard.   *Second Edition.*

JUNIOR ALGEBRA EXAMINATION PAPERS.   By S. W. Finn, M.A.

JUNIOR GREEK EXAMINATION PAPERS. By T. C. Weatherhead, M.A.

JUNIOR GENERAL INFORMATION EXAMINATION PAPERS.   By W. S. Beard.

*A KEY TO THE ABOVE.   *Crown* 8vo.   3s. 6d.

JUNIOR GEOGRAPHY EXAMINATION PAPERS. By W. G. Baker, M.A.

JUNIOR GERMAN EXAMINATION PAPERS.   By A. Voegelin, M.A.

Junior School-Books, Methuen's

Edited by O. D. INSKIP, LL.D., and W. WILLIAMSON, B.A.

A series of elementary books for pupils in lower forms, simply written by teachers of experience.

A CLASS-BOOK OF DICTATION PASSAGES.   By W. Williamson, B.A. *Tenth Edition. Crown* 8vo.   1s. 6d.

THE GOSPEL ACCORDING TO ST. MATTHEW. Edited by E. Wilton South, M.A.   With Three Maps.   *Crown* 8vo.   1s. 6d.

[Continued.

METHUEN'S JUNIOR SCHOOL-BOOKS—continued.

THE GOSPEL ACCORDING TO ST. MARK. Edited by A. E. Rubie, D.D. With Three Maps. *Crown 8vo. 1s. 6d.*

A JUNIOR ENGLISH GRAMMAR. By W. Williamson, B.A. With numerous passages for parsing and analysis, and a chapter on Essay Writing. *Second Edition. Crown 8vo. 2s.*

A JUNIOR CHEMISTRY. By E. A. Tyler, B.A., F.C.S. With 78 Illustrations. *Second Edition. Crown 8vo. 2s. 6d.*

THE ACTS OF THE APOSTLES. Edited by A. E. Rubie, D.D. *Crown 8vo. 2s.*

A JUNIOR FRENCH GRAMMAR. By L. A. Sornet and M. J. Acatos. *Crown 8vo. 2s.*

ELEMENTARY EXPERIMENTAL SCIENCE. PHYSICS by W. T. Clough, A.R.C.S. CHEMISTRY by A. E. Dunstan, B.Sc. With 2 Plates and 154 Diagrams. *Crown 8vo. 2s. 6d.*

A JUNIOR GEOMETRY. By Noel S. Lydon. With 239 Diagrams. *Crown 8vo. 2s.*

*A JUNIOR MAGNETISM AND ELECTRICITY. By W. T. Clough. With many Illustrations. *Crown 8vo.*

ELEMENTARY EXPERIMENTAL CHEMISTRY. By A. E. Dunstan, B.Sc. With 4 Plates and 109 Diagrams. *Crown 8vo. 2s.*

A JUNIOR FRENCH PROSE COMPOSITION. By R. R. N. Baron, M.A. *Crown 8vo. 2s.*

*THE GOSPEL ACCORDING TO ST. LUKE. With an Introduction and Notes by William Williamson, B.A. With Three Maps. *Crown 8vo. 1s. 6d.*

Leaders of Religion

Edited by H. C. BEECHING, M.A., Canon of Westminster   *With Portraits.*
Crown 8vo.   2s. net.

A series of short biographies of the most prominent leaders of religious life and thought of all ages and countries.

CARDINAL NEWMAN. By R. H. Hutton.

JOHN WESLEY. By J. H. Overton, M.A.

BISHOP WILBERFORCE. By G. W. Daniell, M.A.

CARDINAL MANNING. By A. W. Hutton, M.A.

CHARLES SIMEON. By H. C. G. Moule, D.D.

JOHN KEBLE. By Walter Lock, D.D.

THOMAS CHALMERS. By Mrs. Oliphant.

LANCELOT ANDREWES. By R. L. Ottley, D.D. *Second Edition.*

AUGUSTINE OF CANTERBURY. By E. L. Cutts, D.D.

WILLIAM LAUD. By W. H. Hutton, M.A. *Third Edition.*

JOHN KNOX. By F. MacCunn. *Second Edition.*

JOHN HOWE. By R. F. Horton, D.D.

BISHOP KEN. By F. A. Clarke, M.A.

GEORGE FOX, THE QUAKER. By T. Hodgkin, D.C.L.

JOHN DONNE. By Augustus Jessopp, D.D.

THOMAS CRANMER. By A. J. Mason, D.D

BISHOP LATIMER. By R. M. Carlyle and A. J. Carlyle, M.A.

BISHOP BUTLER. By W. A. Spooner, M.A.

Little Blue Books, The

General Editor, E. V. LUCAS.
Illustrated. Demy 16mo.   2s. 6d.

A series of books for children. The aim of the editor is to get entertaining or exciting stories about normal children, the moral of which is implied rather than expressed.

1. THE CASTAWAYS OF MEADOWBANK. By Thomas Cobb.
2. THE BEECHNUT BOOK. By Jacob Abbott. Edited by E. V. Lucas.
3. THE AIR GUN. By T. Hilbert.
4. A SCHOOL YEAR. By Netta Syrett.
5. THE PEELES AT THE CAPITAL. By Roger Ashton.
6. THE TREASURE OF PRINCEGATE PRIORY By T. Cobb.
7. MRS. BARBERRY'S GENERAL SHOP. By Roger Ashton.
8. A BOOK OF BAD CHILDREN. By W. T. Webb.
9. THE LOST BALL. By Thomas Cobb.

Little Books on Art

With many Illustrations. Demy 16mo.   2s. 6d. net.

A series of monographs in miniature, containing the complete outline of the subject under treatment and rejecting minute details. These books are produced with the greatest care. Each volume consists of about 200 pages, and contains from 30 to 40 illustrations, including a frontispiece in photogravure.

GREEK ART. *Second Edition.* H. B. Walters.

BOOKPLATES. E. Almack.

REYNOLDS. J. Sime.

ROMNEY. George Paston.

[Continued.

LITTLE BOOKS ON ART—*continued.*

WATTS. R. E. D. Sketchley.
LEIGHTON. Alice Corkran.
VELASQUEZ. Wilfrid Wilberforce and A. R. Gilbert.
GREUZE AND BOUCHER. Eliza F. Pollard.
VANDYCK. M. G. Smallwood.
TURNER. Frances Tyrell-Gill.
DÜRER. Jessie Allen.
HOPPNER. H. P. K. Skipton.
HOLBEIN. Mrs. G. Fortescue.

BURNE-JONES. Fortunée de Lisle.
REMBRANDT. Mrs. E. A. Sharp
COROT. Alice Pollard and Ethel Birnstingl.
RAPHAEL. A. R. Dryhurst.
MILLET. Netta Peacock.
ILLUMINATED MSS. J. W. Bradley.
CHRIST IN ART. Mrs. Henry Jenner.
JEWELLERY. Cyril Davenport.
*CLAUDE. Edward Dillon.

Little Galleries, The

Demy 16mo.   2s. 6d. net.

A series of little books containing examples of the best work of the great painters. Each volume contains 20 plates in photogravure, together with a short outline of the life and work of the master to whom the book is devoted.

A LITTLE GALLERY OF REYNOLDS.
A LITTLE GALLERY OF ROMNEY.
A LITTLE GALLERY OF HOPPNER.

A LITTLE GALLERY OF MILLAIS.
A LITTLE GALLERY OF ENGLISH POETS.

Little Guides, The

Small Pott 8vo, cloth, 2s. 6d. net.; leather, 3s. 6d. net.

OXFORD AND ITS COLLEGES. By J. Wells, M.A. Illustrated by E. H. New. *Fourth Edition.*
CAMBRIDGE AND ITS COLLEGES. By A. Hamilton Thompson. *Second Edition.* Illustrated by E. H. New.
THE MALVERN COUNTRY. By B. C. A. Windle, D.Sc., F.R.S. Illustrated by E. H. New.
SHAKESPEARE'S COUNTRY. By B. C. A. Windle, D.Sc., F.R.S. Illustrated by E. H. New. *Second Edition.*
SUSSEX. By F. G. Brabant, M.A. Illustrated by E. H. New.
WESTMINSTER ABBEY. By G. E. Troutbeck. Illustrated by F. D. Bedford.
NORFOLK. By W. A. Dutt. Illustrated by B. C. Boulter.
CORNWALL. By A. L. Salmon. Illustrated by B. C. Boulter.
BRITTANY. By S. Baring-Gould. Illustrated by J. Wylie.
HERTFORDSHIRE. By H. W. Tompkins, F.R.H.S. Illustrated by E. H. New.
THE ENGLISH LAKES. By F. G. Brabant, M.A. Illustrated by E. H. New.

KENT. By G. Clinch. Illustrated by F. D. Bedford.
ROME By C. G. Ellaby. Illustrated by B. C. Boulter.
THE ISLE OF WIGHT. By G. Clinch. Illustrated by F. D. Bedford.
SURREY. By F. A. H. Lambert. Illustrated by E. H. New.
BUCKINGHAMSHIRE. By E. S. Roscoe. Illustrated by F. D. Bedford.
SUFFOLK. By W. A. Dutt. Illustrated by J. Wylie.
DERBYSHIRE. By J. C. Cox, LL.D., F.S.A. Illustrated by J. C. Wall.
THE NORTH RIDING OF YORKSHIRE. By J. E. Morris. Illustrated by R. J. S. Bertram.
HAMPSHIRE. By J. C. Cox. Illustrated by M. E. Purser.
SICILY. By F. H. Jackson. With many Illustrations by the Author.
DORSET. By Frank R. Heath. Illustrated.
CHESHIRE. By W. M. Gallichan. Illustrated by Elizabeth Hartley.

Little Library, The

With Introductions, Notes, and Photogravure Frontispieces.
Small Pott 8vo.   Each Volume, cloth, 1s. 6d. net ; leather, 2s. 6d. net.

A series of small books under the above title, containing some of the famous works in English and other literatures, in the domains of fiction, poetry, and belles lettres. The series also contains volumes of selections in prose and verse.

The books are edited with the most sympathetic and scholarly care. Each one contains an introduction which gives (1) a short biography of the author; (2) a critical estimate of the book. Where they are necessary, short notes are added at the foot of the page.

Each volume has a photogravure frontispiece, and the books are produced with great care.

Anon. ENGLISH LYRICS, A LITTLE BOOK OF.

Austen (Jane). PRIDE AND PREJUDICE. Edited by E. V. Lucas. *Two Volumes.*

NORTHANGER ABBEY. Edited by E. V. Lucas.

Bacon (Francis). THE ESSAYS OF LORD BACON. Edited by Edward Wright.

Barham (R. H.). THE INGOLDSBY LEGENDS. Edited by J. B. Atlay. *Two Volumes.*

Barnett (Mrs. P. A.). A LITTLE BOOK OF ENGLISH PROSE.

Beckford (William). THE HISTORY OF THE CALIPH VATHEK. Edited by E. Denison Ross.

Blake (William). SELECTIONS FROM WILLIAM BLAKE. Edited by M. Perugini.

Borrow (George). LAVENGRO. Edited by F. Hindes Groome. *Two Volumes.*

THE ROMANY RYE. Edited by John Sampson.

Browning (Robert). SELECTIONS FROM THE EARLY POEMS OF ROBERT BROWNING. Edited by W. Hall Griffin, M.A.

Canning (George). SELECTIONS FROM THE ANTI-JACOBIN: with George Canning's additional Poems. Edited by Lloyd Sanders.

Cowley (Abraham). THE ESSAYS OF ABRAHAM COWLEY. Edited by H. C. Minchin.

Crabbe (George). SELECTIONS FROM GEORGE CRABBE. Edited by A. C. Deane.

Craik (Mrs.). JOHN HALIFAX, GENTLEMAN. Edited by Anne Matheson. *Two Volumes.*

Crawshaw (Richard). THE ENGLISH POEMS OF RICHARD CRAWSHAW. Edited by Edward Hutton.

Dante (Alighieri). THE INFERNO OF DANTE. Translated by H. F. Cary. Edited by Paget Toynbee, M.A., D.Litt.

THE PURGATORIO OF DANTE. Translated by H. F. Cary. Edited by Paget Toynbee, M.A., D.Litt.

THE PARADISO OF DANTE. Translated by H. F. Cary. Edited by Paget Toynbee, M.A., D.Litt.

Darley (George). SELECTIONS FROM THE POEMS OF GEORGE DARLEY. Edited by R. A. Streatfeild.

Deane (A. C.). A LITTLE BOOK OF LIGHT VERSE.

Dickens (Charles). CHRISTMAS BOOKS. *Two Volumes.*

Ferrier (Susan). MARRIAGE. Edited by A. Goodrich-Freer and Lord Iddesleigh. *Two Volumes.*

THE INHERITANCE. *Two Volumes.*

Gaskell (Mrs.). CRANFORD. Edited by E. V. Lucas.

Hawthorne (Nathaniel). THE SCARLET LETTER. Edited by Percy Dearmer.

Henderson (T. F.). A LITTLE BOOK OF SCOTTISH VERSE.

Keats (John). POEMS. With an Introduction by L. Binyon, and Notes by J. Masefield.

Kinglake (A. W.). EOTHEN. With an Introduction and Notes.

Lamb (Charles). ELIA, AND THE LAST ESSAYS OF ELIA. Edited by E. V. Lucas.

Locker (F.). LONDON LYRICS. Edited by A. D. Godley, M.A. A reprint of the First Edition.

Longfellow (H. W.). SELECTIONS FROM LONGFELLOW. Edited by L. M. Faithfull.

Marvell (Andrew). THE POEMS OF ANDREW MARVELL. Edited by E. Wright.

Milton (John). THE MINOR POEMS OF JOHN MILTON. Edited by H. C. Beeching, M.A., Canon of Westminster.

Moir (D. M.). MANSIE WAUCH. Edited by F. Henderson.

Nichols (J. B. B.). A LITTLE BOOK OF ENGLISH SONNETS.

Rochefoucauld (La). THE MAXIMS OF LA ROCHEFOUCAULD. Translated by Dean Stanhope. Edited by G. H. Powell.

Smith (Horace and James). REJECTED ADDRESSES. Edited by A. D. Godley, M.A.

Sterne (Laurence). A SENTIMENTAL JOURNEY. Edited by H. W. Paul.

Tennyson (Alfred, Lord). THE EARLY POEMS OF ALFRED, LORD TENNYSON. Edited by J. Churton Collins, M.A.

IN MEMORIAM. Edited by H. C. Beeching, M.A.

THE PRINCESS. Edited by Elizabeth Wordsworth.

MAUD. Edited by Elizabeth Wordsworth.

Thackeray (W. M.). VANITY FAIR. Edited by S. Gwynn. *Three Volumes.*

PENDENNIS. Edited by S. Gwynn. *Three Volumes.*

ESMOND. Edited by S. Gwynn.

CHRISTMAS BOOKS. Edited by S. Gwynn.

Vaughan (Henry). THE POEMS OF HENRY VAUGHAN. Edited by Edward Hutton.

[*Continued.*

THE LITTLE LIBRARY—*continued.*

Walton (Izaak). THE COMPLEAT ANGLER. Edited by J. BUCHAN.

Waterhouse (Mrs. Alfred). A LITTLE BOOK OF LIFE AND DEATH. Edited by. *Seventh Edition.*

Wordsworth (W.). SELECTIONS FROM WORDSWORTH. Edited by NOWELL C. SMITH.

Wordsworth (W.) and Coleridge (S. T.). LYRICAL BALLADS. Edited by GEORGE SAMPSON.

Miniature Library, Methuen's

Reprints in miniature of a few interesting books which have qualities of humanity, devotion, or literary genius.

EUPHRANOR: A Dialogue on Youth. By Edward FitzGerald. From the edition published by W. Pickering in 1851. *Demy 32mo. Leather, 2s. net.*

POLONIUS: or Wise Saws and Modern Instances. By Edward FitzGerald. From the edition published by W. Pickering in 1852. *Demy 32mo. Leather, 2s. net.*

THE RUBÁIYÁT OF OMAR KHAYYÁM. By Edward FitzGerald. From the 1st edition of 1859, *Third Edition. Leather, 1s. net.*

THE LIFE OF EDWARD, LORD HERBERT OF CHERBURY. Written by himself. From the edition printed at Strawberry Hill in the year 1764. *Medium 32mo. Leather, 2s. net.*

THE VISIONS OF DOM FRANCISCO QUEVEDO VILLEGAS, Knight of the Order of St. James. Made English by R. L. From the edition printed for H. Herringman, 1668. *Leather. 2s. net.*

POEMS. By Dora Greenwell. From the edition of 1848. *Leather, 2s. net.*

The Oxford Biographies

Fcap. 8vo. Each volume, cloth, 2s. 6d. net; leather, 3s. 6d. net.

These books are written by scholars of repute, who combine knowledge and literary skill with the power of popular presentation. They are illustrated from authentic material.

DANTE ALIGHIERI. By Paget Toynbee, M.A., D.Litt. With 12 Illustrations. *Second Edition.*

SAVONAROLA. By E. L. S. Horsburgh, M.A. With 12 Illustrations. *Second Edition.*

JOHN HOWARD. By E. C. S. Gibson, D.D., Vicar of Leeds. With 12 Illustrations.

TENNYSON. By A. C. Benson, M.A. With 9 Illustrations.

WALTER RALEIGH. By I. A. Taylor. With 12 Illustrations.

ERASMUS. By E. F. H. Capey. With 12 Illustrations.

THE YOUNG PRETENDER. By C. S. Terry. With 12 Illustrations.

ROBERT BURNS. By T. F. Henderson. With 12 Illustrations.

CHATHAM. By A. S. M'Dowall. With 12 Illustrations.

ST. FRANCIS OF ASSISI. By Anna M. Stoddart. With 16 Illustrations.

CANNING. By W. A. Phillips. With 12 Illustrations.

BEACONSFIELD. By Walter Sichel. With 12 Illustrations.

GOETHE. By H. G. Atkins. With 12 Illustrations.

*FENELON. By Viscount St. Cyres. With 12 Illustrations.

School Examination Series

Edited by A. M. M. STEDMAN, M.A. *Crown 8vo. 2s. 6d.*

FRENCH EXAMINATION PAPERS. By A. M. M. Stedman, M.A. *Thirteenth Edition.*
    A KEY, issued to Tutors and Private Students only to be had on application to the Publishers. *Fifth Edition. Crown 8vo. 6s. net.*

LATIN EXAMINATION PAPERS. By A. M. M. Stedman, M.A. *Twelfth Edition.*
    KEY (*Fourth Edition*) issued as above. 6s. net.

GREEK EXAMINATION PAPERS. By A. M. M. Stedman, M.A. *Seventh Edition.*
    KEY (*Second Edition*) issued as above. 6s. net.

GERMAN EXAMINATION PAPERS. By R. J. Morich. *Fifth Edition.*

KEY (*Second Edition*) issued as above. 6s. net.

HISTORY AND GEOGRAPHY EXAMINATION PAPERS. By C. H. Spence, M.A. *Third Edition.*

PHYSICS EXAMINATION PAPERS. By R. E. Steel, M.A., F.C.S.

GENERAL KNOWLEDGE EXAMINATION PAPERS. By A. M. M. Stedman, M.A. *Fifth Edition.*
    KEY (*Third Edition*) issued as above. 7s. net.

EXAMINATION PAPERS IN ENGLISH HISTORY. By J. Tait Plowden-Wardlaw, B.A.

Social Questions of To-day

Edited by H. DE B. GIBBINS, Litt.D., M.A. *Crown 8vo. 2s. 6d.*

A series of volumes upon those topics of social economic, and industrial interest that are foremost in the public mind.

Each volume is written by an author who is an acknowledged authority upon the subject with which he deals.

TRADE UNIONISM—NEW AND OLD. By G. Howell. *Third Edition.*

THE CO-OPERATIVE MOVEMENT TO-DAY. By G. J. Holyoake. *Fourth Edition.*

PROBLEMS OF POVERTY. By J. A. Hobson, M.A. *Fifth Edition.*

THE COMMERCE OF NATIONS. By C. F. Bastable, M.A. *Third Edition.*

THE ALIEN INVASION. By W. H. Wilkins, B.A.

THE RURAL EXODUS. By P. Anderson Graham.

LAND NATIONALIZATION. By Harold Cox, B.A.

A SHORTER WORKING DAY, By H. de Gibbins and R. A. Hadfield.

BACK TO THE LAND. An Inquiry into Rural Depopulation. By H. E. Moore.

TRUSTS, POOLS, AND CORNERS. By J. Stephen Jeans.

THE FACTORY SYSTEM. By R. W. Cooke-Taylor.

THE STATE AND ITS CHILDREN. By Gertrude Tuckwell.

WOMEN'S WORK. By Lady Dilke, Miss Bulley, and Miss Whitley.

SOCIALISM AND MODERN THOUGHT. By M. Kauffmann.

THE PROBLEM OF THE UNEMPLOYED. By J. A. Hobson, M.A.

LIFE IN WEST LONDON. By Arthur Sherwell, M.A. *Third Edition.*

RAILWAY NATIONALIZATION. By Clement Edwards.

WORKHOUSES AND PAUPERISM. By Louisa Twining.

UNIVERSITY AND SOCIAL SETTLEMENTS. By W. Reason, M.A.

Methuen's Standard Library

EDITED BY SIDNEY LEE. *In Sixpenny Volumes.*

MESSRS. METHUEN are publishing a new series of reprints containing both books of classical repute, which are accessible in various forms, and also some rarer books, of which no satisfactory edition at a moderate price is in existence. It is their ambition to place the best books of all nations, and particularly of the Anglo-Saxon race, within the reach of every reader. All the great masters of Poetry, Drama, Fiction, History, Biography, and Philosophy will be represented. Mr. Sidney Lee is the General Editor of the Library, and he contributes a Note to each book. The characteristics of METHUEN'S STANDARD LIBRARY are five :—1. SOUNDNESS OF TEXT. 2. COMPLETENESS. 3. CHEAPNESS. 4. CLEARNESS OF TYPE. 5. SIMPLICITY. In a few cases very long books are issued as Double Volumes at One Shilling net or as Treble Volumes at One Shilling and Sixpence net. The volumes may also be obtained in cloth at One Shilling net, or in the case of a Double or Treble Volume at One and Sixpence net or Two Shillings net.

These are the early Books, all of which are in the Press—

THE WORKS OF WILLIAM SHAKESPEARE. In 10 volumes.

VOL. I.—The Tempest; The Two Gentlemen of Verona; The Merry Wives of Windsor; Measure for Measure; The Comedy of Errors.

VOL. II.—Much Ado About Nothing; Love's Labour's Lost; A Midsummer Night's Dream; The Merchant of Venice; As You Like It.

VOL. III.—The Taming of the Shrew; All's Well that Ends Well; Twelfth Night; The Winter's Tale.

*Vol. IV.—The Life and Death of King John; The Tragedy of King Richard the Second; The First Part of King Henry IV.; The Second Part of King Henry IV.

*Vol. V.—The Life of King Henry V.; The First Part of King Henry VI.; The Second Part of King Henry VI.

*Vol. VI.—The Third Part of King Henry VI.: The Tragedy of King Richard III.; The Famous History of the Life of King Henry VIII.

THE PILGRIM'S PROGRESS. By John Bunyan.

THE NOVELS OF JANE AUSTEN. In 5 volumes.

VOL. I.—Sense and Sensibility.

THE ENGLISH WORKS OF FRANCIS BACON, LORD VERULAM.

Vol. I.—Essays and Counsels and the New Atlantis.

THE POEMS AND PLAYS OF OLIVER GOLDSMITH.

ON THE IMITATION OF CHRIST. By Thomas à Kempis.

[Continued.

METHUEN'S STANDARD LIBRARY—*continued.*

THE WORKS OF BEN JONSON. In about 12 volumes.
  *VOL. I.—The Case is Altered; Every Man in His Humour; Every Man out of His Humour.
  *Vol. II.—Cynthia's Revels; The Poetaster.

THE PROSE WORKS OF JOHN MILTON.
  *VOL. I.—Eikonoklastes and The Tenure of Kings and Magistrates.

SELECT WORKS OF EDMUND BURKE.
  Vol. I.—Reflections on the French Revolution.

THE WORKS OF HENRY FIELDING.
  Vol. I.—Tom Jones. (Treble Volume.)

THE POEMS OF THOMAS CHATTERTON. In 2 volumes.
  *Vol. I.—Miscellaneous Poems.

*THE LIFE OF NELSON. By Robert Southey.

THE MEDITATIONS OF MARCUS AURELIUS. Translated by R. Graves.

THE HISTORY OF THE DECLINE AND FALL OF THE ROMAN EMPIRE. By Edward Gibbon. In 7 volumes.
  The Notes have been revised by J. B. Bury, Litt.D.

THE PLAYS OF CHRISTOPHER MARLOWE.
  *Vol. I.—Tamburlane the Great; The Tragical History of Doctor Faustus.

*THE NATURAL HISTORY AND ANTIQUITIES OF SELBORNE. By Gilbert White.

THE POEMS OF PERCY BYSSHE SHELLEY. In 4 volumes.
  *Vol. I.—Alastor; The Daemon of the World; The Revolt of Islam, etc.
  *Vol. II.—Prometheus Unbound; The Cenci; The Masque of Anarchy; Peter Bell the Third; Ode to Liberty; The Witch of Atlas; Ode to Naples; Œdipus Tyrannus.
  The text has been revised by C. D. Locock.

*THE LITTLE FLOWERS OF ST. FRANCIS. Translated by W. Heywood.

THE WORKS OF SIR THOMAS BROWNE. In 6 volumes.
  *Vol. I.—Religio Medici and Urn Burial.

THE POEMS OF JOHN MILTON. In 2 volumes.
  *Vol. I.—Paradise Lost.
  *Vol. II.—Miscellaneous Poems and Paradise Regained.

SELECT WORKS OF SIR THOMAS MORE.
  *Vol. I.—Utopia and Poems.

*THE ANALOGY OF RELIGION, NATURAL AND REVEALED. By Joseph Butler, D.D.

*THE PLAYS OF PHILIP MASSINGER.
  Vol. I.—The Duke of Milan; The Bondman; The Roman Actor.

*THE POEMS OF JOHN KEATS. In 2 volumes.
*THE REPUBLIC OF PLATO. Translated by Taylor and Sydenham.

Technology, Textbooks of

Edited by PROFESSOR J. WERTHEIMER, F.I.C.
Fully Illustrated.

HOW TO MAKE A DRESS. By J. A. E. Wood. *Third Edition. Crown 8vo. 1s. 6d.*

CARPENTRY AND JOINERY. By F. C. Webber. *Third Edition. Crown 8vo. 3s. 6d.*

PRACTICAL MECHANICS. By Sidney H. Wells. *Third Edition. Crown 8vo. 3s. 6d.*

PRACTICAL PHYSICS. By H. Stroud, D.Sc., M.A. *Crown 8vo. 3s. 6d.*

MILLINERY, THEORETICAL AND PRACTICAL. By Clare Hill. *Second Edition. Crown 8vo. 2s.*

PRACTICAL CHEMISTRY. Part I. By W. French, M.A. *Crown 8vo. Third Edition. 1s. 6d.*

PRACTICAL CHEMISTRY. Part II. By W. French, M.A., and T. H. Boardman, M.A. *Crown 8vo. 1s. 6d.*

TECHNICAL ARITHMETIC AND GEOMETRY. By C. T. Millis, M.I.M.E. *Crown 8vo. 3s. 6d.*

AN INTRODUCTION TO THE STUDY OF TEXTILE DESIGN. By Aldred F. Barker. *Demy 8vo. 7s. 6d.*

BUILDERS' QUANTITIES. By H. C. Grubb. *Crown 8vo. 4s. 6d.*

REPOUSSÉ METAL WORK. By A. C. Horth. *Crown 8vo. 2s. 6d.*

Theology, Handbooks of

Edited by R. L. OTTLEY, D.D., Professor of Pastoral Theology at Oxford, and Canon of Christ Church, Oxford.

The series is intended, in part, to furnish the clergy and teachers or students of Theology with trustworthy Text-books, adequately representing the present position of the questions dealt with; in part, to make accessible to the reading public an accurate and concise statement of facts and principles in all questions bearing on Theology and Religion.

THE XXXIX. ARTICLES OF THE CHURCH OF ENGLAND. Edited by E. C. S. Gibson, D.D. *Third and Cheaper Edition in one Volume. Demy 8vo. 12s. 6d.*

AN INTRODUCTION TO THE HISTORY OF RELIGION. By F. B. Jevons, M.A., Litt.D. *Third Edition. Demy 8vo. 10s. 6d.*

[*Continued.*

HANDBOOKS OF THEOLOGY—*continued.*

THE DOCTRINE OF THE INCARNATION. By R. L. Ottley, D.D. *Second and Cheaper Edition. Demy 8vo.* 12s. 6d.

AN INTRODUCTION TO THE HISTORY OF THE CREEDS. By A. E. Burn, B.D. *Demy 8vo.* 10s. 6d.

THE PHILOSOPHY OF RELIGION IN ENGLAND AND AMERICA. By Alfred Caldecott, D.D. *Demy 8vo.* 10s. 6d.

A HISTORY OF EARLY CHRISTIAN DOCTRINE. By J. F. Bethune Baker, M.A. *Demy 8vo.* 10s. 6d.

Westminster Commentaries, The

General Editor, WALTER LOCK, D.D., Warden of Keble College, Dean Ireland's Professor of Exegesis in the University of Oxford.

The object of each commentary is primarily exegetical, to interpret the author's meaning to the present generation. The editors will not deal, except very subordinately, with questions of textual criticism or philology; but, taking the English text in the Revised Version as their basis, they will try to combine a hearty acceptance of critical principles with loyalty to the Catholic Faith.

THE BOOK OF GENESIS. Edited with Introduction and Notes by S. R. Driver, D.D. *Fourth Edition Demy 8vo.* 10s. 6d.

THE BOOK OF JOB. Edited by E. C. S. Gibson, D.D. *Second Edition. Demy 8vo.* 6s.

THE ACTS OF THE APOSTLES. Edited by R. B. Rackham, M.A. *Demy 8vo. Second and Cheaper Edition.* 10s. 6d.

THE FIRST EPISTLE OF PAUL THE APOSTLE TO THE CORINTHIANS. Edited by H. L. Goudge, M.A. *Demy 8vo.* 6s.

THE EPISTLE OF ST. JAMES. Edited with Introduction and Notes by R. J. Knowling, M.A. *Demy 8vo.* 6s.

PART II.—FICTION

Albanesi (E. Maria). SUSANNAH AND ONE OTHER. *Fourth Edition. Crown 8vo.* 6s.

THE BLUNDER OF AN INNOCENT. *Second Edition. Crown 8vo.* 6s.

CAPRICIOUS CAROLINE. *Second Edition. Crown 8vo.* 6s.

LOVE AND LOUISA. *Second Edition. Crown 8vo.* 6s.

PETER, A PARASITE. *Crown 8vo.* 6s.

THE BROWN EYES OF MARY. *Crown 8vo.* 6s.

Anstey (F.), Author of 'Vice Versâ.' A BAYARD FROM BENGAL. Illustrated by BERNARD PARTRIDGE. *Third Edition. Crown 8vo.* 3s. 6d.

Bacheller (Irving), Author of 'Eben Holden.' DARREL OF THE BLESSED ISLES. *Third Edition. Crown 8vo.* 6s.

Bagot (Richard). A ROMAN MYSTERY. *Third Edition. Crown 8vo.* 6s.

THE PASSPORT. *Second Ed. Cr. 8vo.* 6s.

Balfour (Andrew). See Shilling Novels.

Baring-Gould (S.). ARMINELL. *Fifth Edition. Crown 8vo.* 6s.

URITH. *Fifth Edition. Crown 8vo.* 6s.

IN THE ROAR OF THE SEA. *Seventh Edition. Crown 8vo.* 6s.

CHEAP JACK ZITA. *Fourth Edition. Crown 8vo.* 6s.

MARGERY OF QUETHER. *Third Edition. Crown 8vo.* 6s.

THE QUEEN OF LOVE. *Fifth Edition. Crown 8vo.* 6s.

JACQUETTA. *Third Edition. Crown 8vo.* 6s.

KITTY ALONE. *Fifth Edition. Cr. 8vo.* 6s.

NOÉMI. Illustrated. *Fourth Edition. Crown 8vo.* 6s.

THE BROOM-SQUIRE. Illustrated. *Fourth Edition. Crown 8vo.* 6s.

DARTMOOR IDYLLS. *Crown 8vo.* 6s.

THE PENNYCOMEQUICKS. *Third Edition. Crown 8vo.* 6s.

GUAVAS THE TINNER. Illustrated. *Second Edition. Crown 8vo.* 6s.

BLADYS. Illustrated. *Second Edition. Crown 8vo.* 6s.

PABO THE PRIEST. *Crown 8vo.* 6s.

WINEFRED. Illustrated. *Second Edition. Crown 8vo.* 6s.

ROYAL GEORGIE. Illustrated. *Cr. 8vo.* 6s.

MISS QUILLET. Illustrated. *Crown 8vo.* 6s.

CHRIS OF ALL SORTS. *Crown 8vo.* 6s.

IN DEWISLAND. *Second Edition. Crown 8vo.* 6s.

LITTLE TU'PENNY. *A New Edition.* 6d. See also Shilling Novels.

Barlow (Jane). THE LAND OF THE SHAMROCK. *Crown 8vo.* 6s. See also Shilling Novels.

Barr (Robert). IN THE MIDST OF ALARMS. *Third Edition. Crown 8vo.* 6s.

'A book which has abundantly satisfied us by its capital humour.'—*Daily Chronicle.*

THE MUTABLE MANY. *Third Edition.*
Crown 8vo. 6s.
'There is much insight in it, and much
excellent humour.'—*Daily Chronicle.*
THE COUNTESS TEKLA. *Third Edition.*
Crown 8vo. 6s.
'Of these mediæval romances, which are
now gaining ground, "The Countess Tekla"
is the very best we have seen. —*Pall Mall
Gazette.*
THE LADY ELECTRA. *Second Edition.*
Crown 8vo. 6s.
THE TEMPESTUOUS PETTICOAT.
Third Edition. Crown 8vo. 6s.
See also Shilling Novels.
Begbie (Harold). THE ADVENTURES
OF SIR JOHN SPARROW. *Crown 8vo. 6s.*
Belloc (Hilaire). EMMANUEL BURDEN,
MERCHANT. With 36 Illustrations by
G. K. CHESTERTON. *Second Edition.*
Crown 8vo. 6s.
Benson (E. F.). See Shilling Novels.
Benson (Margaret). SUBJECT TO
VANITY. *Crown 8vo. 3s. 6d.*
Besant (Sir Walter). See Shilling Novels.
Bourne (Harold C.). See V. Langbridge.
Burton (J. Bloundelle). THE YEAR
ONE: A Page of the French Revolution.
Illustrated. *Crown 8vo. 6s.*
THE FATE OF VALSEC. *Crown 8vo. 6s.*
A BRANDED NAME. *Crown 8vo. 6s.*
See also Shilling Novels.
Capes (Bernard), Author of 'The Lake of
Wine.' THE EXTRAORDINARY CON-
FESSIONS OF DIANA PLEASE. *Third
Edition. Crown 8vo. 6s.*
A JAY OF ITALY. *Third Ed. Cr. 8vo. 6s.*
Chesney (Weatherby). THE TRAGEDY
OF THE GREAT EMERALD. *Crown
8vo. 6s.*
THE MYSTERY OF A BUNGALOW.
Second Edition. Crown 8vo. 6s.
See also Shilling Novels.
Clifford (Hugh). A FREE LANCE OF
TO-DAY. *Crown 8vo. 6s.*
Clifford (Mrs. W. K.). See Shilling Novels
and Books for Boys and Girls.
Cobb (Thomas). A CHANGE OF FACE.
Crown 8vo. 6s.
Corelli (Marie). A ROMANCE OF TWO
WORLDS. *Twenty-Fifth Edition. Crown
8vo. 6s.*
VENDETTA. *Twenty-First Edition. Crown
8vo. 6s.*
THELMA. *Thirty-Second Edition. Crown
8vo. 6s.*
ARDATH: THE STORY OF A DEAD
SELF. *Fifteenth Edition. Crown 8vo. 6s.*
THE SOUL OF LILITH. *Twelfth Edition.*
Crown 8vo. 6s.
WORMWOOD. *Fourteenth Edition. Crown
8vo. 6s.*
BARABBAS: A DREAM OF THE
WORLD'S TRAGEDY. *Fortieth Edi-
tion. Crown 8vo. 6s.*

The tender reverence of the treatment
and the imaginative beauty of the writing
have reconciled us to the daring of the conception. This "Dream of the World's
Tragedy" is a lofty and not inadequate
paraphrase of the supreme climax of the
inspired narrative.'—*Dublin Review.*
THE SORROWS OF SATAN. *Forty-
Ninth Edition. Crown 8vo. 6s.*
'A very powerful piece of work. . . .
The conception is magnificent, and is likely
to win an abiding place within the memory
of man. . . . The author has immense command of language, and a limitless audacity.
. . . This interesting and remarkable romance
will live long after much of the ephemeral
literature of the day is forgotten. . . . A
literary phenomenon . . . novel, and even
sublime.'—W. T. STEAD in the *Review of
Reviews.*
THE MASTER CHRISTIAN. 165*th
Thousand. Crown 8vo. 6s.*
'It cannot be denied that "The Master
Christian" is a powerful book ; that it is one
likely to raise uncomfortable questions in all
but the most self-satisfied readers, and that
it strikes at the root of the failure of the
Churches—the decay of faith—in a manner
which shows the inevitable disaster heaping
up. . . . The good Cardinal Bonpré is a
beautiful figure, fit to stand beside the good
Bishop in "Les Misérables." It is a book
with a serious purpose expressed with absolute
unconventionality and passion. . . . And this
is to say it is a book worth reading.'—
Examiner.
TEMPORAL POWER: A STUDY IN
SUPREMACY. 130*th Thousand. Crown
8vo. 6s.*
'It is impossible to read such a work as
"Temporal Power" without becoming con-
vinced that the story is intended to convey
certain criticisms on the ways of the world
and certain suggestions for the betterment
of humanity. . . . If the chief intention of
the book was to hold the mirror up to shams,
injustice, dishonesty, cruelty, and neglect
of conscience, nothing but praise can be given
to that intention.'—*Morning Post.*
GOD'S GOOD MAN: A SIMPLE LOVE
STORY. 134*th Thousand. Crown 8vo. 6s.*
Cotes (Mrs. Everard). See Sara Jeannette
Duncan.
Cotterell (Constance). THE VIRGIN
AND THE SCALES. *Second Edition.*
Crown 8vo. 6s.
Crane (Stephen) and **Barr (Robert).**
THE O'RUDDY. *Crown 8vo. 6s.*
Crockett (S. R.), Author of 'The Raiders,'
etc. LOCHINVAR. Illustrated. *Second
Edition. Crown 8vo. 6s.*
THE STANDARD BEARER. *Crown 8vo.
6s.*
Croker (B. M.). ANGEL. *Fourth Edition.*
Crown 8vo. 6s.

PEGGY OF THE BARTONS. *Sixth Edit.* *Crown 8vo.* 6s.

THE OLD CANTONMENT. *Crown 8vo.* 6s.

A STATE SECRET. *Third Edition. Crown 8vo.* 3s. 6d.

JOHANNA. *Second Edition. Crown 8vo.* 6s.

THE HAPPY VALLEY. *Third Edition. Crown 8vo.* 6s.

A NINE DAYS' WONDER. *Crown 8vo.* 6s.

Dawson (A. J.). DANIEL WHYTE. *Crown 8vo.* 3s. 6d.

Doyle (A. Conan), Author of 'Sherlock Holmes,' 'The White Company,' etc. ROUND THE RED LAMP. *Ninth Edition. Crown 8vo.* 6s.

Duncan (Sara Jeannette) (Mrs. Everar. Cotes). THOSE DELIGHTFUL AMERICANS. Illustrated. *Third Edition. Crown 8vo.* 6s.

THE POOL IN THE DESERT. *Crown 8vo.* 6s.

A VOYAGE OF CONSOLATION. *Crown 8vo.* 3s. 6d.

Findlater (J. H.). THE GREEN GRAVES OF BALGOWRIE. *Fifth Edition. Crown 8vo.* 6s.

Findlater (Mary). A NARROW WAY. *Third Edition. Crow 8vo.* 6s.

THE ROSE OF JOY. *Second Edition. Crown 8vo.* 6s.

See also Shilling Novels.

Fitzpatrick (K.) THE WEANS AT ROWALLAN. Illustrated. *Second Edition. Crown 8vo.* 6s.

Fitzstephen (Gerald). MORE KIN THAN KIND. *Crown 8vo.* 6s.

Fletcher (J. S.). LUCIAN THE DREAMER. *Crown 8vo.* 6s.

Fraser (Mrs. Hugh), Author of 'The Stolen Emperor.' THE SLAKING OF THE SWORD. *Crown 8vo.* 6s.

*THE SHADOW OF THE LORD. *Crown 8vo.* 6s.

Gerard (Dorothea), Author of 'Lady Baby.' THE CONQUEST OF LONDON. *Second Edition. Crown 8vo.* 6s.

HOLY MATRIMONY. *Second Edition. Crown 8vo.* 6s.

MADE OF MONEY. *Crown 8vo.* 6s.

THE BRIDGE OF LIFE. *Crown 8vo.* 6s.

*THE IMPROBABLE IDYLL. *Crown 8vo.* 6s.

See also Shilling Novels.

Gerard (Emily). THE HERONS' TOWER. *Crown 8vo.* 6s.

Gissing (George), Author of 'Demos,' 'In the Year of Jubilee,' etc. THE TOWN TRAVELLER. *Second Edition. Crown 8vo.* 6s.

See also Shilling Novels.

Gleig (Charles). BUNTER'S CRUISE. Illustrated. *Crown 8vo.* 3s. 6d.

Harrod (F.) (Frances Forbes Robertson). THE TAMING OF THE BRUTE. *Crown 8vo.* 6s.

Herbertson (Agnes G.). PATIENCE DEAN. *Crown 8vo.* 6s.

Hichens (Robert). THE PROPHET OF BERKELEY SQUARE. *Second Edition. Crown 8vo.* 6s.

TONGUES OF CONSCIENCE. *Second Edition. Crown 8vo.* 6s.

FELIX. *Fourth Edition. Crown 8vo.* 6s.

THE WOMAN WITH THE FAN. *Sixth Edition. Crown 8vo.* 6s.

BYEWAYS. *Crown 8vo.* 3s. 6d.

THE GARDEN OF ALLAH. *Eleventh Edition. Crown 8vo.* 6s.

THE BLACK SPANIEL. *Crown 8vo.* 6s.

Hobbes (John Oliver), Author of 'Robert Orange.' THE SERIOUS WOOING. *Crown 8vo.* 6s.

Hope (Anthony). THE GOD IN THE CAR. *Tenth Edition. Crown 8vo.* 6s.

'A very remarkable book, deserving of critical analysis impossible within our limit; brilliant, but not superficial; well considered, but not elaborated; constructed with the proverbial art that conceals, but yet allows itself to be enjoyed by readers to whom fine literary method is a keen pleasure.'— *The World.*

A CHANGE OF AIR. *Sixth Edition. Crown 8vo.* 6s.

'A graceful, vivacious comedy, true to human nature. The characters are traced with a masterly hand.'— *Times.*

A MAN OF MARK. *Fifth Edition. Crown 8vo.* 6s.

'Of all Mr. Hope's books, "A Man of Mark" is the one which best compares with "The Prisoner of Zenda."'— *National Observer.*

THE CHRONICLES OF COUNT ANTONIO. *Seventh Edition. Crown 8vo.* 6s.

'It is a perfectly enchanting story of love and chivalry, and pure romance. The Count is the most constant, desperate, and modest and tender of lovers, a peerless gentleman, an intrepid fighter, a faithful friend, and a magnanimous foe.'— *Guardian.*

PHROSO. Illustrated by H. R. MILLAR. *Sixth Edition. Crown 8vo.* 6s.

'The tale is thoroughly fresh, quick with vitality, stirring the blood.'— *St. James's Gazette.*

SIMON DALE. Illustrated. *Sixth Edition. Crown 8vo.* 6s.

'There is searching analysis of human nature, with a most ingeniously constructed plot. Mr. Hope has drawn the contrasts of his women with marvellous subtlety and delicacy.'— *Times.*

THE KING'S MIRROR. *Fourth Edition. Crown 8vo.* 6s.

'In elegance, delicacy, and tact it ranks with the best of his novels, while in the wide range of its portraiture and the subtilty of its analysis it surpasses all his earlier ventures.—*Spectator.*

QUISANTE. *Fourth Edition. Crown 8vo.* 6s.

'The book is notable for a very high literary quality, and an impress of power and mastery on every page.'—*Daily Chronicle.*

THE DOLLY DIALOGUES. *Crown 8vo.* 6s.

A SERVANT OF THE PUBLIC. *Second Edition. Crown 8vo.* 6s.

Hope (Graham), Author of 'A Cardinal and his Conscience,' etc., etc. THE LADY OF LYTE. *Second Ed. Crown 8vo.* 6s.

Hough (Emerson). THE MISSISSIPPI BUBBLE. Illustrated. *Crown 8vo.* 6s.

Housman (Clemence). AGLOVALE DE GALIS. *Crown 8vo.* 6s.

Hyne (C. J. Cutcliffe), Author of 'Captain Kettle.' MR. HORROCKS, PURSER. *Third Edition. Crown 8vo.* 6s.

Jacobs (W. W.). MANY CARGOES. *Twenty-Seventh Edition. Crown 8vo.* 3s. 6d.

SEA URCHINS. *Eleventh Edition. Crown 8vo.* 3s. 6d.

A MASTER OF CRAFT. Illustrated. *Sixth Edition. Crown 8vo.* 3s. 6d.

'Can be unreservedly recommended to all who have not lost their appetite for wholesome laughter.'—*Spectator.*

'The best humorous book published for many a day.'—*Black and White.*

LIGHT FREIGHTS. Illustrated. *Fourth Edition. Crown 8vo.* 3s. 6d.

'His wit and humour are perfectly irresistible. Mr. Jacobs writes of skippers, and mates, and seamen, and his crew are the jolliest lot that ever sailed.'—*Daily News.*

'Laughter in every page.'—*Daily Mail.*

James (Henry). THE SOFT SIDE. *Second Edition. Crown 8vo.* 6s.

THE BETTER SORT. *Crown 8vo.* 6s.

THE AMBASSADORS. *Second Edition. Crown 8vo.* 6s.

THE GOLDEN BOWL. *Third Edition. Crown 8vo.* 6s.

Janson (Gustaf). ABRAHAM'S SACRIFICE. *Crown 8vo.* 6s.

Keays (H. A. Mitchell). HE THAT EATETH BREAD WITH ME. *Crown 8vo.* 6s.

Langbridge (V.) and Bourne (C. Harold). THE VALLEY OF INHERITANCE. *Crown 8vo.* 6s.

Lawless (Hon. Emily). See Shilling Novels.

Lawson (Harry), Author of 'When the Billy Boils.' CHILDREN OF THE BUSH. *Crown 8vo.* 6s.

Le Queux (W.). THE HUNCHBACK OF WESTMINSTER. *Third Edition. Crown 8vo.* 6s.

THE CLOSED BOOK. *Third Edition. Crown 8vo.* 6s.

THE VALLEY OF THE SHADOW. Illustrated. *Third Edition. Crown 8vo.* 6s.

BEHIND THE THRONE. *Crown 8vo.* 6s.

Levett-Yeats (S.). ORRAIN. *Second Edition. Crown 8vo.* 6s.

Linton (E. Lynn). THE TRUE HISTORY OF JOSHUA DAVIDSON, Christian and Communist. *Twelfth Edition. Medium 8vo.* 6d.

Long (J. Luther), Co-Author of 'The Darling of the Gods.' MADAME BUTTERFLY. *Crown 8vo.* 3s. 6d.

SIXTY JANE. *Crown 8vo.* 6s.

Lyall (Edna). DERRICK VAUGHAN, NOVELIST. *42nd Thousand. Cr. 8vo.* 3s. 6d.

M'Carthy (Justin H.), Author of 'If I were King.' THE LADY OF LOYALTY HOUSE. *Third Edition. Crown 8vo.* 6s.

THE DRYAD. *Second Edition. Crown 8vo.* 6s.

Macnaughtan (S.). THE FORTUNE OF CHRISTINA MACNAB. *Third Edition. Crown 8vo.* 6s.

Malet (Lucas). COLONEL ENDERBY'S WIFE. *Third Edition. Crown 8vo.* 6s.

A COUNSEL OF PERFECTION. *New Edition. Crown 8vo.* 6s.

LITTLE PETER. *Second Edition. Crown 8vo.* 3s. 6d.

THE WAGES OF SIN. *Fourteenth Edition. Crown 8vo.* 6s.

THE CARISSIMA. *Fourth Edition. Crown 8vo.* 6s.

THE GATELESS BARRIER. *Fourth Edition. Crown 8vo.* 6s.

'In "The Gateless Barrier" it is at once evident that, whilst Lucas Malet has preserved her birthright of originality, the artistry, the actual writing, is above even the high level of the books that were born before.'—*Westminster Gazette.*

THE HISTORY OF SIR RICHARD CALMADY. *Seventh Edition.*

'A picture finely and amply conceived. In the strength and insight in which the story has been conceived, in the wealth of fancy and reflection bestowed upon its execution, and in the moving sincerity of its pathos throughout, "Sir Richard Calmady" must rank as the great novel of a great writer.'—*Literature.*

'The ripest fruit of Lucas Malet's genius. A picture of maternal love by turns tender and terrible.'—*Spectator.*

'A remarkably fine book, with a noble motive and a sound conclusion.'—*Pilot.*

Mann (Mrs. M. E.). OLIVIA'S SUMMER. *Second Edition. Crown 8vo.* 6s.

A LOST ESTATE. *A New Edition. Crown 8vo.* 6s.

THE PARISH OF HILBY. *A New Edition. Crown 8vo.* 6s.

THE PARISH NURSE. *Second Edition. Crown 8vo.* 6s.

GRAN'MA'S JANE. *Crown 8vo.* 6s.

MRS. PETER HOWARD. *Crown 8vo. 6s.*
A WINTER'S TALE. *A New Edition.*
Crown 8vo. 6s.
ONE ANOTHER'S BURDENS. *A New Edition. Crown 8vo. 6s.*
See also Books for Boys and Girls.

Marriott (Charles), Author of 'The Column.' GENEVRA. *Second Edition. Cr. 8vo. 6s.*

Marsh (Richard). THE TWICKENHAM PEERAGE. *Second Edition. Crown 8vo. 6s.*
A DUEL. *Crown 8vo. 6s.*
THE MARQUIS OF PUTNEY. *Crown 8vo. 6s.*
See also Shilling Novels.

Mason (A. E. W.), Author of 'The Courtship of Morrice Buckler,' 'Miranda of the Balcony,' etc. CLEMENTINA. Illustrated. *Crown 8vo. Second Edition. 6s.*

Mathers (Helen), Author of 'Comin' thro' the Rye.' HONEY. *Fourth Edition. Crown 8vo. 6s.*
GRIFF OF GRIFFITHSCOURT. *Crown 8vo. 6s.*
THE FERRYMAN. *Crown 8vo. 6s.*

Maxwell (W. B.), Author of 'The Ragged Messenger.' VIVIEN. *Third Edition. Crown 8vo. 6s.*

Meade (L. T.). DRIFT. *Second Edition. Crown 8vo. 6s.*
RESURGAM. *Crown 8vo. 6s.*
See also Shilling Novels.

Meredith (Ellis). HEART OF MY HEART. *Crown 8vo. 6s.*

'Miss Molly' (The Author of). THE GREAT RECONCILER. *Crown 8vo. 6s.*

Mitford (Bertram). THE SIGN OF THE SPIDER. Illustrated. *Sixth Edition. Crown 8vo. 3s. 6d.*
IN THE WHIRL OF THE RISING. *Third Edition. Crown 8vo. 6s.*
THE RED DERELICT. *Second Edition. Crown 8vo. 6s.*

Montresor (F. F.), Author of 'Into the Highways and Hedges.' THE ALIEN. *Third Edition. Crown 8vo. 6s.*

Morrison (Arthur). TALES OF MEAN STREETS. *Sixth Edition. Crown 8vo. 6s.*
'A great book. The author's method is amazingly effective, and produces a thrilling sense of reality. The writer lays upon us a master hand. The book is simply appalling and irresistible in its interest. It is humorous also; without humour it would not make the mark it is certain to make.'—*World.*
A CHILD OF THE JAGO. *Fourth Edition. Crown 8vo. 6s.*
'The book is a masterpiece.'—*Pall Mall Gazette.*
TO LONDON TOWN. *Second Edition. Crown 8vo. 6s.*
'This is the new Mr. Arthur Morrison, gracious and tender, sympathetic and human.'—*Daily Telegraph.*

CUNNING MURRELL. *Crown 8vo. 6s.*
'Admirable. . . . Delightful humorous relief . . . a most artistic and satisfactory achievement.'—*Spectator.*
THE HOLE IN THE WALL. *Third Edition. Crown 8vo. 6s.*
'A masterpiece of artistic realism. It has a finality of touch that only a master may command.'—*Daily Chronicle.*
'An absolute masterpiece, which any novelist might be proud to claim.'—*Graphic.*
'"The Hole in the Wall" is a masterly piece of work. His characters are drawn with amazing skill. Extraordinary power.'—*Daily Telegraph.*
DIVERS VANITIES. *Crown 8vo. 6s.*

Nesbit (E.). (Mrs. E. Bland). THE RED HOUSE. Illustrated. *Fourth Edition. Crown 8vo. 6s.*
See also Shilling Novels.

Norris (W. E.). THE CREDIT OF THE COUNTY. Illustrated. *Second Edition. Crown 8vo. 6s.*
THE EMBARRASSING ORPHAN. *Crown 8vo. 6s.*
NIGEL'S VOCATION. *Crown 8vo. 6s.*
BARHAM OF BELTANA. *Second Edition. Crown 8vo. 6s.*
See also Shilling Novels.

Ollivant (Alfred). OWD BOB, THE GREY DOG OF KENMUIR. *Eighth Edition. Crown 8vo. 6s.*

Oppenheim (E. Phillips). MASTER OF MEN. *Third Edition. Crown 8vo. 6s.*

Oxenham (John), Author of 'Barbe of Grand Bayou.' A WEAVER OF WEBS. *Second Edition. Crown 8vo. 6s.*
THE GATE OF THE DESERT. *Fourth Edition. Crown 8vo. 6s.*

Pain (Barry). THREE FANTASIES. *Crown 8vo. 1s.*
LINDLEY KAYS. *Third Edition. Crown 8vo. 6s.*

Parker (Gilbert). PIERRE AND HIS PEOPLE. *Sixth Edition.*
'Stories happily conceived and finely executed. There is strength and genius in Mr. Parker's style.'—*Daily Telegraph.*
MRS. FALCHION. *Fifth Edition. Crown 8vo. 6s.*
'A splendid study of character.'—*Athenæum.*
THE TRANSLATION OF A SAVAGE. *Second Edition. Crown 8vo. 6s.*
THE TRAIL OF THE SWORD. Illustrated. *Eighth Edition. Crown 8vo. 6s.*
'A rousing and dramatic tale. A book like this is a joy inexpressible.' — *Daily Chronicle.*
WHEN VALMOND CAME TO PONTIAC: The Story of a Lost Napoleon. *Fifth Edition. Crown 8vo. 6s.*
'Here we find romance—real, breathing, living romance. The character of Valmond is drawn unerringly.'—*Pall Mall Gazette.*

AN ADVENTURER OF THE NORTH:
The Last Adventures of 'Pretty Pierre.'
Third Edition. Crown 8vo. 6s.
'The present book is full of fine and moving
stories of the great North.' — *Glasgow
Herald.*
THE SEATS OF THE MIGHTY. Illus-
trated. *Thirteenth Edition. Crown 8vo. 6s.*
'Mr. Parker has produced a really fine
historical novel.'—*Athenæum.*
'A great book.'—*Black and White.*
THE BATTLE OF THE STRONG. a
Romance of Two Kingdoms. Illustrated.
Fourth Edition. Crown 8vo. 6s.
'Nothing more vigorous or more human
has come from Mr. Gilbert Parker than
this novel.'—*Literature.*
THE POMP OF THE LAVILETTES.
Second Edition. Crown 8vo. 3s. 6d.
'Unforced pathos, and a deeper knowledge
of human nature than he has displayed be-
fore.'—*Pall Mall Gazette.*
Pemberton (Max). THE FOOTSTEPS
OF A THRONE. Illustrated. *Third
Edition. Crown 8vo. 6s.*
I CROWN THEE KING. With Illustra-
tions by Frank Dadd and A. Forrestier.
Crown 8vo. 6s.
Phillpotts (Eden). LYING PROPHETS.
Crown 8vo. 6s.
CHILDREN OF THE MIST. *Fifth Edi-
tion. Crown 8vo. 6s.*
THE HUMAN BOY. With a Frontispiece.
Fourth Edition. Crown 8vo. 6s.
'Mr. Phillpotts knows exactly what
school-boys do, and can lay bare their
inmost thoughts; likewise he shows an all-
pervading sense of humour.'—*Academy.*
SONS OF THE MORNING. *Second
Edition. Crown 8vo. 6s.*
'A book of strange power and fascination.'
—*Morning Post.*
THE RIVER. *Third Edition. Cr. 8vo. 6s.*
'"The River" places Mr. Phillpotts in
the front rank of living novelists.'—*Punch.*
'Since "Lorna Doone" we have had
nothing so picturesque as this new romance.'
—*Birmingham Gazette.*
'Mr. Phillpotts's new book is a master-
piece which brings him indisputably into the
front rank of English novelists.'—*Pall Mall
Gazette.*
'This great romance of the River Dart.
The finest book Mr. Eden Phillpotts has
written.'—*Morning Post.*
THE AMERICAN PRISONER. *Third
Edition. Crown 8vo. 6s.*
THE SECRET WOMAN. *Fourth Edition.
Crown 8vo. 6s.*
KNOCK AT A VENTURE. *Second
Edition. Crown 8vo. 6s.*
See also Shilling Novels.
Pickthall (Marmaduke). SAÏD THE
FISHERMAN. *Fifth Edition. Crown
8vo. 6s.*

BRENDLE. *Crown 8vo 6s.*
'Q,' Author of 'Dead Man's Rock.' THE
WHITE WOLF. *Second Edition. Crown
8vo. 6s.*
Rhys (Grace). THE WOOING OF
SHEILA. *Second Edition. Crown 8vo.
6s.*
THE PRINCE OF LISNOVER. *Crown
8vo. 6s.*
Rhys (Grace) and Another. THE DI-
VERTED VILLAGE. With Illustrations
by DOROTHY GWYN JEFFREYS. *Crown
8vo. 6s.*
Ridge (W. Pett). LOST PROPERTY.
Second Edition. Crown 8vo. 6s.
ERB. *Second Edition. Crown 8vo. 6s.*
A SON OF THE STATE. *Crown 8vo.
3s. 6d.*
A BREAKER OF LAWS. *Crown 8vo.
3s. 6d.*
MRS GALER'S BUSINESS. *Second
Edition. Crown 8vo. 6s.*
SECRETARY TO BAYNE, M.P. *Crown
8vo. 3s. 6d.*
Ritchie (Mrs. David G.). THE TRUTH-
FUL LIAR. *Crown 8vo. 6s.*
Roberts (C. G. D.). THE HEART OF
THE ANCIENT WOOD. *Crown 8vo.
3s. 6d.*
Russell (W. Clark). MY DANISH
SWEETHEART. Illustrated. *Fifth
Edition. Crown 8vo. 6s.*
HIS ISLAND PRINCESS. Illustrated.
Second Edition. Crown 6vo. 6s.
See also Shilling Novels.
Sergeant (Adeline). ANTHEA'S WAY.
Crown 8vo. 6s.
THE PROGRESS OF RACHEL. *Crown
8vo. 6s.*
THE MYSTERY OF THE MOAT. *Second
Edition. Crown 8vo. 6s.*
MRS. LYGON'S HUSBAND. *Cr. 8vo. 6s.*
See also Shilling Novels.
Shannon (W. F.). THE MESS DECK.
Crown 8vo. 3s. 6d.
See also Shilling Novels.
Sonnichsen (Albert). DEEP SEA VAGA-
BONDS. *Crown 8vo. 6s.*
Thompson (Vance). SPINNERS OF
LIFE. *Crown 8vo. 6s.*
Urquhart (M.). A TRAGEDY IN COM-
MONPLACE. *Second Ed. Crown 8vo. 6s.*
Waineman (Paul). BY A FINNISH
LAKE. *Crown 8vo. 6s.*
THE SONG OF THE FOREST. *Crown
8vo. 6s.* See also Shilling Novels.
Watson (H. B. Marriott). ALARUMS
AND EXCURSIONS. *Crown 8vo. 6s.*
CAPTAIN FORTUNE. *Second Edition.
Crown 8vo. 6s.*
TWISTED EGLANTINE. With 8 Illus-
trations by FRANK CRAIG. *Second Edition.
Crown 8vo. 6s.* See also Shilling Novels.
Wells (H. G.) THE SEA LADY. *Crown
8vo. 6s.*

Weyman (Stanley), Author of 'A Gentleman of France.' UNDER THE RED ROBE. With Illustrations by R. C. WOODVILLE. *Nineteenth Edition.* *Crown 8vo. 6s.*

White (Stewart E.). Author of 'The Blazed Trail.' CONJUROR'S HOUSE. A Romance of the Free Trail. *Second Edition. Crown 8vo. 6s.*

White (Percy). THE SYSTEM. *Third Edition. Crown 8vo. 6s.*

THE PATIENT MAN. *Crown 8vo. 6s.*

Williamson (Mrs. C. N.), Author of 'The Barnstormers.' THE ADVENTURE OF PRINCESS SYLVIA. *Crown 8vo. 3s. 6d.*

THE WOMAN WHO DARED. *Crown 8vo. 6s.*

THE SEA COULD TELL. *Second Edition. Crown 8vo. 6s.*

THE CASTLE OF THE SHADOWS. *Third Edition. Crown 8vo. 6s.*
See also Shilling Novels.

Williamson (C. N. and A. M.). THE LIGHTNING CONDUCTOR: Being the Romance of a Motor Car. Illustrated. *Twelfth Edition. Crown 8vo. 6s.*

THE PRINCESS PASSES. Illustrated. *Fourth Edition. Crown 8vo. 6s.*

MY FRIEND THE CHAUFFEUR. With 16 Illustrations. *Second Ed. Crown 8vo. 6s.*

*Wyllarde (Dolf), Author of 'Uriah the Hittite.' THE FORERUNNERS. *Crown 8vo. 6s.*

Methuen's Strand Library

Crown 8vo. Cloth, 1s. net.

ENCOURAGED by the great and steady sale of their Sixpenny Novels, Messrs. Methuen have determined to issue a new series of fiction at a low price under the title of 'METHUEN'S STRAND LIBRARY.' These books are well printed and well bound in *cloth*, and the excellence of their quality may be gauged from the names of those authors who contribute the early volumes of the series.

Messrs. Methuen would point out that the books are as good and as long as a six shilling novel, that they are bound in cloth and not in paper, and that their price is One Shilling *net*. They feel sure that the public will appreciate such good and cheap literature, and the books can be seen at all good booksellers.

The first volumes are—

Balfour (Andrew). VENGEANCE IS MINE.
TO ARMS.
Baring-Gould (S.). MRS. CURGENVEN OF CURGENVEN.
DOMITIA.
THE FROBISHERS.
Barlow (Jane). Author of 'Irish Idylls.' FROM THE EAST UNTO THE WEST
A CREEL OF IRISH STORIES.
THE FOUNDING OF FORTUNES.
Barr (Robert). THE VICTORS.
Bartram (George). THIRTEEN EVENINGS.
Benson (E. F.), Author of Dodo.' THE CAPSINA.
Besant (Sir Walter). A FIVE-YEARS' TRYST.
Bowles (G. Stewart). A STRETCH OFF THE LAND.
Brooke (Emma). THE POET'S CHILD.
Bullock (Shan F.). THE BARRYS.
THE CHARMER.
THE SQUIREEN.
THE RED LEAGUERS.
Burton (J. Bloundelle). ACROSS THE SALT SEAS.
THE CLASH OF ARMS.
DENOUNCED.
Chesney (Weatherby). THE BAPTIST RING.
THE BRANDED PRINCE.
THE FOUNDERED GALLEON.
JOHN TOPP.

Clifford (Mrs. W. K.). A FLASH OF SUMMER.
Collingwood (Harry). THE DOCTOR OF THE 'JULIET.'
Cornfield (L. Cope). SONS OF ADVERSITY.
Crane (Stephen). WOUNDS IN THE RAIN.
Denny (C. E.). THE ROMANCE OF UPFOLD MANOR.
Dickson (Harris). THE BLACK WOLF'S BREED.
Embree (E. C. F.). THE HEART OF FLAME.
Fenn (G. Manville). AN ELECTRIC SPARK.
Findlater (Mary). OVER THE HILLS.
Forrest (R. E.). THE SWORD OF AZRAEL.
Francis (M. E.). MISS ERIN.
Gallon (Tom). RICKERBY'S FOLLY.
Gerard (Dorothea). THINGS THAT HAVE HAPPENED.
Glanville (Ernest). THE DESPATCH RIDER.
THE LOST REGIMENT.
THE INCA'S TREASURE.
Gordon (Julien). MRS. CLYDE.
WORLD'S PEOPLE.
Goss (C. F.). THE REDEMPTION OF DAVID CORSON.
Hales (A. G.). JAIR THE APOSTATE.
Hamilton (Lord Ernest). MARY HAMILTON.

Harrison (Mrs. Burton). A PRINCESS-OF THE HILLS. Illustrated.
Hooper (I.). THE SINGER OF MARLY.
Hough (Emerson). THE MISSISSIPPI BUBBLE.
'Iota' (Mrs. Caffyn). ANNE MAULE-VERER.
Kelly (Florence Finch). WITH HOOPS OF STEEL.
Lawless (Hon. Emily). MAELCHO.
Linden (Annie). A WOMAN OF SENTI-MENT.
Lorimer (Norma). JOSIAH'S WIFE.
Lush (Charles K.). THE AUTOCRATS.
Macdonnell (A.). THE STORY OF TERESA.
Macgrath (Harold). THE PUPPET CROWN.
Mackie (Pauline Bradford). THE VOICE IN THE DESERT.
M'Queen Gray (E.) MY STEWARDSHIP.
Marsh (Richard). THE SEEN AND THE UNSEEN.
GARNERED.
A METAMORPHOSIS.
MARVELS AND MYSTERIES.
BOTH SIDES OF THE VEIL.
Mayall (J. W.). THE CYNIC AND THE SYREN.
Meade (L. T.). OUT OF THE FASHION.
Monkhouse (Allan). LOVE IN A LIFE.
Moore (Arthur). THE KNIGHT PUNC-TILIOUS.
Nesbit (Mrs. Bland). THE LITERARY SENSE.
Norris (W. E.). AN OCTAVE.
Oliphant (Mrs.). THE PRODIGALS.
THE LADY'S WALK.
SIR ROBERT'S FORTUNE.
THE TWO MARY'S.

Penny (Mrs. F. A.). A MIXED MARRI-AGE.
Phillpotts (Eden). THE STRIKING HOURS.
FANCY FREE.
Randal (J.). AUNT BETHIA'S BUTTON.
Raymond (Walter). FORTUNE'S DAR-LING.
Rhys (Grace). THE DIVERTED VILL-AGE.
Rickert (Edith). OUT OF THE CYPRESS SWAMP.
Roberton (M. H.). A GALLANT QUAKER.
Saunders (Marshall). ROSE A CHAR-LITTE.
Sergeant (Adeline). ACCUSED AND ACCUSER.
BARBARA'S MONEY.
THE ENTHUSIAST.
A GREAT LADY.
THE LOVE THAT OVERCAME.
THE MASTER OF BEECHWOOD.
UNDER SUSPICION.
THE YELLOW DIAMOND.
Shannon (W. F.). JIM TWELVES.
Strain (E. H.). ELMSLIE'S DRAG NET.
Stringer (Arthur). THE SILVER POPPY.
Stuart (Esmé). CHRISTALLA.
Sutherland (Duchess of). ONE HOUR AND THE NEXT.
Swan (Annie). LOVE GROWN COLD.
Swift (Benjamin). SORDON.
Tanqueray (Mrs. B. M.), THE ROYAL QUAKER.
Trafford-Taunton (Mrs. E. W.). SILENT DOMINION.
Waineman (Paul). A HEROINE FROM FINLAND.
Watson (H. B. Marriott-). THE SKIRTS OF HAPPY CHANCE.

Books for Boys and Girls

Crown 8vo. 3s. 6d.

THE GETTING WELL OF DOROTHY. By Mrs. W. K. Clifford. Illustrated by Gordon-Browne. *Second Edition.*
THE ICELANDER'S SWORD. By S. Baring-Gould.
ONLY A GUARD-ROOM DOG. By Edith E. Cuthell.
THE DOCTOR OF THE JULIET. By Harry Collingwood.
LITTLE PETER. By Lucas Malet. *Second Edition.*
MASTER ROCKAFELLAR'S VOYAGE. By W. Clark Russell.

THE SECRET OF MADAME DE MONLUC. By the Author of "Mdlle. Mori."
SYD BELTON : Or, the Boy who would not go to Sea. By G. Manville Fenn.
THE RED GRANGE. By Mrs. Molesworth.
A GIRL OF THE PEOPLE. By L. T. Meade.
HEPSY GIPSY. By L. T. Meade. *2s. 6d.*
THE HONOURABLE MISS. By L. T. Meade.
THERE WAS ONCE A PRINCE. By Mrs. M. E. Mann.
WHEN ARNOLD COMES HOME. By Mrs. M. E. Mann.

The Novels of Alexandre Dumas

Price 6d. Double Volumes, 1s.

THE THREE MUSKETEERS. With a long Introduction by Andrew Lang. Double volume.
THE PRINCE OF THIEVES. *Second Edition.*
ROBIN HOOD. A Sequel to the above.

THE CORSICAN BROTHERS.
GEORGES.
CROP-EARED JACQUOT ; JANE ; Etc.
TWENTY YEARS AFTER. Double volume.
AMAURY.

THE CASTLE OF EPPSTEIN.
THE SNOWBALL, and SULTANETTA.
CECILE; OR, THE WEDDING GOWN.
ACTÉ.
THE BLACK TULIP.
THE VICOMTE DE BRAGELONNE.
Part I. Louis de la Vallière. Double Volume.
Part II. The Man in the Iron Mask. Double Volume.
THE CONVICT'S SON.
THE WOLF-LEADER.
NANON; OR, THE WOMEN' WAR. Double volume.
PAULINE; MURAT; AND PASCAL BRUNO.
THE ADVENTURES OF CAPTAIN PAMPHILE.
FERNANDE.
GABRIEL LAMBERT.
CATHERINE BLUM.
THE CHEVALIER D'HARMENTAL. Double volume.
SYLVANDIRE.
THE FENCING MASTER.
THE REMINISCENCES OF ANTONY.
CONSCIENCE.
*THE REGENT'S DAUGHTER. A Sequel to Chevalier d'Harmental.

Illustrated Edition.

THE THREE MUSKETEERS. Illustrated in Colour by Frank Adams. 2s. 6d.
THE PRINCE OF THIEVES. Illustrated in Colour by Frank Adams. 2s.

ROBIN HOOD THE OUTLAW. Illustrated in Colour by Frank Adams. 2s.
THE CORSICAN BROTHERS. Illustrated in Colour by A. M. M'Lellan. 1s. 6d.
THE WOLF-LEADER. Illustrated in Colour by Frank Adams. 1s. 6d.
GEORGES. Illustrated in Colour by Munro Orr. 2s.
TWENTY YEARS AFTER. Illustrated in Colour by Frank Adams. 3s.
AMAURY. Illustrated in Colour by Gordon Browne. 2s.
THE SNOWBALL, and SULTANETTA. Illustrated in Colour by Frank Adams. 2s.
THE VICOMTE DE BRAGELONNE. Illustrated in Colour by Frank Adams. 3s. 6d.
*CROP-EARED JACQUOT; JANE; Etc. Illustrated in Colour by Gordon Browne. 1s. 6d.
THE CASTLE OF EPPSTEIN. Illustrated in Colour by Stewart Orr. 1s. 6d.
ACTÉ. Illustrated in Colour by Gordon Browne. 1s. 6d.
*CECILE; OR, THE WEDDING GOWN. Illustrated in Colour by D. Murray Smith. 1s. 6d.
*THE ADVENTURES OF CAPTAIN PAMPHILE. Illustrated in Colour by Frank Adams. 1s. 6d.
*FERNANDE. Illustrated in Colour by Munro Orr. 2s.
*THE BLACK TULIP. Illustrated in Colour by A. Orr. 1s. 6d.

Methuen's Sixpenny Books

Austen (Jane). PRIDE AND PREJUDICE.
Baden-Powell (Major-General R. S. S.). THE DOWNFALL OF PREMPEH.
Bagot (Richard). A ROMAN MYSTERY.
Balfour (Andrew). BY STROKE OF SWORD.
Baring-Gould (S.). FURZE BLOOM.
CHEAP JACK ZITA.
KITTY ALONE.
URITH.
THE BROOM SQUIRE.
IN THE ROAR OF THE SEA.
NOÉMI.
A BOOK OF FAIRY TALES. Illustrated.
LITTLE TU'PENNY.
THE FROBISHERS.
*WINEFRED.
Barr (Robert). JENNIE BAXTER, JOURNALIST.
IN THE MIDST OF ALARMS.
THE COUNTESS TEKLA.
THE MUTABLE MANY.
Benson (E. F.). DODO.
Bloundelle-Burton (J.). ACROSS THE SALT SEAS.
Brontë (Charlotte). SHIRLEY.
Brownell (C. L.). THE HEART OF JAPAN.

Caffyn (Mrs.), 'Iota.' ANNE MAULEVERER.
Clifford (Mrs. W. K.). A FLASH OF SUMMER.
MRS. KEITH'S CRIME.
Connell (F. Norreys). THE NIGGER KNIGHTS.
*Cooper (E. H.). A FOOL'S YEAR.
Corbett (Julian). A BUSINESS IN GREAT WATERS.
Croker (Mrs. B. M.). PEGGY OF THE BARTONS.
A STATE SECRET.
ANGEL. JOHANNA.
Dante (Alighieri). THE VISION OF DANTE (CARY).
Doyle (A. Conan). ROUND THE RED LAMP.
Duncan (Sarah Jeannette). A VOYAGE OF CONSOLATION.
THOSE DELIGHTFUL AMERICANS.
Eliot (George). THE MILL ON THE FLOSS.
Findlater (Jane H.). THE GREEN GRAVES OF BALGOWRIE.
Gallon (Tom). RICKERBY'S FOLLY.
Gaskell (Mrs.). CRANFORD.
MARY BARTON.
NORTH AND SOUTH.